THE JEWISHNESS OF ISRAELIS

SUNY Series in Israeli Studies
Edited by Russell Stone

The Jewishness of Israelis

Responses to the Guttman Report

Edited by
Charles S. Liebman and Elihu Katz

STATE UNIVERSITY OF NEW YORK PRESS

Published by
State University of New York Press, Albany

Printed in the United States of America

For information, address State University of New York Press,
State University Plaza, Albany, N.Y., 12246

Production by Cathleen Collins
Marketing by Bernadette LaManna

Library of Congress Cataloging-in-Publication Data

The Jewishness of Israelis : responses to the Guttman report / edited
by Charles S. Liebman and Elihu Katz.
p. cm. – (SUNY series in Israeli studies)
Includes bibliographical references and index.
ISBN 0-7914-3305-6 (alk. paper). – ISBN 0-7914-3306-4 (pbk. :
alk. paper)
1. Judaism–Israel–Public opinion. 2. Orthodox Judaism–Israel–
Public opinion. 3. Israelis–Religious life. 4. Public opinion–
Israel. 5. Social surveys–Israel. I. Liebman, Charles S.
II. Katz, Elihu, 1926- . III. Series.
BM390.J49 1997
296'.095694–dc20 96-2904
CIP

10 9 8 7 6 5 4 3 2 1

To our esteemed friend
S. Z. ABRAMOV

Contents

Figures

Tables

Foreword

From its founding in 1984, AVI CHAI committed itself to the perpetuation of the Jewish people, Judaism, and the centrality of the State of Israel to the Jewish people. We state our objective as follows:

> To encourage mutual understanding and sensitivity among Jews of different religious backgrounds and commitments to observance; and
> To encourage those of the Jewish faith towards greater commitment to Jewish observance and life-style by increasing their understanding, appreciation, and practice of Jewish traditions, customs and laws.

Early in 1986, the board of AVI CHAI asked our chairman and executive director to meet with nearly fifty individuals whose knowledge of Israeli society spanned a wide range of professional disciplines and personal philosophies. We hoped that these interviews could help us understand the landscape in order to play a constructive role in attenuating the societal tensions connected to beliefs, observances, and social interaction among Israeli Jews. But this information, while providing useful background, did not prove to be a sufficient basis for sound philanthropic initiatives, in our opinion.

Subsequently in that year, our board undertook to begin a "preliminary investigation to develop the design stage of a sociological, behavioral study of the people of Israel." We hoped that a comprehensive, sociological study that could define actual behavior and attitudes would present us with enough understanding of the complex societal dialectical tensions to develop our programmatic agenda.

Despite this intent, the consideration of a study lay moribund while we tried a few other approaches between 1987 and 1990. First, we commissioned a literature search of published studies, both in Hebrew and

English. Parallel to the literature review, we commissioned, under the direction of Charles Liebman, a series of case studies designed to offer anecdotal insights into the interrelationships between Israeli Jews of different levels of observance. The eleven studies were later published in 1990, by Keter Books, in both English and Hebrew. The title in English is *Conflict and Accommodation between Jews in Israel: Religious and Secular.*

In 1989, seeking further information and suggestions for action, we decided to solicit papers from a diverse group of outstanding Israelis. These papers, presented to the board in 1990, had a potpourri of interesting approaches but again did not provide us with sufficient "hard" data. People thought they knew what the Israeli public did and felt, but there was no reliable basis for their conclusions. In point of fact, we later discovered that the conventional wisdom was erroneous.

Later in 1990, we finally undertook the commissioning of the study that forms the basis of this volume. We decided that the director of this project must be an Israeli social scientist with a reputation for professional integrity, widely respected in the academic community, with an institutional research framework in which to conduct the project. Professor Elihu Katz, scientific director of the Louis Guttman Institute of Applied Social Science in Israel, recipient of the Israel Prize for his work in the field of communication, was an obvious choice.

That summer, frequent meetings were held by a steering committee composed of Professor Katz, Dr. Shlomit Levy (designated as the principal investigator), and Hanna Levinsohn (senior staff member), on behalf of Guttman, and on behalf of AVI CHAI, the Chairman Zalman C. Bernstein, Trustee David Weiss, and our professional staff.

In December we entered into the grant letter that formalized the Steering Committee and dealt at some length, among other issues, with our mutual desire to ensure the confidentiality of the data and the conditions under which all, or part, of the data could be published, when, and by whom. AVI CHAI assured the Guttman Institute of complete independence in analysis and interpretation of the data. The Steering Committee held a series of meetings and finally agreed upon the sample size; that residents of Judea and Samaria would be added and separately tabulated; and all the interviews would be conducted face-to-face. It was also determined that Hebrew-speaking adults over twenty years of age would be the focus of the analysis, although we all understood that this would exclude much of the recent large immigration from the Soviet Union.

Professor Katz pointed out that our desire to provide attitudinal information in order to understand where we might initiate programs for reducing societal tensions, combined with data on religious observance, made for two separate "forests." He suggested that we explore both forests at the same time by a common set of questions, to which would be added, for 1,200 respondents, additional religious practice questions, and for the other 1,200, additional social interaction questions. Fortunately, as it turned out, we had earlier decided to double the usual in-depth study size of 1,200 to 2,400 (in addition to 150 interviews in Judea and Samaria).

Once the data had been gathered we asked Guttman "to focus its analysis on the following seven areas: trends in religious practice and belief; variations in religious practice and belief among several age groups in comparison with one another; attitudes towards the religious 'status quo' and towards *haredim*, including attitudes toward army service; geographical analysis; areas of social interaction among people of different levels of observance and ethnicity; reactions to the religious establishment, with consideration whether an attitude of dislike is linked to level of observance; and areas of mutual contact 'desired' by groups of different backgrounds and levels of observance."

The report of the Guttman Institute, which arrived just prior to our September 1992 board meeting, was a daunting, 400-page tome, replete with table after table. The data and the Guttman Institute analysis were a surprise, since it was clear that there exists a higher degree of commonality than had been generally portrayed. The facts indicated that a large majority of the Jewish population seemed to have found a meeting ground that they found comfortable despite the venomous sting of the extremities (non-Zionist *haredim* and the ideological secularists). In line with our historical policy of publishing information developed for our board, which had content of general interest, the AVI CHAI board decided to release the entire study.

Now we faced the problem that the report, written for our board under the pressure of a deadline, needed to be edited and then translated into Hebrew. This decision gave us the time to address ourselves to the unwieldiness of a 400-page document. We asked the Guttman Institute to produce a *Highlights* booklet summarizing the full report, with graphs and tables. This booklet, would be distributed in Hebrew and in English, although the full report, in both languages, would also be made available. Producing these four documents naturally took some time. (The *Highlights* booklet has also been translated into Russian, French and Spanish.)

Because this study would surely be of interest to all those concerned with this vital Israeli issue, our board decided to launch the distribution of the study with a conference on "The Jewishness of Israelis," at the Van Leer Institute in Jerusalem in December of 1993. The conference, as some commented, was attended by the "largest number of outstanding Israeli academics ever in one room." In preparation for the conference, papers had been solicited from a coterie of Israeli academics from various social sciences and humanities, as well as some religious figures.

The media provided extensive coverage, not only before and after the conference but for a substantial period thereafter. In fact, quotes from the study continue to appear in the press to this day. Additionally, the study was used and is being used as the basic reference source by academics in Israel and throughout the Diaspora in analyzing "The Jewishness of Israelis." Interestingly enough, but not surprisingly, by culling the data, enterprising advertising and marketing people are also using the study as the basis for consumer-product campaigns, among other innovative twists for supporting ideas and projects.

Based on the study, our trustees and staff presented a large menu of potential program initiatives. We have since embarked upon a few. To date, our emphasis has been on Jewish education, both for junior high schools and teacher training, as well as education in Judaism and Zionism for officers in the Israel Defense Forces. We hope that we, as well as others, will use the data and its analysis to enable those who are in fact the dominant majority in Israeli society to feel emboldened in their search for the Jewish character of the State.

The board of AVI CHAI, more convinced than ever that facts and analysis are necessary to understand the evolving sociological mosaic of Israel, plans to commission a comparable study at the end of this decade. In the meantime, we have commissioned Guttman to prepare an in-depth study of high-school-age youth, the findings of which may well be at variance with the picture presented in the adult study.

This volume is an independent study by Charles Liebman and Elihu Katz based on the Guttman Report and on the responses to that Report in Israeli society. By decision of our board, the AVI CHAI Foundation resolved to encourage the authors as well as assist them in any way it could in the preparation of this volume. We saw a preliminary Table of Contents but at no point were we consulted about the substance of the material nor do we bear any responsibility for the views expressed in this book. They are exclusively those of the authors.

We are grateful for the opportunity of this Foreword to tell the AVI CHAI story behind the study.

AVI CHAI
Adar I 5755
February 1995

Preface

The question of the religious attitudes and behavior of Israelis Jews has long exercised the Israeli public. People are interested in religious behavior, especially in comparing their own with that of others, but there are social and political reasons that also account for this interest. First of all, media reports and surveys of Israeli public opinion suggest that there is a great deal of tension between religious and nonreligious Jews. Part of this tension is attributed to the necessity for people whose styles of life are different to live and work together. But it is exacerbated by the sense of many Israelis that religious Jews constitute a small minority of the population and possess undue influence in Israeli politics. The standard estimate of the percentage of religious Jews in Israel hovers around 20 percent of all Jews, though it is sometimes reported as even lower. That being the case, it is often charged by both the media and politicians of the secular left that "religious" legislation, that is, legislation that imposes restrictions on public life in Israel such as closing of theaters and coffee houses on the Sabbath (restrictions which have recently been eased), or banning public transportation on the Sabbath, or the requirement that all marriages between Jews be performed in accordance with Jewish religious law, is unfair and "undemocratic." This legislation is generally termed, "religious coercion." The label alone gives a good sense of how it is viewed in the media and by large numbers of Israelis. Religious parties, it is charged, represent less than one-fifth of the population but form a balance of power between the two major parties and thereby succeed in imposing their demands on all Israelis.

The Guttman Institute study on the religious attitudes, beliefs, and behavior of Israeli Jews provided the fullest source of data about how Israeli Jews behave religiously, what they believe, how they view Jews of different religious orientations, and what role they feel religion ought to play in public life. It is, therefore, not at all surprising that the study received widespread attention.

The report eschewed the labels of "religious" and "secular." It suggested, at least by indirection, that Israeli Jews cannot be dichotomized in this manner. Instead, it reported its findings in terms of levels of religious observance. It found that Israeli Jews can be ranged along a continuum in terms of their religious practice. In general, the report found, Israelis were far more traditional in their behavior and beliefs than had heretofore been imagined, and, in the words of the report itself, "the rhetoric of polarization" within Israeli society between observant and nonobservant was exaggerated, at least from a behavioral point of view.

Although the report occasioned an enormous amount of commentary and discussion, it received relatively little attention in the United States, even in Jewish circles. Our original purpose in preparing this volume was to afford the English-speaking reader access to the major findings of the Guttman Institute report and to a cross section of the commentary accorded that report by both the Israeli media and leading Israeli intellectuals. We anticipated producing an edited volume in which our own contribution would be rather modest.

As the volume developed we found that the primary materials we had intended to present required interpretation. Indeed, a more careful look at the material suggested that its findings had, at least in part, been misunderstood. Furthermore, we found that our own reflections on the report led us in directions we had not, heretofore, anticipated. As we became more involved in the project of presentation, the volume became more and more of a commentary and reflection by us on both the Guttman Report and on its reception in Israeli society rather than a detached exposition of the report and its reception. In other words, there is more of Liebman and Katz in this volume than we had initially intended. Nevertheless, we hope there is enough primary material to allow the reader to judge our interpretive effort for him/herself.

The first chapter simply reproduces the *Highlights* booklet referred to in the Foreword by the AVI CHAI Foundation. In addition, the Appendix contains ten of the papers presented at the Van Leer conference, held in December of 1993. That conference brought together leading Israeli intellectuals to discuss the report and its implications for Israeli society. We chose those papers, half the number actually circulated, which in our opinion represented the range of responses by the Van Leer invitees, to the report.

Chapters 2 through 6 represent our own contribution. Chapters 2 and 3 are written by Liebman. Chapter 2 is an analysis of how the Israeli media treated the report. The analysis points to the manner in which a scientific report is popularized and the almost inevitable distortion that takes place in the process of the popularization. This chapter, therefore, may be of special interest to those concerned with studies of the media. Chapter 3 is an analysis of the papers presented at the Van Leer conference. The analysis refers to papers found in the Appendix as well as to other papers and oral presentations that were delivered at that conference.

Chapter 4 was written by Elihu Katz, who is both an editor of this volume as well as a coauthor of the Guttman Report. It is an effort to explain what it is that the report did and did not demonstrate given the limitations of survey research and the methodology employed by the Guttman Institute. It constitutes a corrective and a response to some of the critics.

Chapters 5 and 6, also by Liebman, are an effort to understand the major finding of the Guttman Report in the context of religious developments in other societies, and the specific nature of Israeli society. The chapters provide a very broad interpretive framework for the Guttman Report findings and speculate on the consequences of new developments in Israeli society for religious attitudes and behavior of Israeli Jews. The final section suggests the possibility that the Israeli political map will be redrawn with attitudes toward the religious tradition providing its major coordinates.

We are very grateful to the AVI CHAI Foundation. The foundation, which commissioned the original report, suggested that we undertake the preparation of this volume. It was more than forthcoming, with information, written materials, and secretarial assistance at every stage of our work without ever suggesting, much less imposing, a particular perspective or point of view. We hope that our study gives them *nachas*. We are also grateful to the Yehuda Avner Chair in Religion and Politics at Bar-Ilan University for its assistance.

Charles S. Liebman
Elihu Katz

1

Beliefs, Observances and Social Interaction Among Israeli Jews

The Guttman Institute Report

SHLOMIT LEVY,
HANNA LEVINSOHN,
AND ELIHU KATZ

This is a study of religious observance, social interaction, and beliefs and values of Jews in Israel. Specifically, it explores the actual observance of mitzvot,[1] social and demographic differences in religious behavior, the role of religion in public life, Jewish identification, Jewish beliefs and values as well as general social values, and issues of interaction among social groups that differ in the character of their religious observance and ethnic origin.

The present research is the most comprehensive that has been conducted on the topic of religious behavior of Jews in Israel, with respect both to the representativeness of the sample population and the range of topics covered.

The Samples and Fieldwork

The research population consists of Jewish adults[2] twenty years of age and over, residing in all types of communities in Israel.[3] Two samples, each of which comprised about 1,200 respondents (1,195 and 1,204), were selected to ensure proper representation of the population and coverage of a broad range of issues. Different questionnaires were designed for the two samples, one focusing primarily on Jewish religious behavior and social values, and the other focusing primarily on social interaction among Jews. There were eighty-five common questions asked of both samples.

Fieldwork was conducted between October 20 and December 16, 1991. The respondents were interviewed in their homes by interviewers of the Louis Guttman Institute of Applied Social Research, who were especially trained for this purpose, under the supervision of the institute's field supervisors.

In addition, certain supplementary questions were asked of respondents in fieldwork from February 14 to March 22, 1993. These questions were designed to examine prevailing images of religious beliefs and behaviors so that they might be contrasted with the actual beliefs and behaviors revealed in the main study.

The following are selected findings described in the various chapters of the monograph, which is available upon request.[4] These Highlights, naturally, are not a substitute for the full monograph of 145 pages of analysis, plus bibliography and appendices, which include the complete text of the questionnaires and 149 pages of cross-tabulations. Like the monograph, these Highlights divide into: Observances, Social Interaction, Religion in Public Life, and Beliefs and Values.

OBSERVANCES

Fourteen percent of Israeli Jews define themselves as strictly observant, and 24 percent more say they are observant to a great extent. Approximately 40 percent report themselves somewhat observant, and about 20 percent totally nonobservant [Figure 1.1].

This distribution of religious observance has remained essentially unchanged over the past twenty-five years. It extends also to specific observances; for example, the proportion of synagogue attendance corresponds, by and large, to Guttman Institute observations since 1969.[5]

Nevertheless, when asked to estimate the proportion of Israelis that observe the religious tradition in the same way that you do, respondents at each level of religiosity overestimate the number of others who behave as they do. The majority are not well acquainted with the facts regarding religious observance of the Israeli public and at each level of religiosity overestimate the proportion of Israelis that observe the religious tradition in the same way that they do. In other words, regardless of the extent of their observance, Israelis feel well supported in their positions. This sense of support rises with the decline in observance; that is, the less observant feel that there are even more of them.

When asked about affiliation with a particular religious trend, nearly half reported no affiliation. Only in recent years has the Israeli public become aware of the existence of denominations in religious affiliation.[6]

Fig. 1.1. Self-Defined Religiosity (percent of respondents)

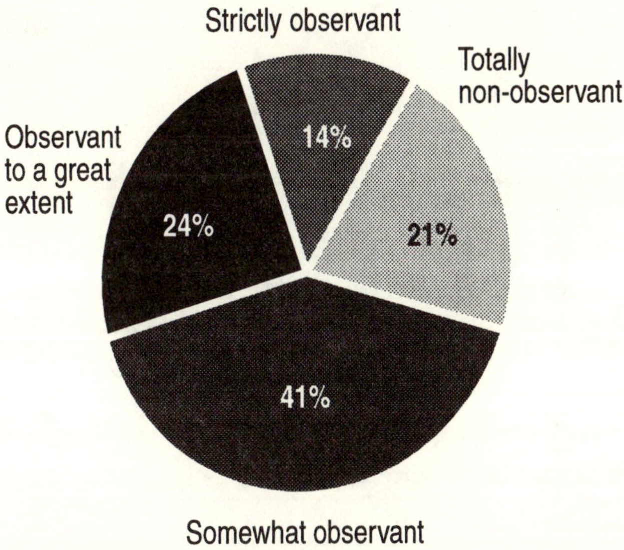

Observance By Background Traits

Self-defined religious observance does not vary much among different age groups, between men and women, and between old-time residents and newcomers [Figure 1.2].

Ethnic origin makes a difference, both in observance and in some attitudes. Those from Eastern ethnic backgrounds (Asian-African, known as Sephardim) are, in general, more sympathetic to religious tradition, while those from Western ethnic backgrounds (Ashkenazim) are, in general, less sympathetic. There is a high concentration (70%) of Jews of Eastern origin in the category, "observant to a great extent," just as there is a high concentration of Western Jews among the "totally nonobservant." Israelis born to Eastern parents are generally less observant than their Eastern-born parents, while the Western-born and their Israeli offspring do not differ with respect to religious observance [Figure 1.3].

Religious observance varies with levels of education, both general and religious. Respondents with low levels of general education are the most observant, while the nonobservant concentrate among the better educated, especially those with full university education [Figure 1.4].

Fig. 1.2. Religious Observance by Age (percent of respondents)

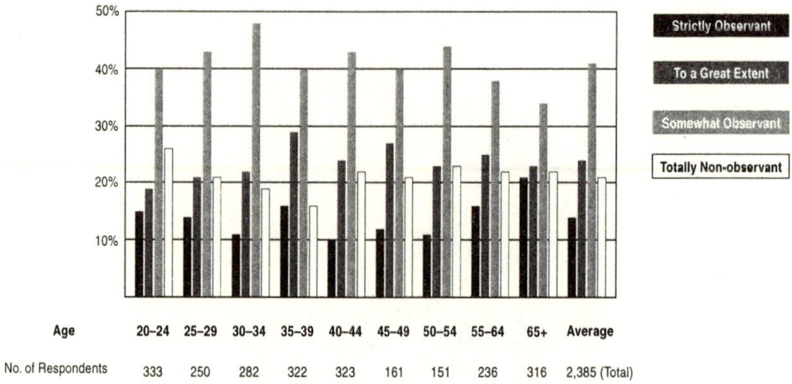

Fig. 1.3. Religious Observance by Ethnicity

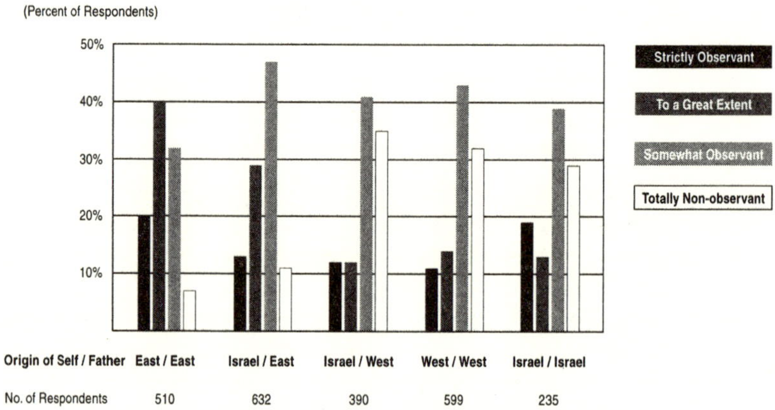

In a religious school setting, however, increased levels of education lead to increased observance. It should be noted that religious schooling refers to only 37 percent of the population, since 63 percent reported that they had no religious schooling.

Stability of Religious Observance and Attitudes Over TIme

In addition to the relative stability of religious observance over time and the striking similarity in the distribution of observance across age groups,

Fig. 1.4. Observance by Years of Schooling (general and religious)

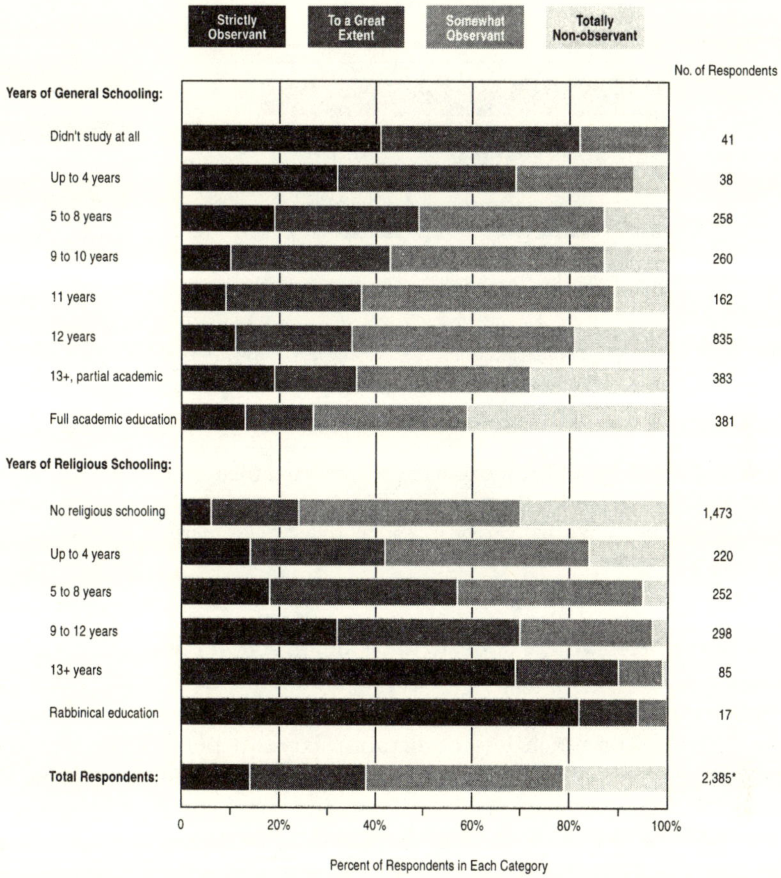

Note: "Total Respondents" do not sum to the separate categories, since there is some overlap.

respondents also report high correlations between own and parents' observance. Only 20 percent report themselves to be radically different from their parents in this respect [Figure 1.5].

Behaviorally speaking, then, it is fair to conclude that intergenerational continuity outweighs change, to which one should add that there is somewhat more movement toward lesser rather than greater observance. Thus, fewer respondents from strictly observant homes follow their parents as closely as those from totally nonobservant homes.

Fig. 1.5. Own Observance Relative to Parents' Observance*

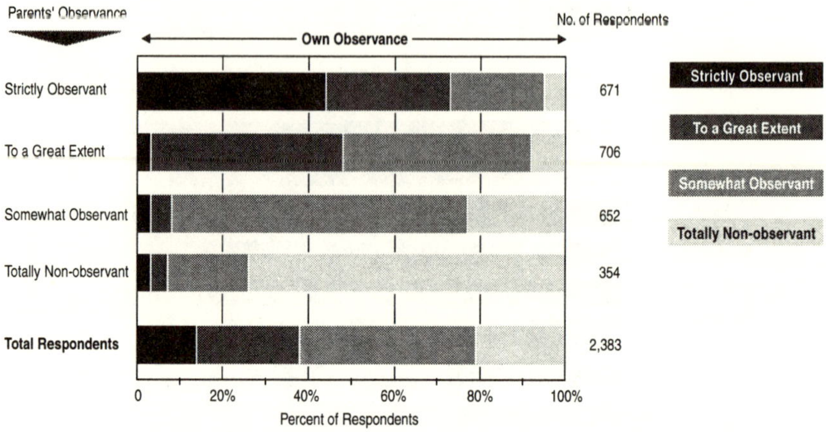

*For example, of the 671 respondents who reported their parents as "strictly observant," 44% reported themselves as equally observant, 29% consider themselves observant "to a great extent," 22% say they are "somewhat observant," and 6% say they are "totally observant."

Nevertheless, there appears to be an attraction toward increased religious observance. A third say that they would like to be somewhat more or much more observant, while only 5 percent say that they would want to be a little less or much less observant. Sixty-two percent say that they would want to remain the same. The more observant the respondent, the greater the wish to be even more observant. Interestingly, 10 percent of the totally nonobservant also express a wish to be somewhat more observant, and one half of the nonobservant would prefer their children to be somewhat observant rather than totally nonobservant.

Observing Shabbat

Until very recently, the Seventh Day—the Shabbat—was the whole of the Israeli weekend and had to double as a religious holiday replete with mitzvot, as well as to serve as a day off in the Western sense. For the past few years, Friday has been added to the weekend, and the five-day work week now encompasses about half the work force. As a day off, Friday also carries a burden of traditional duties having to do with preparation for the Sabbath. Public observance of Shabbat begins at sundown on Friday, when shops, most public transportation, and most places of entertainment are closed until after sundown on Saturday.

Table 1.1. Observance of Shabbat

	*(Percent of Respondents)**			
	Always	*Occasionally*	*Never*	*Total*
Prescriptive Mitzvot				
(Self or Others in Home)				
Light Shabbat candles	56	24	20	100
Have a special meal on Friday night	54	26	20	100
Light Shabbat candles with blessing	51	21	28	100
Recite Kiddush on Friday night	46	21	32	100
Recite Kiddush on Shabbat morning	28	16	56	100
Pray at synagogue on Friday night	24	22	53	100
Pray for the welfare of Israel	23	24	53	100
Pray at a synagogue on Shabbat morning	23	22	56	100
Recite Havdalah	23	17	60	100
Conduct Seuda Shlishit	21	17	62	100
Proscriptive Mitzvot				
Refrain from working in public	42	19	39	100
Refrain from working inside the home	37	21	43	100
Refrain from lighting fire	37	14	50	100
Refrain from going out to paid entertainment	28	14	59	100
Refrain from traveling	26	16	57	100
Refrain from turning on electricity/phone	22	14	64	100
Refrain from hosting persons who must travel in order to reach you	18	11	70	100
Refrain from being a guest at a nonobservant home	18	14	67	100

*May not total exactly, due to rounding.

Two thirds of the population mark the Shabbat as a special day by observing some mitzvot "always" or "occasionally," such as lighting candles or participating in a special meal on Friday night; almost half recite Kiddush [Table 1.1]. It should be noted that more households mark Shabbat by lighting candles than is generally perceived to be the case. Overall, 77 percent say that marking Shabbat in some way is a very important or important principle in their lives, including 39 percent of those who consider themselves "totally nonobservant."

Most Israelis desire that Friday night remain a quiet, home-centered evening (68%), and Friday-night rituals have far more adherents than

Shabbat-day observances. Only a minority (20–30%) never observe mitzvot such as candle-lighting, Kiddush, or a festive meal. Even some of the nonobservant mark Shabbat eve in a traditional manner (especially by lighting candles and having a special meal).

On the other hand, only a minority attend synagogue on Shabbat morning, and this fact is, by and large, more accurately perceived by the public than the more widespread Shabbat-eve practices.

Prescriptive mitzvot ('ase) have more adherents than proscriptive ones (lo ta'ase). Only 20–40 percent always observe Shabbat proscriptions against work, lighting fire, travel, paid entertainment, electricity, and telephone, while regular observance of prescriptive mitzvot ranges from 20–60 percent. Only about one-fourth (22–26%) always observe the prohibitions against turning electricity on or off and traveling on the Sabbath.

Scale analysis of the prescriptive mitzvot for Shabbat suggests that synagogue attendance on Shabbat morning is probably the first precept to be dropped en route to nonobservance, while lighting Shabbat candles is the durable commandment (last to go) [Table 1.2]. As for Shabbat proscriptions, the first departure from strict observance is using electricity. The next step is travel, followed in turn by paid entertainment, lighting a fire, and working inside the home, while the last to go is performing work in public.[7] Thus, working in public on Shabbat best defines nonobservance of proscriptive mitzvot [Table 1.3].

In short, the Israeli Shabbat is best characterized in terms of (1) in-home rituals of welcoming Shabbat, (2) refraining from work in public, and (3) relaxing and spending time with the family on a free day (not necessarily at home, except for the strictly observant).

With respect to Shabbat observance, the Western groups, both first and second generation, are more consistent than the Eastern groups in the sense of performing all or nothing.

However, nonobservant Western groups are more likely to perform certain rituals symbolically (e.g., by lighting candles without a blessing or eating a festive meal) rather than in the manner prescribed. Most of these are Westerners who define themselves as "somewhat observant." In the long run such symbolic patterns may be indicative of those who see themselves as traditional (masorti) in Israeli society. Compared to the Western groups, the less observant of Eastern origin tend to augment the symbolic candles or special meal with Kiddush.

A generational change is evident between Eastern-born respondents and their Israeli offspring. The latter are less observant and more similar in their religious behavior to other Israeli-born respondents. This applies especially to proscriptive mitzvot of Shabbat, such as refraining from travel, using electricity, and so on. Nevertheless, Israeli-born of Eastern origin are far more observant than their Western counterparts [Figure 1.3].

Table 1.2. Scale of Observance of Shabbat Prescriptive Mitzvot*
(For each mitzvah, 1 = always 2 = occasionally or never)

	Most Observant				*PROFILE*				*Least Observant*
	#1	*#2*	*#3*	*#4*	*#5*	*#6*	*#7*	*#8*	*#9*
Light Shabbat candles	1	1	1	1	1	1	1	1	2
Shabbat candles with blessing	1	1	1	1	1	1	1	2	2
Special meal on Friday night	1	1	1	1	1	1	2	2	2
Recite Kiddush on Shabat eve	1	1	1	1	1	2	2	2	2
Recite Havdalah	1	1	1	1	2	2	2	2	2
Pray on Shabbat eve	1	1	1	2	2	2	2	2	2
Pray on Shabbat morning	1	1	2	2	2	2	2	2	2
Pray for the State	1	2	2	2	2	2	2	2	2
Number of Respondents	365	57	14	56	264	72	140	51	785
Percent of Sample	15%	2%	1%	2%	11%	3%	6%	2%	33%

Total Number of Scalable Respondents: 1,804 (75% of sample)

*Profile #1, for example, refers to 15% of the sample, who "always" adhere to all eight mitzvot of which the scale consists. The scalogram encompasses 75% of all respondents; the remaining 25% have "deviant" profiles that do not fit the scale. Note that the predominant types are #1 (all), #9 (none), and #5 which consists of adherence to Shabbat eve practices only.

Table 1.3. Scale of Observance of Shabbat Proscriptive Mitzvot*
(For each mitzvah, 1 = always 2 = occasionally or never)

	Most Observant			*PROFILE*			*Least Observant*
	#1	*#2*	*#3*	*#4*	*#5*	*#6*	*#7*
Refrain from working in public	1	1	1	1	1	1	2
Refrain from working inside the home	1	1	1	1	1	2	2
Refrain from lighting fire	1	1	1	1	2	2	2
Refrain from paid entertainment	1	1	1	2	2	2	2
Refrain from traveling	1	1	2	2	2	2	2
Refrain from turning on electricity	1	2	2	2	2	2	2
Number of Respondents	446	54	58	104	73	105	1,189
Percent of Sample	19%	2%	2%	6%	3%	4%	50%

Total Number of Scalable Respondents: 2,029 (86% of sample)

*Profile #1, for example, refers to 19% of the sample, who "always" adhere to all six mitzvot of which the scale consists. The scalogram encompasses 86% of all respondents; the remaining 14% have "deviant" profiles that do not fit the scale. Comparing Table 2 and Table 3, note that 33% of respondents fall into the least observant Profile #9 in the Prescriptive scale, whereas 50% of respondents fall into the least observant Profile #7, in the Proscriptive Scale.

Keeping Kosher

Two-thirds report that they always eat kosher food at home. However, since kosher food is predominant in Israel, a more stringent indicator of kashrut is having separate utensils for meat and dairy foods. This practice is maintained by approximately one half of the population, who also wait an interval between eating meat and dairy foods. Even when abroad, half report observing kashrut always, but a higher proportion of respondents never observe kashrut abroad compared to never observing kashrut in Israel [Figure 1.6]. About 40 percent strictly observe all of the kashrut behaviors studied. Public perception of the observance of kashrut, however, underestimates the extent of its prevalence.

Scale analysis of kashrut practices confirms that the most vulnerable practice (first to go) is keeping separate utensils for meat and dairy foods, and most tenacious (last to go) is avoidance of explicitly nonkosher food [Table 1.4].

Quality of food (healthy, clean) is considered by the respondents no less important a reason for observing kashrut than observing the mitzvah for its own sake.

Celebrating Holidays

Holidays are more widely observed than Shabbat and most aspects of kashrut. Indeed, more than the other domains of observance, major holidays are a consensual domain, embracing both observant and nonobservant. This may be because holidays are special events that occur only once a year, compared to everyday or even weekly routines. Moreover, many of the holidays have a unifying power, national or existential, in addition to their more strictly religious definition. The public is well aware of the pervasive observance of major holidays.

Indeed, a wide consensus prevails with respect to the celebration of the major holidays, both religious/national (Passover, Hanukkah) and religious/existential (Yom Kippur): 78 percent always participate in a Passover Seder mostly of the traditional type [Figure 1.7]; 72 percent always light Hanukkah candles; on Yom Kippur 71 percent always fast and 69 percent join in at least some of the prayers.

Passover observance is very widespread. Even most (78%) of the totally nonobservant always or frequently participate in a Seder of some kind. Beyond celebration of the Seder, about 70 percent of Israeli Jews, including more than one fifth of the nonobservant, refrain from hametz on Passover.

Fewer respondents (36–38%) always observe Sukkot (having a kosher sukkah) or Purim (listening to the Megillah of Esther). Customs

Fig. 1.6. Kashrut Observance

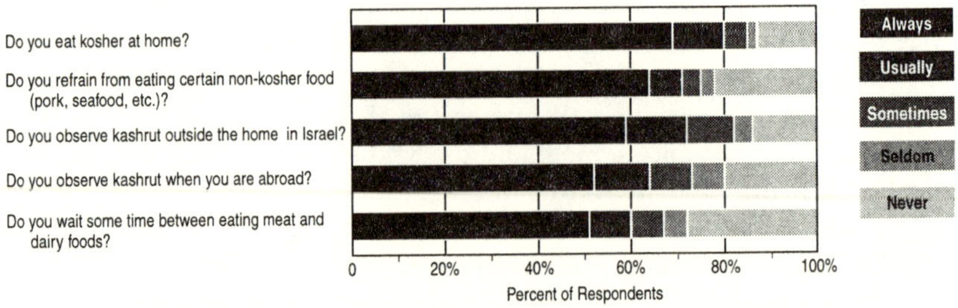

Fig. 1.7. Observance of Holidays

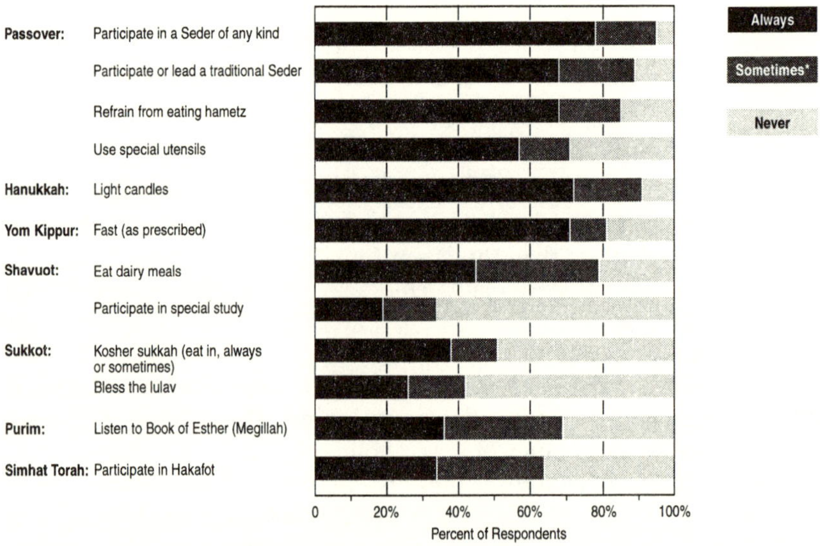

*Combines "Often," "Sometimes," and "Seldom."

relating to holidays, such as eating dairy foods on Shavuot, are often more widely observed than particular mitzvot, such as blessing the lulav on Sukkot.

Those of Eastern origin, whether born abroad or in Israel, tend to be more observant of the holidays than those of Western background. Noteworthy is the fact that lighting Hanukkah candles, participating in a Seder, and building a sukkah (not necessarily a kosher one) are more

Table 1.4. Scale of Kashrut Observance*
(For each item, 1 = always 2 = usually or sometimes 3 = seldom or never)

	PROFILE									
	#1	*#2*	*#3*	*#4*	*#5*	*#6*	*#7*	*#8*	*#9*	*#10*
Kosher food at home	1	1	1	1	2	2	2	2	3	3
Kosher food outside the home in Israel	1	1	1	2	2	2	2	2	2	3
Observe interval between meat and dairy foods	1	1	2	2	2	2	3	3	3	3
Refrain from nonkosher food (pork, seafood, etc.)	1	1	1	1	1	2	2	3	3	3
Separate utensils**	1	2	2	2	2	2	2	2	2	2
Number of Respondents	849	199	94	14	13	66	60	117	22	260
Percent of Sample	37%	8%	4%	1%	1%	3%	3%	5%	1%	11%

Total Number of Respondents: 1,694 (74% of sample)

*Profile #1, for example, refers to 37% of respondents in the sample, who "always" perform the five kashrut observances of which the scale consists. The scalogram encompasses 74% of all respondents; the remaining 26% have "deviant" profiles that do not fit the scale.

**Note that all items are scored at three levels, except "separate utensils" which is scored dichotomously (yes or no).

prevalent among Israeli-born respondents of Western origin than among their foreign-born parents. This is apparently a function of age and the presence of small children in the family, as well as an expression of the desire for Jewish continuity even among this relatively nonobservant sector of Israeli society.

Marking the Life Cycle

Over 80 percent feel it is important to them that life-cycle events be invested with a Jewish religious character: brit milah (92%); bar mitzvah (83%); wedding (87%); burial, shivah and kaddish for parents (88–91%). Only a small minority (4–7%) consider such ceremonies not at all important. Even a majority of the totally nonobservant consider it important to mark these turning points (birth, maturity, marriage, death) with Jewish ceremony.

Attending Synagogue and Prayer

A majority (about 60%) of Israeli Jews go to synagogue on high holidays or on special occasions during the year. About one-quarter attend regularly, most weekly. About one fifth report that they never go to synagogue. Present synagogue attendance of Israelis is very similar to that reported by the Guttman Institute a quarter of a century ago. Those born in the East attend synagogue most regularly.

Almost a fifth (22%) of men and 10 percent of women say that they pray daily. Asked, Do you know how to pray from a prayer book? 46 percent replied "not at all" or "only a little."

Other Observances: Mezuzah, Kippah, Tefillin, Mikveh

Four perennial observances exemplify the wide range of similarities and differences in religious behavior: mezuzah, kippah, tefillin, mikveh.

There is no difference at all between the strictly observant and the totally nonobservant in affixing a mezuzah. Virtually all respondents (98%) have a mezuzah on their front doors; the great majority have one on each of the required doors. Almost all of the nonobservant (92%) have a mezuzah at least on the entrance door of their homes, with 36 percent of them having a mezuzah on each of the doors traditionally required to have one. Seventy-four percent (46% definitely) believe that the mezuzah protects the home.

Wearing a kippah moves between the extremes of always (22%) and never (37%), with a plurality using a head-covering on a variety of special occasions. Among those who do wear a kippah, 62 percent use a knitted kippah, 30 percent a black kippah, and 8 percent use other types of head-covering.

Over half (56%) of married women never use a head-covering, compared to 13 percent who always do so. About a third (30%) use a head-covering occasionally, mainly when lighting Shabbat candles, when praying, and on a variety of special occasions.

Seventy-nine percent of Jewish men own tefillin, and about a quarter use them regularly. About half do not use them at all. For their part, 16 percent of women go to a mikveh regularly, and an additional 8 percent go occasionally. This proportion is unchanged since 1969, as is also noted with respect to certain other practices–synagogue attendance, for example.

Scope of Observance and Reasons for Nonobservance

If performance is taken as the measure of observing mitzvot regardless of intent or frequency, virtually all Israeli Jews are observant in some way. The ubiquitous mezuzah is an example. Additional evidence comes from scalogram analysis of ten observances from three different domains, Shabbat, kashrut, and holidays, which reveals that 93 percent of Israelis observe at least one of the relevant mitzvot from these domains. That is, only a small minority (7%) of respondents are objectively nonobservant in terms of these ten cross-domain precepts, compared to one fifth who describe themselves as "totally nonobservant." In other words, 93 percent of Israeli Jews perform at least one of these precepts, without necessarily considering themselves religious.

Respondents were asked to accept or reject four different explanations for nonobservance and to rate the importance of each as an explanation. The rank order ranges from 67 percent who said that people lack proper education to 38 percent who said that ethical people don't need mitzvot. In between, the explanations that mitzvot are hard to observe and mitzvot may be observed selectively were supported by about half of the respondents. For the strictly observant, the predominant explanation is that people lack proper education and, perhaps surprisingly, over half of the totally nonobservant agree. The nonobservant give more weight to ethical people don't need mitzvot. In sum, nonobservance in the eyes of both the strictly observant and the totally nonobservant is not so much a matter of difficulty of performance as it is a matter of different outlook, related to education and ethics. In fact, about half of the nonobservant agree with all four of the explanations offered for nonobservance [Table 1.5].

Table 1.5. Reasons for Nonobservance
(Percent of Respondents Replying "Very Important" or "Important")

	Self-Defined Religiosity				
	Strictly Observant	*Observant to a Great Extent*	*Somewhat Observant*	*Not at all Observant*	*Total*
"People lack proper education"	76	77	66	52	67
"Selective observance is adequate"	48	64	58	42	55
"It is difficult to observe"	45	56	58	46	53
"Ethical people don't need mitzvot"	24	36	39	58	38

SOCIAL INTERACTION

Intergroup Relations: Attitudes

Relations among Jews of different religious backgrounds and commitments to observance are considered much more problematic by Israelis than interethnic relations. Although there are ups and downs in the assessment of the quality of these relations, ethnicity has been judged the less problematic for many years [Figure 1.8].

The study substantiates that ethnic background hardly segregates Israeli society today. Two thirds think that relations between Ashkenazim and Sephardim are good. Relations of veteran Israelis with Ethiopian and Russian newcomers are also rated good by two-thirds of the population.

By contrast, less than one third regard relations between religious and nonreligious as good [Figure 1.9]. It is the less observant (with a preponderance of the Western-born and their offspring, and the higher educated) who are least positive in their assessment.

Although respondents place somewhat more blame for poor relations at the door of the religious, the predominant image is that in both groups some do and some don't show respect and acceptance of the other group. The nonobservant accuse the observant of disrespect, more than the other way around.

Stereotypes of the quality of intergroup relations along religious lines are more problematic [Figure 1.10] than the actual attitudes of respondents speaking for themselves. There appears to be high readiness of

Fig. 1.8. Changes Over Time in Feelings of Social Solidarity, 1977–1990

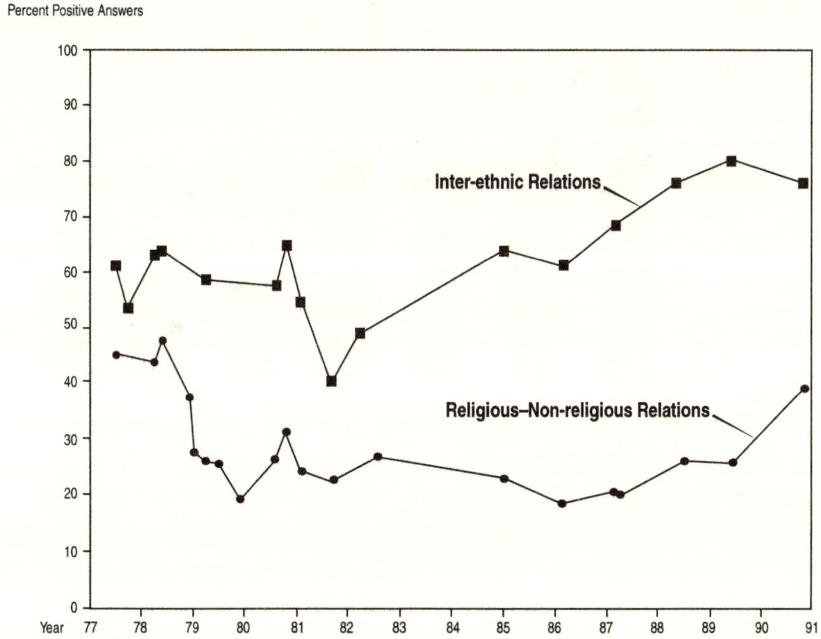

Adapted from: Levy, Shlomit (1992): *Social Problem Indicators for Israel: State and Society*. Jerusalem: The Louis Guttman Israel Institute of Applied Social Research.

mutual acceptance of both ethnic and religious differences, except that religious differences are perceived to be something of a barrier in the most intimate relationships, especially marriage.

On a personal level, in other words, attitudes of respondents to a variety of groups, including the religious and nonreligious, are reported as largely nonproblematic. Three-fourths of Israelis assert that it would be acceptable for people of different religious perspectives to live in their neighborhoods. But they view with equal antipathy those groups on the extreme ends of the religious spectrum, the Haredim and the antireligious.

When it comes to personal attitudes toward the extreme groups of Haredim and antireligious, the full force of the religiosity variable comes into play: the more observant the respondent, the more he/she appreciates the Haredim and the less he/she appreciates the antireligious. The assessment of the Haredim by the nonobservant, and the antireligious by the observant, is not only negative, it borders on very strong rejection.

Fig. 1.9. Assessment of Intergroup Relations (Percent of Respondents Replying "Very Good" and "Pretty Good")

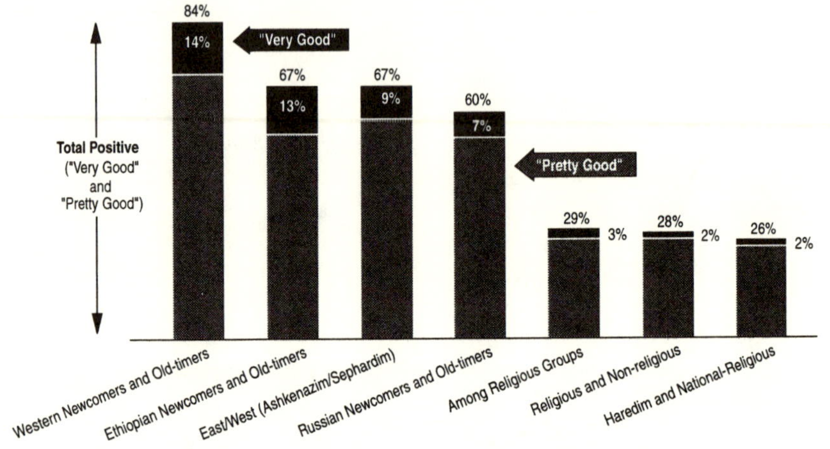

Fig. 1.10. Personal Attitudes toward Various Groups (Percent of Respondents Replying "Very Positive" and "Positive")

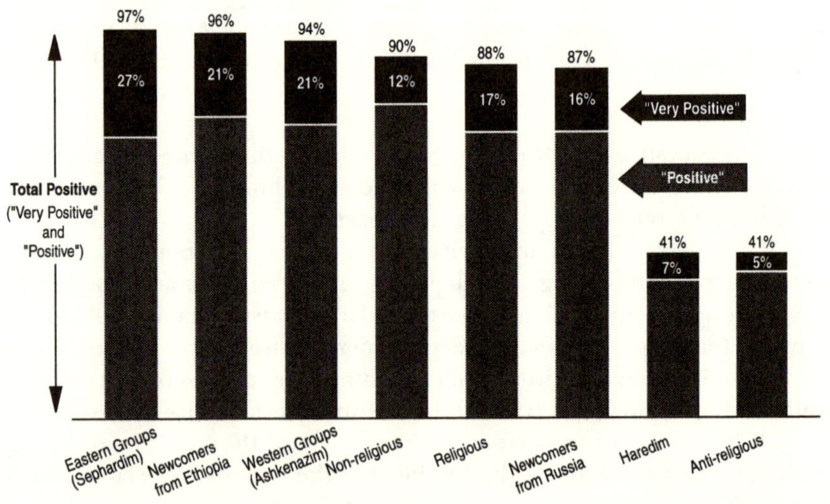

Fig. 1.11. Acceptance of Child's Marriage to "Other" (Percent of Respondents Replying Positively*)

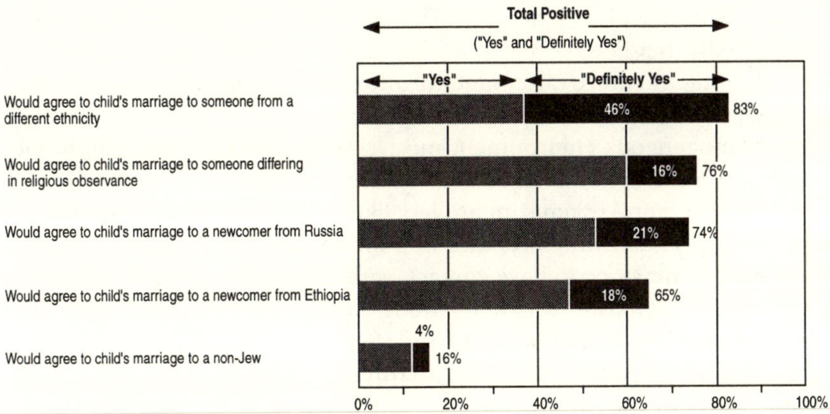

*Percentages based on 90% of the respondents who answered the question.

The more impersonal the social setting, the greater is the acceptance and the actual presence of people who differ in religious observance.

Even when close family is considered, only a minority are opposed to the marriage of their children to someone different in ethnicity (17%) or religious observance (24%). (In contrast, there is virtual unanimity in opposition to a child's marriage to a non-Jew.) However, the proportion who definitely agree to interethnic marriage is far higher (46%) than in the case of marriage involving difference in the degree of religious observance (16%) [Figure 1.11]. The likelihood of success of a marriage in which one spouse is religious and the other is not is judged to be considerably lower than the likelihood of success attributed to interethnic marriage.

Intergroup Relations: Interaction

In the course of their daily lives, three quarters of the population report that they occasionally or frequently interact with people who differ from them in terms of religious observance.

In general, it is the *less* religious respondents, those who describe themselves as "totally nonobservant" or "somewhat observant," who have least contact with people who differ from themselves in observance. The ostensible closure of the strictly observant is expressed only in those social settings that specify continuity of religious identity, namely, children's education and close family. In this sense, the strictly observant are similar to the totally nonobservant. Thus, the more observant prefer more homogeneous environments but actually have less homogeneous environments. Or, to put it otherwise, the more observant say they are less ready for interaction with religiously different others but actually have more contact with them.

Among the more observant, the most self-segregated group is the Israeli-born generation of Western parentage, whose expressed preference for a homogeneous environment most closely coincides with the homogeneity of their actual interactions. In other words, the younger generation of observant Ashkenazim are less likely than their observant parents and less likely than the observant in both generations of Eastern ethnicity to want contact, or to have contact, with others who are different from themselves religiously, whether among family, friends, neighbors, children's classmates, or fellow workers.

The nonobservant of Western ethnicity differ from their observant counterparts in that they are more likely to agree to the presence of religiously different others but, in fact, have less contact with them.

On the frequent occasions when persons of different degrees of religiosity do meet, more than half report that they discuss religious issues and lifestyle differences between the observant and the nonobservant. But in response to the question: Does meeting with people who are different from you in religious observance influence your attitude toward them? 84 percent say that it does not, either positively or negatively. Still, when influence does take place, it is judged more positive (11%) than negative (4%).

Helping Others (Man-to-Man Mitzvot)

Extending help to others, in time and money, counts as a mitzvah, and the large majority of Israelis (75%) are aware that Judaism attributes importance to assisting those in need. About a fifth of Israeli Jews report that they engage in voluntary public work on a regular basis; 43 percent say they are not involved at all. Twenty-seven percent visit sick persons who are neither family nor friends in hospitals and other mitzvah situations. Many fewer are systematically helping new immigrants, families in distress, or serving in the Civil Guard, although many express readiness to do so if asked.

Contributing money to charity is much more pervasive than contributing time. A high proportion do so often or sometimes.

Devoting time, as well as contributing money to others, is strongly associated with self-defined religiosity. In general, the higher the level of observance, the greater the level of community service. The more the need is defined in religious terms, the greater the gap between the observant and the nonobservant.

Fig. 1.12. State and Religion (percent of respondents)

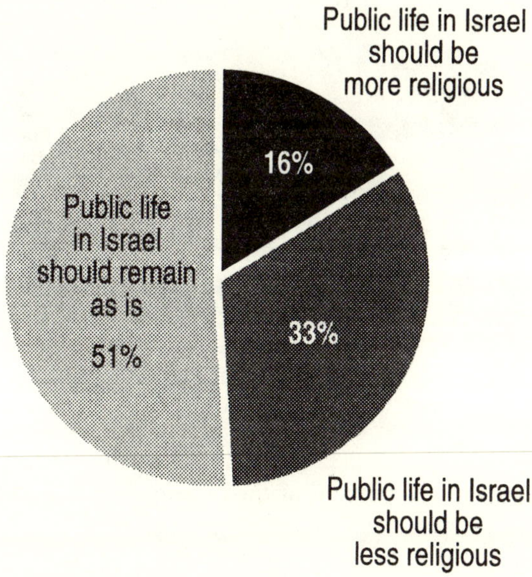

Religion in Public Life

From the work of the Guttman Institute since the 1960s, we know that almost half of Israeli Jews believe it to be a concern of government that public life comply with Jewish religious tradition. However, the majority of respondents since the mid-1970s have been critical of the present relationship between state and religion. When asked, In your opinion, how successful is the present integration of religion and state in Israel? 60–75 percent of respondents in the last fifteen years have held the opinion that the present situation is unsatisfactory in this respect. The less the religious observance, the lower the positive assessment; the proportion of approval drops from 50 percent among the strictly observant to 10 percent among the not at all observant.

In answer to a related question, half of the respondents think that public life in the state of Israel should remain as is, neither more nor less religious. Those who think that change is required are more likely to say that public life should be less religious (33%) than more religious (16%) [Figure 1.12]. Each of the two extreme groups, strictly observant and totally nonobservant, pulls in its own direction.

When a more legalistic question is put to respondents about the status quo that governs the place of religion in Israel, two thirds of respondents

Fig. 1.13. Attitudes toward Separation of State and Religion and Instituting Civil Marriage (percent of respondents)

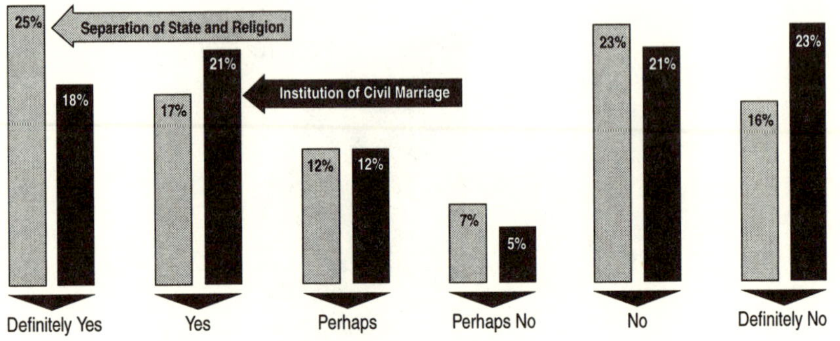

support change. These include, for different reasons, well over half of the strictly observant and 78 percent of the nonobservant. Forty-two percent favor separation of state and religion [Figure 1.13].

Four in ten Israeli Jews favor instituting civil marriage (18% definitely yes), and they concentrate among the nonobservant of Western origin. An equal number oppose it. If instituted, however, over half of the respondents believe that they would not utilize it themselves, and only 16 percent claim that they would definitely choose this kind of marriage.

About two thirds of the population (one third definitely and one third moderately) are in favor of liberalization of rules governing the opening of theaters and public transportation on Friday night.

Three fourths express strong support for kosher food in public institutions and in the army, and an additional 17 percent agree that perhaps it should be so. Most object, however, to making kosher licenses contingent on other forms of observance.

As noted earlier, the Hebrew equivalents of Conservative and Reform denominations are not well recognized by Israelis.[8] Nevertheless, the study attempted to ask whether Conservative and Reform movements should be given status equal to that of the Orthodox. Findings suggest that a majority would favor such a change. However, when asked if there were a Conservative or Reform synagogue in your neighborhood, how often do you think you would attend, 55 percent said never, as compared to only 19 percent of Israelis who never attend synagogue.

Army Service

Israeli Jews affirm that service in the Army is a fundamental expression of commitment to society. As a result, the conscription of yeshivah stu-

Fig. 1.14. Army Service for Yeshivah Students and Religious Girls (percent of respondents)

dents and religious girls is another of the most controversial topics. A great majority of the public does not approve of the exemption from army service given to male yeshivah students and to religious girls; 90 percent support conscription of yeshivah students, and 70 percent support conscription of religious girls [Figure 1.14]. Even a majority of the strictly observant (59%) support recruitment of yeshivah students, but only 23 percent of them support recruitment of religious girls; and an additional 22 percent favor an alternate form of national service [Table 1.6].

In all religiosity groupings, the drafting of yeshivah students is supported more than the drafting of religious girls.

The Rabbinate

About three quarters do not consult a rabbi either on personal matters or on matters of observance. Regular consultation on personal matters is much more characteristic of strictly observant respondents than of the other religiosity groups. Consulting always or often is reported by 38 percent of the strictly observant, as against 11 percent of the mostly observant, and none of the somewhat and the nonobservant.

Eastern-born respondents tend more than any other ethnic group to consult a rabbi on both personal matters (38%) and questions of observance (39%). Among their Israeli offspring the inclination to consult a rabbi is more on matters of observance than on personal matters (34% versus 24%). A similar trend, but with smaller differences, prevails among the Western-born and their Israeli offspring.

Although they would like it to be otherwise, Israeli Jews view the Rabbinate as ritual functionaries who neither address themselves to current societal problems nor provide guidance in people's personal lives. Almost two thirds think that the official Rabbinate should address itself

Table 1.6. Attitudes toward Army Service by Religious Observance (Percent of Responses)

	Self-Defined Religiosity				
	Strictly Observant	*To a Great Extent*	*Somewhat Observant*	*Totally Nonobservant*	*Total*
Are you for, or against, the drafting of yeshivah students into the army?					
Definitely for	30%	47%	60%	69%	55%
For	29	43	36	29	35
Opposed	16	7	4	2	6
Strongly opposed	25	3	0	0	4
Total	100%	100%	100%	100%	100%
Number of respondents	158	276	509	247	1,190
Are you for, or against, the drafting of religious girls into the army?					
Definitely for	11%	26%	44%	53%	37%
For	12	34	36	36	33
Opposed	16	20	11	4	12
Strongly opposed	39	7	2	1	8
Only national service	22	13	7	6	10
Total	100%	100%	100%	100%	100%
Number of respondents	161	278	510	245	1,194

Fig. 1.15. Israelis' Belief in Principles of the Jewish Faith (percent of responses)

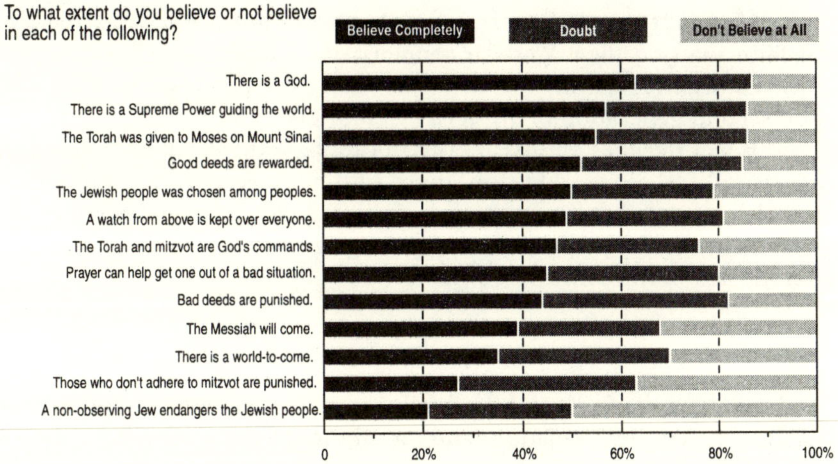

to current problems, but only 30 percent think that the Rabbinate is now successfully doing so. Positive responses increase with the increase in religious observance.

BELIEFS AND VALUES

Principles of Faith

Sixty percent of respondents firmly believe in the existence of God or a supreme power that guides the world [Figure 1.15]. Even among the nonobservant, one fifth hold these beliefs.

About half of Israeli Jews firmly believe the Torah was given to Moses on Mt. Sinai, that Divine Providence watches over everyone, that the Torah and mitzvot are God's commands, and that good deeds are rewarded. Over 40 percent believe that bad deeds are punished, and a smaller number (27%) believe that those who do not observe mitzvot will be punished. More than a third believe in a world-to-come and in the coming of the Messiah.

These principles of faith are very highly intercorrelated, that is, one belief leads to another. Multivariate analysis reveals that the same structure of interrelations among beliefs holds, by and large, across religious and ethnic groups.

The more observant the respondents, the more they report belief in each of the principles. However, the strictly observant and the totally nonobservant are at polar ends with respect to only two main issues: the world-to-come, including the coming of the Messiah, and the origin of mitzvot (as God's command, as well as punishment for nonobservance).

More of those of Eastern ethnicity believe in each of the principles of faith than do their Western counterparts. The second generation of Eastern origin is slightly less believing than their parents, while the first and second generation of Western origin do not differ at all.

Belief declines with years of education: without taking account of specifically religious education, those with more years of schooling tend to believe somewhat less in the principles of faith. But belief is not correlated with age; respondents of different age groups are similar in their belief in each of the principles of faith.

General and Jewish Values

To honor parents and to raise a family are at the top of the ranking of values for the entire population (and for all the religious groupings who report at least some observance). Among the nonobservant, values of self-fulfillment, such as to be at peace with oneself, and interpersonal values stemming from general ethics rank higher than to honor parents and to raise a family. However, the vast majority among the nonobservant, as well as among respondents from the other religious groupings, also regards these precepts as very important guiding principles.

Multivariate analysis of the interrelations among Jewish values (importance) and performance (observance) suggests that the public, in general, acts to a great extent in accordance with its values.

By calculating the distance among the Jewish values, Smallest Space Analysis (SSA) reveals a circular structure consisting of wedges for each domain, with a common origin in the value of belongingness (important to feel part of the Jewish people) [Figure 1.16]. The right side of the circle arrays the importance attributed to the mitzvot between Man-and-God in a consecutive series consisting of life-cycle rituals, mitzvot and beliefs, Torah study, and marking Shabbat and holidays. The left side groups family values, self-fulfillment, belongingness, and mitzvot between Man-and-Man.

The SSA diagram also maps the optimal location of each of the four types of self-defined religiosity by superimposing them on the structure of Jewish values in Figure 1.16. This makes it possible to identify those values most closely associated with each level of observance. It is as if those who define themselves as "strictly observant" want to be characterized as having one foot in Torah studies and another foot in mitzvot. The "mostly observant" may be found on the borderline between valuing life-cycle rituals and valuing Man-to-God mitzvot. The

Fig. 1.16. The Circular Structure of Jewish Values and the Loci of Self-Defined Observance (SSA-I)

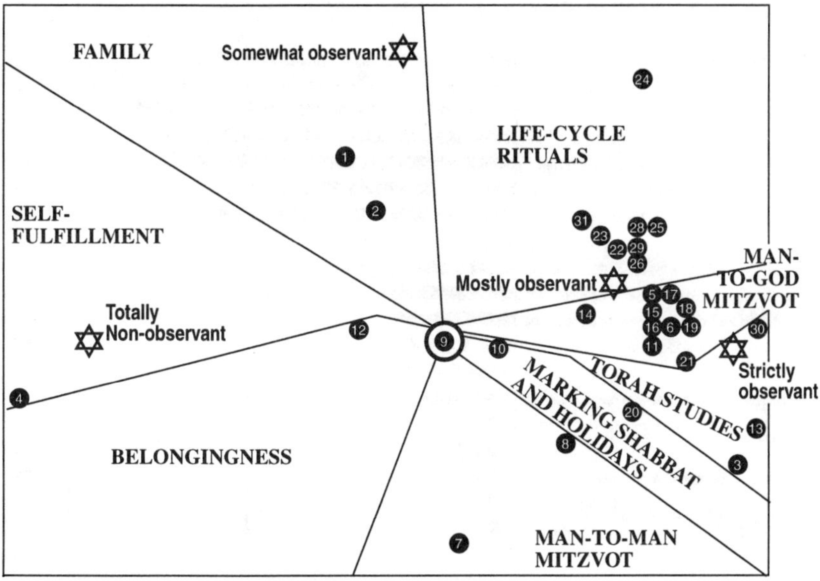

LEGEND

Family:
1-To raise a family
2-To honor parents

Life-Cycle Rituals:
22-Brit Milah
23-Bar Mitzvah in some way
24-Bat Mitzvah
25-Religious Bar Mitzvah
26-Religious wedding
27-Religious burial
28-Sit Shivah
29-Kaddish
31-Not marry non-Jew

Man-to-God Mitzvot:
5-Believe in God
6-Observe Mitzvot
11-Traditional Holidays
14-Passover Seder
15-Yom Kippur fast
16-Soul-searching on Yom Kippur
17-Kashrut outside home
19-Religious Shabbat
21-Observe as parents

Torah Studies:
3-Study Bible
13-Study Talmud
30-Study Torah

Marking Shabbat and Holidays:
10-Mark Holidays in some way
20-Mark Shabbat in some way

Belongingness:
9-Feeling part of the Jewish people
12-Live in Israel

Self-fulfillment:
4-At peace with oneself

Man-to-Man Mitzvot:
7-Help needy
8-Contribute to charity

"somewhat observant" are located in the area of family values, between the domains of family and life-cycle rituals. The "totally nonobservant" fall in the value area of self-fulfillment, concerned with being at peace with oneself and, at the same time, attributing importance to belonging to the Jewish people.

Fig. 1.17. Ranking Jewish Values by the "Totally Nonobservant"

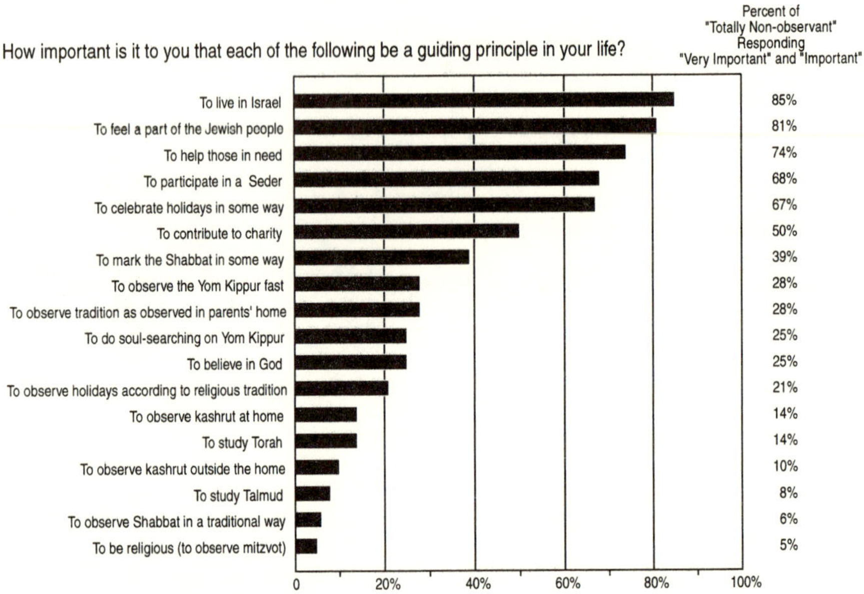

Adherence to general ethical values, as well as to values implying belongingness to the Jewish people, and attributing importance to Jewish holidays and Jewish life-cycle ceremonies are considered as guiding principles across all sectors of society. Values related to observance of mitzvot are not shared across sectors (except for a few mitzvot governing interpersonal relations) [Figure 1.17] and are guiding principles only in the eyes of the observant.

Factors that Motivate Jewish Identification

Living in Israel, upbringing at home, and observances related to the life cycle, Shabbat, and holidays, are all viewed as factors that influence the feelings of Israelis that they are part of the Jewish people.

At the top of a list of factors that motivate Jewish identification, respondents name the Zionist experience (the history of Israel in recent times, the respondent's living in Israel) and parental influence [Table 1.7]. Current history is followed by celebrating national/religious holidays (Passover Seder and Hanukkah), family gathering on

Table 1.7. Motivating Factors in Jewish Identification

	Assessment of Influence		
	Subjective (Percent Replying)		*Objective*
To what extent does each of the following influence your feeling that you are part of the Jewish people?	*"Influences a Lot" and "Influences"*	*"Influences a Lot"*	*Correlation with Jewish Identification**
The establishment of Israel	95	68	.55
Living in Israel	94	67	.59
Upbringing in parents' home	89	56	.59
The history of Jewish settlement in Israel	84	36	.51
Participating in a Passover Seder	82	50	.57
Celebrating Hanukkah	82	46	.60
Being with family on Shabbat or Holidays	81	46	.60
Participating in a Brit Milah ceremony	80	47	.59
To assist fellow Jews in need	78	38	.54
Saying/hearing Kaddish/Yizkor	75	45	.56
The Jewish religion	75	44	.58
Special meals on Shabbat and holidays	75	40	.52
Celebrating Purim	73	38	.54
Jewish history of over 3,000 years	72	30	.45
"Kol Nidrei" prayer	67	42	.50
Lighting Shabbat candles	67	16	.53

*Feeling part of the Jewish people.

Shabbat and participating in life-cycle ceremonies such as Brit Milah and Kaddish. At the bottom of the list but still affirmed by two thirds to three quarters of respondents are specific religious observances, the Jewish religion, and ancient history. These self-assessments imply that the Jewish tradition motivates Jewish identification through holidays and certain life-cycle rituals more than through specific religious observances. This result coincides with results reported earlier on observances and values.

An objective analysis correlating the importance attributed to each motivating factor of Jewish identification with the respondents' overall sense of belonging to the Jewish people, suggests that religious and national factors may have almost equal influence after all. In other words, the objective ranking differs from the subjective ranking in that the former gives equal weight to the religious and national factors, while the latter places more emphasis on recent national events as a motivator of Jewish identification than on the Jewish religious tradition.

Earlier research revealed that a tie to Israel alone (recent history), when not accompanied by others of the motivating factors, may actually be associated with a lower level of Jewish identification.[9] This proposition finds support in the rather lower feeling of belongingness to the Jewish people expressed by the totally nonobservant in the present study.

It is noteworthy that 84 percent of the respondents report visiting the Western Wall: 11 percent often, 35 percent sometimes, and 35 percent seldom. The Wall is considered a visible symbol of the continuity of history and heritage.

Israel and the Diaspora

Israelis overwhelmingly take pride in being Jewish (94%) and believe it is important to live in Israel (93%). They also feel a connectedness to fellow Jews around the world (96%). The observant exceed the nonobservant not only in this aspect of Jewish peoplehood but, interestingly, also in answer to the question, Do you consider yourself a Zionist? Sixty percent of the strictly observant answered definitely yes compared to 40 percent of the nonobservant.

Three-fourths of Israelis believe that Jews in Israel and Jews in the Diaspora share a common fate. More than half believe the Jews are a chosen people. About two thirds agree to the proposition that Israel would not be able to survive without a strong relationship with the Jewish people worldwide. A somewhat larger majority agree to the reciprocal proposition that the Jewish people in the Diaspora would not be able to survive without the existence of the State of Israel. In other words, the percentage of respondents who believe that the survival of Diaspora Jewry is dependent on the existence of the state of Israel is somewhat higher than those who believe that the existence of the state is dependent on a strong relationship with Diaspora Jewry.

It is of interest to note that the reverse situation prevailed in 1975, when more respondents thought that Israel could not survive without a strong relationship with the Jewish Diaspora than those who agreed to the reciprocal proposition, that the Jewish people in the Diaspora could not survive without Israel. It appears that during the past eighteen years Israelis have gained more confidence in the independence of the state and its centrality for the Jewish people. These views are shared across all sectors of the population. In effect, most Israeli Jews see the state of Israel as the state of the Jewish people as a whole, essential for the survival of Jews in the Diaspora but also dependent upon them.

SUMMARY

In sum, the study finds that there are certain traditional attitudes, values, and practices that embrace a vast majority of Israeli Jews: the commitment to Jewish continuity, the celebration of major holidays, the performance of life-cycle rituals. Certain practices, such as marking the Shabbat eve, encompass about two-thirds of the population, by virtue of the fact that the large group of somewhat observant augments the ranks of the strictly and mostly observant. Israeli Jews are strongly committed to the continuing Jewish character of their society, even while they are selective in the forms of their observance. They believe that public life should respect the tradition but are critical of the status quo governing state and religion.

While there is a sense of tension in the relations between groups of different degrees of religiosity and an antipathy to the ultra-Orthodox and the antireligious, the study strongly suggests that the rhetoric of secular and religious polarization generally used to characterize Israeli society is misleading from a behavioral point of view. It would be more accurate to say that Israeli society has a strong traditional bent and, as far as religious practice is concerned, that there is a continuum from the strictly observant to the nonobservant rather than a great divide between a religious minority and a secular majority.

NOTES

1. A glossary of Hebrew terminology appears at the end of this chapter.
2. Only Hebrew-speaking persons were interviewed.

3. Excluding kibbutzim; data were gathered utilizing the same questionnaires on a sample of the settlers in Gaza, Golan, Judea, and Samaria. Although the data on the settlers are not incorporated here, they are available upon request.

4. Shlomit Levy, Hanna Levinsohn, Elihu Katz, "Beliefs, Observances and Social Interaction Among Israeli Jews," Jerusalem: The Louis Guttman Israel Institute of Applied Social Research, 1993. The present chapter is a somewhat edited version of "Highlights from the Guttman Institute Report," distributed by the AVI CHAI Foundation and the Guttman Institute. We wish to acknowledge the guidance of Professor Jacob Katz, Professor Zecharia Dor-Shav, and Dr. Peri Kedem in the design of the study.

5. For purposes of comparison over time, we allude at various points to the Continuing Survey of The Guttman Institute, founded in 1967; Shlomit Levy, *Social Problem Indicators for Israel: State and Society*, Jerusalem: Louis Guttman Israel Institute of Applied Social Research, 1992 (Hebrew); Hanna Levinsohn, *Attitudes of the Israeli Public on Issues of Religion and Jewish Tradition*, Jerusalem: Louis Guttman Israel Institute of Applied Social Research, 1990 (Hebrew); and Yehuda Ben-Meir and Peri Kedem, "A Measure of Religiosity for the Jewish Population of Israel," *Megamot* 24 (3), 1979, pp. 353–62 (Hebrew).

6. The Hebrew equivalents of Conservative and Reform denominations are not well recognized by Israelis. The word *masorti*, in particular, is ambiguous and probably does not specifically connote Conservative Judaism. "The term *Haredi* (pl. *Haredim*) literally means 'fearful' and recalls the Scriptural reference to the righteous person who fears the word of God. In the nineteenth century, the term was a synonym for an Orthodox Jew. Today, in Israel, Orthodox Jews are divided into Religious-Zionists, also called National-Religious, and Haredim, whom the press refers to as 'ultra-Orthodox.' Haredim are generally characterized by their strict interpretation of Jewish law, their rejection of secular culture, and their ambivalent attitude toward the Jewish State, which in the case of some Haredim is hostile" (from Charles S. Liebman, ed., *Religious and Secular*, Keter Publishing House/AVI CHAI, 1991.) Lines between Haredim and National-Religious are not as neatly drawn as most believe. In fact, the present study shows that more Haredim are likely to define themselves as "Zionist" than as "non-Zionist." The findings, however, may also be affected by the lower level of respondent cooperation within the Haredi sector.

7. Work in public means doing work outside the home that others will notice, such as gardening, hanging laundry, and so on.

8. See note 6 for a discussion of the difficulties involved in wording such questions.

9. See the doctoral thesis of Shlomit Levy, "Components of the Jewish Identity as Motivators for Jewish Identification among Jewish Youth and Adults in Israel 1967–1982," Jerusalem: Hebrew University, 1985 (Hebrew, with Abstract and Table of Contents in English).

GLOSSARY

Ashkenazi (pl. Ashkenazim)

Jews of European origin, "Ashkenaz" being a Biblical geographical term that was later applied to Germany and the regions of Jewish settlement north of the Roman Empire.

Bar/Bat Mitzvah

Literally, "son/daughter of the commandment," referring to coming-of-age with regard to adult responsibilities for observance of mitzvot (13 for a boy, 12 for a girl). In common parlance, the term is used to describe the celebration of reaching this stage of life.

Brit Milah

Ritual circumcision performed on male infants on the eighth day after birth, representing entry into the Biblical covenant between Abraham and God.

Haggadah

Ritual text of the Passover Seder ceremony that is read at home celebrations on the first night of the holiday.

Hakafot

Festive processions around the synagogue with the Torah scrolls, held on the holiday of Simhat Torah.

Hametz

Leavened grain products that are prohibited during the Festival of Passover.

Hanukkah

Eight-day holiday commemorating the rededication of the Temple in Jerusalem by the Maccabees in the year 165 B.C.E. and marking the overthrow of Hellenist rule in Israel. Observed by home candle-lighting ceremonies with an eight-branched candelabrum.

Havdalah

Ceremony that indicates the conclusion of the Sabbath, using the symbols of wine, spices, and a multiwicked candle.

Kaddish

Prayer in the Aramaic language that calls upon the community to sanctify God's Name, requiring a minyan for recitation. The prayer is recited at every daily service, and by mourners, for example, for 11 months following the death of a parent, and yearly on the anniversary of the parent's death.

Kashrut (Kosher)

Jewish dietary laws, specifying permitted and forbidden foods, separation of meat and dairy products, etc.

Kibbutz (pl. Kibbutzim)

Cooperative settlements in Israel.

Kiddush

Sanctification of Shabbat and other holidays through a blessing recited over wine at night and the following day.

Kippah (pl. Kippot)

A skullcap, worn by males out of reverence for God and as a form of religious identity.

Kol Nidrei

Prayer for the annulment of vows, recited on the eve of Yom Kippur; used also to refer to the Yom Kippur evening service.

Lulav

A palm branch, combined with other species of plants, for use during holiday prayers on the Festival of Sukkot.

Ma'ariv

Evening prayer service (also known as *Arvit*).

Masorti

Traditional Jew, as opposed to "secular" or "religious" Jew in contemporary Israeli parlance. The term has also been adopted in Israel by the Movement for Conservative Judaism.

Megillah of Esther

Scroll containing the Biblical Book of Esther, read in the synagogue on the holiday of Purim.

Mezuzah

Parchment containing verses *(Shema Yisrael)* from the Biblical book of Deuteronomy, encased in a protective box and attached to the doorposts of Jewish homes, offices, and institutions.

Mikveh

A ritual bath, primarily used by married women for immersion at the conclusion of the menstrual cycle, prior to resumption of marital relations.

Mincha

Afternoon prayer service.

Minyan

Quorum of ten adult males (over the age of 13), required for public prayer services.

Mitzvah (pl. Mitzvot)

Biblical or rabbinic commandment, categorized as prescriptive (*'aseh*—positive) or proscriptive (*lo ta'aseh*—negative).

Purim

Holiday commemorating the Jews' salvation from enemies in ancient Persia who sought to destroy them, as related in the Biblical Book of Esther.

Seder

Literally, "Order;" sacrosanct service celebrating the Exodus from Egypt, held as a home ceremony over a meal on the first night of Passover.

Sephardi (pl. Sephardim)

Jews of Spanish and Portuguese origin who were expelled from the Iberian Peninsula in the late fifteenth and early sixteenth centuries and settled throughout the Mediterranean region, including North Africa.

Seudah Shlishit

Literally, "The Third Meal"; held between the afternoon and evening (concluding) services of Shabbat, in order to fulfill the requirement of feasting three times on this holy day.

Shabbat

The seventh day; biblically ordained day of rest extending from sunset on Friday until after sunset on Saturday.

Shacharit

Morning prayer service.

Shavuot

Festival commemorating the giving of the Ten Commandments on Mount Sinai and celebrating the "first fruits" of the spring harvest. The holiday occurs 50 days after Passover.

Shivah

Literally, "seven;" the week of mourning at home observed by those who have lost an immediate relative (parent, child, sibling, or spouse.) It is a mitzvah for condolence calls to be made during this period.

Shmitah

Literally, "release;" the Sabbatical year, referring to the seventh year in every seven-year cycle in which, according to Biblical command, debts are forgiven and the land is left fallow.

Simchat Torah

Literally, "the rejoicing of the law;" the concluding day of the Sukkot festival season on which the annual reading of the entire Torah is completed and immediately started anew, amid great festivities.

Sukkah

A booth erected as a temporary outdoor home for meals and dwelling during the festival of Sukkot, in commemoration of the makeshift homes used by the Israelites in the wilderness, after the Exodus from Egypt.

Sukkot

Festival of Tabernacles (Booths), commemorating God's watching over the Jewish people during the period of the wilderness, after leaving Egypt, and celebrating the plentitude of the autumn harvest.

Tefillin

Phylacteries; leather boxes containing passages from the Bible written on parchment and attached by leather straps to the head and arm of males 13 years and older during week-day morning prayers. The tefillin symbolize commitment of mind, heart and might to fulfill Biblical precepts.

Torah

Literally, "teaching" or "the law;" referring to the Five Books of Moses and at times denoting the entire Scripture and traditional Jewish learning.

Tisha B'Av

The ninth day of the summer month of Av, during which both the First and Second Temples in Jerusalem were destroyed (586 B.C.E. and 70 C.E.); observed as a day of fasting and mourning.

Tzaddikim

Literally, "the righteous;" referring to outstanding righteous human beings; in this context to rabbinic sages of antiquity. Tombs of such sages are seen as places of petitionary prayer.

Yeshiva

School at various levels, from primary to theological seminary, for study of traditional religious texts.

Yizkor

Memorial prayer for the dead, recited in the synagogue during morning services on Yom Kippur and other major holidays.

2

The Media and the Guttman Report

CHARLES S. LIEBMAN

This chapter and the chapter that follows survey how two critical sectors of the Israeli public, the media and the academic community, greeted the Guttman Report. The media and the academics are very important because they serve as the major conduits through which the results of the Guttman study were communicated to the general public. Both the full text of the Guttman Report and a summary of the report, published as a separate pamphlet under the title *Highlights from the Guttman Institute Report* (hereafter referred to as *Highlights* and reprinted in this volume as chapter 1) were on sale to the public. But the distribution facilities of the Guttman Institute and the Avi-Chai Foundation border on the nonexistent, and the public is not accustomed to purchasing material of this sort anyway.

THE GUTTMAN CONCEPTION

The media's interpretation is critical in the short run; the academic community is probably more important in the long run. We turn our attention first to the media. In doing so, this chapter is not only attentive to the text of the media reports but to the more subtle question of how the results of a scientific report become popularized and the attendant and inevitable distortion that accompanies that popularization.

Barbie Zelizer, relying on earlier scholars, describes journalists as an interpretive community. She observes that

> journalists present events through explanatory frames that construct reality but do not reveal the secrets, sources or methods of such a process. Audiences tend to protest this only when they

> dislike what is being portrayed . . . the selection, formation, and presentation of events ultimately hinge on how journalists decide to construct the news in one way and not another. . . .[1]

Avi-Chai, with Guttman Institute approval, prepared a press release that it distributed together with *Highlights* to all Israeli newspapers. Some reporters did request and thereupon received copies of the full report. However, coverage of the Guttman Report in the press and on television and radio suggests that, with some exceptions, reporters and editors relied heavily on a press release for their basic information of the report's contents. The press release comprised five and a half single-spaced pages of text, so even though the media was in fact reporting on a press release it had to select from among the wealth of information reported in the release. *Highlights* facilitated the journalists in this regard as well by quoting three key statements from the report on its front cover. The quotes really constituted a shortened version of the press release. The first three paragraphs of the press release were as follows:

> "The rhetoric of secular and religious polarization used to characterize Israeli society is highly misleading. It is truer to say that Israeli society has a strong traditional bent, with a continuum from the 'strictly observant' to the 'non-observant,' rather than a great divide between a religious minority and a secular majority. Israeli Jews are strongly committed to the continuing Jewish character of their society, even while they are selective in the forms of their observance. They believe that public life should respect tradition, but they are critical of the 'status quo' governing State and Religion."
>
> These are some of the conclusions of this most detailed and in-depth study ever done in Israel, encompassing 2,400 personal interviews, on the subject of "Beliefs, Observances and Social Interaction among Israeli Jews" carried out by The Guttman Institute of Applied Social Research, at the initiative of the AVI CHAI Foundation in Jerusalem.
>
> AVI CHAI is a private foundation which focuses in Israel on efforts to encourage mutual understanding and sensitivity among Jews of different religious backgrounds and commitments to observance. The study was carried out under the direction of Dr. Shlomit Levy, Hanna Levinsohn, and Prof. Elihu Katz, Scientific Director of the Institute.

The three paragraphs found on the front page of *Highlights*, designed to look like direct quotes from the report, are also to be found in the first paragraph of the press release. They are reproduced here in their entirety:

> . . . the rhetoric of secular and religious polarization generally used to characterize Israeli society is highly misleading.
>
> . . . Israeli society has a strong traditional bent, and, as far as religious practice is concerned . . . there is a continuum from the "strictly observant" to the "non-observant," rather than a great divide between a religious minority and a secular majority.
>
> Israeli Jews are strongly committed to the continuing Jewish character of their society, even while they are selective in the forms of their observance. They believe that public life should respect the tradition, but are critical of the "status quo" governing State and Religion.

These statements represent a conception of the Guttman Report results. They condense a 136-page report with additional tables of roughly the same number of pages into a very concise package that conveys, explicitly and implicitly, a very clear message. To paraphrase the message and condense it even further, it says:

> . . . *contrary to what everyone thought, the religious and secular in Israel are not polarized. Virtually all Israelis tend to be traditional in their religious practice. They are also committed to the Jewish character of Israeli society although they are critical of the religious status quo.*

This is how the authors of the report, in subsequent interviews, summarized their message. We will call this the Guttman conception. The term is not meant to suggest that this conception is unfair or biased. My own sense is that, with one caveat, it is a fair conceptualization of the report. However, the public also assumes that that which is currently true is likely to continue to be true. As we shall see in the final two chapters, evidence in the report itself suggests that this is not the case.

Most journalists who reported the results of the Guttman study copied or slightly revised the key statements from *Highlights* or similar statements from the press release and thereby reinforced the Guttman conception. Alternate conceptualizations did emerge, more often among intellectuals (see chapter 3) than among journalists.

THE SCOPE AND NATURE OF THE MEDIA COVERAGE

The Guttman Report enjoyed extensive coverage in the media. There were over fifty-six references to the report, most of them major stories, in the press and on radio and television over a six-week period from December 6, 1993, to January 21, 1994.[2] This probably represents wider coverage than any previous survey research report had ever enjoyed. Every one of the nine Hebrew- (and English-) language daily newspapers, except *Ma'Ariv*, carried a lead story about the report and/or a major feature story. The one national weekly then in print and many of the local weeklies did the same. All five radio stations and the major Israeli television channel described the Guttman Report; two television programs and one radio program utilized the report as the basis for extended discussions.

The extensive nature of the coverage deserves some mention. In one sense it confirms that which the Guttman Report asserts; Israeli Jews, who constitute over 80 percent of Israeli society, are committed to Jewishness, if not to Judaism, and, consequently, a report about the beliefs, attitudes, and observances of Israeli Jews is deemed interesting. That is probably part of the answer but not, I suspect, the whole one, because the Israeli press does not, under ordinary circumstances, pay much attention to the prosaic side of Jewishness. It is my impression that by and large the nonreligious media report challenges to Jewish life and tradition in a favorable light and describe efforts by the religious establishment to impose religious forms of life in a negative light.[3] The media do this because most journalists are secular rather than religious and also because journalists believe they are mirroring what most Israelis want to hear and read. If this is true, then the media, implicitly if not explicitly, saw the Guttman Report as a challenge to its own conceptions or assumptions about the nature of Jewish life in Israel and the norms and values of most Israelis. The Guttman Report, more precisely the Guttman conception of the report, contradicted that which journalists believed to be true. To their credit, perhaps because of their curiosity about whether their own perceptions were correct, or because journalists like to stir up controversy and they believed they had a story likely to arouse controversy, but perhaps as a sign of their indolence, most of the media descriptions were presented in terms of the Guttman conception.

Not every reference described the report in whole or in part. A number of the media reports mentioned the Guttman data to make some point that bore little relationship to the report itself.[4] But even peripheral mention added to the prestige of the report. This was especially prevalent at the second or third mention of the report, from mid-January through mid-February. After that, references to the report virtually ceased.

In deciding how to treat the story of the Guttman Report, the media, consciously or unconsciously, had to choose between a number of options. The first option, the easiest way out as we noted, a course that most of the media followed, was to publish or rewrite the first few paragraphs of the release or the statements on the cover of *Highlights*. The hook that the media utilized, more often than not, to attract reader attention was the surprising nature of the findings. The terms "shocked" and "astounded" were often employed. The media did not always specify who it was that was shocked or astounded. When it did do so, the most common reference was to scholars.

When journalists reported the results of the Guttman Institute study by copying or slightly rewording the opening paragraphs of the press release or the cover of *Highlights* they were accepting, as we said, the Guttman conception of the Guttman Report. There were four other options that might have been exercised by the media or by anyone wishing to bypass the Guttman conception.

In a few cases journalists simply selected the data that fit their own preconceptions about how Israeli Jews behave or ought to behave and limited themselves to reporting this data. This seemed to characterize some of the radical secularists among the journalists.

A few others, also unhappy with the results, challenged the results of the report by suggesting that the methods employed in administering the survey were inappropriate or biased. Since this meant challenging the highly prestigious Guttman Institute, which undertook the survey, this option could only be chosen by journalists of great hubris or profound ignorance of survey research.

A third option was to reinterpret the Guttman data. The data could then be presented as confirmation of a different conceptual framework without explicitly challenging the Guttman conception. This was the option that the religious media, in general, and the *haredi* (ultra-Orthodox) media, in particular, chose.

The fourth and most sophisticated option was to challenge the Guttman conception in explicit terms. This was rarely attempted by journalists. It was more commonly undertaken by academics, as we shall see in the following chapter, and in the essays of the Van Leer participants, which are reproduced in the Appendix.

The media coverage is presented here, more or less in chronological order. As will be seen, all of the options described earlier found expression in one media report or another.

THE *HAREDI* PRESS AND THE GUTTMAN CONCEPTION

The Guttman Report was completed in the summer of 1993, but its release was withheld. The summary, *Highlights from the Guttman Institute Report* (reprinted in chapter 1), was distributed, in confidence, to about sixty academics who indicated they would attend the Van Leer conference described in the next chapter. Apparently one or more of the conference participants leaked a copy of *Highlights* to *Davar*. At the time, *Davar* was the daily paper published by the Israeli Labor Federation. It no longer exists.

The first news of the Guttman survey appeared on December 5. The Labor newspaper devoted two stories to the report. The front page story was headlined, "In Israel They Believe They Are Members Of A Chosen People" (alluding to responses to one of the survey's questions on belief). The *Davar* story was written without the benefit of the press release that had yet to be formulated, but it followed the same general outline as the Guttman conception. It emphasized the survey respondents' sense of the central role that the state of Israel plays in contemporary Judaism and the strong ties that Israelis have to all the Jewish people. The story then focused on selected aspects of the beliefs and attitudes found in the report. The word "they" in the headline seems to exclude the journalist and his audience. But the somewhat abrasive tone of the headline, suggesting wide-eyed superstitious masses who do not share the values of the writer and his readers, was not at all typical of the article's text.

A second story on page 5 was headed, "There Is A God."[5] It began as follows:

> Contrary to the notion that the general tendency of the public is to secularism, two-thirds of the Jews in Israel observe the tradition.

The remainder of the story followed that vein. The hook was obvious—we thought one thing was correct, but it turns out that something different is correct.

There is an additional point worth noting about *Davar*'s coverage. References are to Jews in Israel; "Jewish residents of Israel" is how the front page story refers to them. As we shall see, some of the media made no distinction between the survey sample, composed of Jews in Israel, and all Israelis. This reinforces the point to be made in the final two chapters concerning the taken-for-granted status of Judaism and Jewishness in Israel, even among those who feel alienated from the Jewish tradition and would prefer to dejudaize the public forum.

The stories in *Davar* were picked up the following day by *Ha'Modia*, the oldest and best established of the three *haredi* dailies.[6] The first story appeared under a front page headline, "Jews Believe." *Ha'Modia*'s treatment is significant because of the way in which it conceptualized the Guttman Report and its implications—a conceptualization that all the *haredi* press was to adopt. The lead story, based according to its author on the story in *Davar*, emphasized that the report vindicated *haredi* leaders in their assertion that most Israeli Jews, "the nation residing in Zion" (*ha'am hayoshev b'tzion*), support religion and observe Jewish tradition. But, *Ha'Modia* continued, the secular media conceal or distort this fact. This and subsequent stories provided corroboration to a basic *haredi* message—the demonic behavior of the secular media.[7]

The secular press along with a handful of politicians whose names are not always specified, play a prominent role in the *haredi* worldview. *Haredim*, on the one hand, decry the Israeli environment, which is characterized by violations of religious prescriptions, deliberate and blatant disrespect for Jewish tradition, and general licentiousness. On the other hand, wholesale condemnation of other Jews is contrary to the Jewish tradition and far less acceptable since the Yom Kippur War. Since that time, as I have argued elsewhere,[8] a process of integration and at least partial legitimation of *haredim* in Israeli society has been taking place. This process has proven most beneficial for *haredim* in gaining access to public funds. But no less and probably more importantly, it fits the reality that many and probably most *haredim* themselves sense. In their own eyes they both are and are not part of Israeli society. The balance between being "part of" and being "isolated from" differs from one *haredi* to another, from one context to another, and from one period to another. But the sense of being "part of" has been growing among more and more *haredim* and in more and more contexts.

Nevertheless, the *haredi* paradox remains. They live in an Israeli Jewish society that they would like to affirm and an environment that they insist on viewing as demonic, both because much of what takes place there is an anathema in their eyes and because if they were to desist resisting the environment they would undermine their cultural autonomy. The solution, heretofore, was to explain and thereby excuse the behavior of the vast majority of nonobservant Jews as a consequence of their ignorance. Blame is attributed to the secular media and a handful of "leftist" politicians who deliberately promote this ignorance and its consequences.

The Guttman Report permitted the *haredi* media to carry their argument one step further. The report demonstrated that the public was not necessarily composed of sinners who acted out of ignorance. On the contrary, the public was composed of Jews who acted properly, but the secular media deliberately kept this a secret. And lest one suspect that this was an invention of a *haredi* mind, the reader is reminded each time the Guttman Report is described in a *haredi* publication that the authors of the report are secular Jews.[9] Indeed, illustrating another of the paradoxes that characterize the *haredi* world (we *haredim* are the source of truth and secularists are deceitful if not misguided, but somehow the secular world is more objective), the author of one story reminds the reader that the research that he is reporting was not undertaken

> by a *haredi* or religious institution. Therefore one can relate to its findings and conclusions as highly objective.

The first story in *Ha'Modia* maintained that the Guttman Report vindicated *haredi* leaders who had always maintained that Israeli Jews tended toward observance. In contrast, a second story acknowledged that the secular are more observant than we *haredim* had thought. And, the author goes on to add, those who do not observe, act that way from ignorance. After reminding readers that the authors of the report are not religious, the journalist arrives at his main point. The worst enemy is the media who provide an image of a secular majority and thereby serve the secular "exactly as it serves the left, as though the majority of the citizens of the state of Israel were left wing."

The notion that the religious public constitute a majority of the society but are mislead by the secular media into the belief that they are a minority is also found in the weekly pamphlet published by Habad (the followers of the Lubavitch *rebbe*) and distributed in many synagogues throughout Israel. Its December 13 issue notes that the Guttman Report challenges the notion that there has been a growing alienation from the values of Judaism in the last few years. This misconception is attributed to the media "controlled almost entirely by people of extreme secularist ideology." They incite the public against religious institutions.

This attack on the secular media was comparatively mild. Two examples of more vituperative attacks are of particular interest. On December 10, *Ha'Modia* utilized the Guttman Report to further develop its conceptual scheme. The report served as the basis for an attack on Israeli democracy or the lack thereof. Israel, the journalist claimed, pretends to be a democracy. But the

> vast majority of the public is ground down under the nailed boot of a tiny minority, a handful of leftists who arrogantly captured all the media outlets, and do as they see fit to the public.

The author then points to the recent closing of an afternoon daily, *Hadashot*. That newspaper, so it was claimed, had lost many readers after it violated censorship regulations by publishing material demonstrating that Israel's secret security forces had lied. The writer cited the loss of readership as evidence that

> the Israeli public, even the secular, is pro-Jewish, pro-religion, in favor of tradition. It isn't left-wing, Arabist, and also not Sturmerist [a reference to *Der Sturmer*, the antisemitic Nazi newspaper].

Further evidence that the majority of the society is pro-Jewish is then introduced by the Guttman Report, which the journalist reminds his readers was prepared by "a staff of secular professors" and published in the "known Canaanite paper, *Davar.*" The author chooses bits of data from the report that best support the argument for high levels of observance among the public and concludes that the media, along with a few leftists, distorts and misleads the public.

An association of the secular media and the political Left is vividly expressed in a similar story that appeared a few weeks later in a *haredi* weekly, *Yerushalayim.* The author of the article cites the Guttman Report figures as so startling that even the Israeli media could not ignore them. The data demonstrate, says the writer, that the charge of religious coercion "is a big ugly lie." [Apparently the writer's train of thought is that since a majority of the society is religious, religious coercion cannot, by definition, exist.] The "atheist leftists . . . haters of religion and anti-semites" who scream against religious coercion are a tiny minority, the writer affirms. If Israel were a democracy this could not happen, but Israel is not a democracy and the "haters of religion and the leftists" rule "without restraint." They control the media and thereby create the false impression that the observant are a minority.

The *haredi* articles lend themselves to an analysis that takes us too far afield from our present concerns. Nevertheless, a couple of points beg mentioning because they are relevant to developments in Israeli Jewish life to which we return in the final two chapters. First, by attacking Israel because it only pretends to be a democracy but really is not, the *haredi* press has, by indirection, offered some legitimacy to the label democracy; although it is equally clear that it has little understanding that democracy also includes protection of individual rights. Second, the demonization of the political Left is especially characteristic of the *haredi* world in the last few years. Indeed, it is another sign of its integration into Israeli culture—albeit into one segment of that culture. The association of radical secularism with radical leftism (an association that has a great deal of truth though hardly all the truth) serves the same purposes as the demonization of the secular press but also provides a legitimation for *haredi* alliances with the secular Right. Finally, what is most striking about the *haredi* media treatment of Jewish-Israeli society is its reification of "the nation." That is, the concept "nation" is reified to the point where the notion of a divided nation is inconceivable. Whereas the Guttman Report talks about the continuum between religious and nonreligious, or more observant and less observant, and points to rather sharp divisions on issues of religious politics as opposed to religious observance, the *haredi* press seems unwilling, more likely incapable, of making such distinctions.

Yom L'Yom, the daily paper of Shas, the Sephardic religious party, printed a short story on December 21, under the headline: "Survey Results: No Split Between Religious and Non-Religious." Shas is led by Sephardic *haredi* rabbis, but many of its voters are traditional rather than strictly observant. Indeed, the Sephardim represent the core of religiously permissive traditionalists whom the Guttman Report finds to constitute the majority of Israeli Jews. They are the constituents and potential constituents of Shas, and it is no surprise that Shas was pleased by the results of the report or that the Guttman conception suited its needs. The following day, December 22, the paper carried a longer story under the headline, "This Is Secularism?," which adopted the same conceptual framework that first appeared in *Ha'Modia*. *Yom L'Yom*, however, employed far more moderate tones, as is appropriate to a party that was an on-again, off-again coalition partner of the government elected in 1992. The first paragraph noted that the notion of a "secular majority" was undermined by the Guttman survey. After presenting a few figures about high levels of observance, the paper reminded its readers that the survey was not conducted by "Shas or other religious, so there is no room to accuse anyone of forging the figures." The article concludes by saying that we now know how to relate to those who would erase the Jewish character of the state of Israel in the name of an ostensible secular majority.

THE SECULAR MEDIA AND THE GUTTMAN CONCEPTION

At the time of the Guttman Report publication, five Hebrew-language radio stations reached a national audience. Four of them were under some form of government control; one, the IDF channel, was geared especially to an army audience. The fifth station, "Channel 7" was a pirate channel identified with the political Right and with a militant version of religious-Zionism.

On December 7 one of the government stations broadcast news of the Guttman Report based on the story in *Davar*. It borrowed its lead from the cover of *Highlights*: "there is no basis to the rhetoric of secular and religious polarization in Israeli society." The broadcast provided some additional statistics on observance of the tradition and the responsibility that Jews feel to the entire Jewish nation. The statement that Israeli Jews believe that the tradition ought to be respected was balanced, as it was in *Highlights*, by the statement that Israelis are critical of the status quo concerning religion and state. (I suspect that the radio station obtained a copy of *Highlights*, perhaps *Davar*'s copy.)

A second government station carried the Guttman Report story on its news broadcasts the following day. (In both cases references were to Israeli and not Jewish-Israeli society.)

The December 19 news report on the IDF channel adopted its own interpretation of the Guttman Report. It began its coverage by highlighting the fact that 90 percent of Israeli citizens (once again ignoring the non-

Jewish population) supported the drafting of yeshiva students. One might have explained this bit of selectivity by recalling that it was broadcast by an army station, and anything affecting the army presumably took priority. But the next statistic the station presented was that a "majority of the public supports public transportation on the Sabbath and opening more movie theaters on Friday night." A more detailed report then followed. It repeated the figure of massive support for drafting yeshiva students and added the additional figure of 70 percent in favor of drafting religious girls, 42 percent in favor of separating religion and state, and two thirds reporting they would like to use public transportation on the Sabbath and attend more movies on Friday night. The announcer then pointed to the survey results indicating that Sephardim (Jews of Eastern origin, primarily North African) were more positive toward religion than Ashkenazim (Jews of Western, primarily European, background), and that whereas 40 percent of the population favored instituting civil marriage ceremonies, only 16 percent preferred a civil to a religious marriage ceremony.

There was nothing inaccurate in any of the details of the broadcast, but it certainly misled the listener with regard to the overall findings of the Guttman Report. The Israeli news agency, *Itim*, adopted the same strategy. It distributed a short news story that focused on the 90 percent figure in favor of drafting yeshiva students. On December 27, that story was also published in *Al Hamishmar*, the left-wing daily which since then ceased publication, and in *Yediot Aharonot*, Israel's most popular daily. But the story in *Yediot* was a supplement to a much lengthier and more complete story that had appeared a few days earlier.

The Avi Chai press release was finally distributed on December 20 and 21 and led to broad coverage of the Guttman Report during that week. In most cases, stories in the press and on radio featured those aspects of the press release found in *Highlights*, but the headline in each paper reflected slightly different orientations. "Most Israeli Jews Observe Some 'Mitzvot'" was the cautious headline in the English-language daily, *Jerusalem Post*. The lead sentence was also carefully balanced:

> Two-thirds of the country's Jews mark shabbat with some form of ritual observance and more than 70 percent fast on Yom Kippur, but almost half say that they either do not know or barely know how to pray from a prayer book.

Not surprisingly, the *Jerusalem Post*, read by Israel's foreign colony as well as tourists, made note of the fact that the survey was confined to Israeli Jews.

The religious-Zionist daily, *Ha'Zofe*, kept very close to the press release. This is not surprising since in ideological terms, the Guttman conception of the report should have been most satisfying to the more religiously moderate religious-zionists. The same was true of the pirate station, channel 7. Since the unity of Jewish society is an especially important theme to its sponsors, the press release's emphasis on the absence of divisions among religious and secular Jews coincided with the station's ideological orientation.

Yediot Aharonot is Israel's largest-selling daily. Its first report of the Guttman study appeared December 21 and relied heavily on the press release, both in content and in conception. For example, the headline read "80 Percent Observe Tradition." The writer, however, did uncover an inconsistency and called the Guttman Institute's attention to the fact that according to the report the percentage of those who reported that they pray regularly is identical to the percentage of those who reported that they recite the prayer for the welfare of the state of Israel. Since few *haredim* recite this prayer, it suggests that they are grossly underrepresented in the sample. Elihu Katz responds to this point in chapter 4.

A national weekly (*Shishi*) and local weeklies, some independent and some sponsored by the national press, also carried the Guttman Report story in their weekend edition. They generally followed the tone of the press release. The lead-in, as we noted earlier, was often the surprising nature of the statistics on belief and observance. A number of the weekend stories stressed the "surprisingly" or "startlingly" high rate of belief and observance–sometimes specifying that it is the researchers who are "in shock," but in one case, suggesting that it is the journalist himself. The writer in the weekly *Shishi* (the paper, now defunct, was a successor to *Hadashot*), for example, seems quite genuine in referring to the "startling findings" that 63 percent of Israelis (note the inclusive and inaccurate term "Israelis" rather than "Jewish Israelis") "fully believe there is a God." He suggests that it is he who is astounded and then offers his interpretation, one that is quite consistent with the *Highlights* and the press release. He says:

> If I understand something about the data, the results of the study tell us about the very close tie between the citizens of Israel and Judaism and religion, including the laws of the religion. This tie does not dictate full observance of the religious commandments.

The best-researched story along these lines, despite the inaccurate headline, "We Fast on Kippur (But Only Because of the Diet)" appeared in the Jerusalem weekly of *Yediot Aharonot*. (The two largest Israeli papers print their own local supplements on the weekend.) The secondary headline read:

> A new and surprising study by the Guttman Institute reveals that Israeli society still views itself as traditional, despite objection to the interference of the religious establishment in private lives. The *haredi* are celebrating, learned researchers are in shock, but there are those who see the data as testimony to the maturity of the average Israeli, who lights candles but doesn't ask why. . . .

The story, other than a lead paragraph that likened Israel to Saudi Arabia, was devoid of sensationalism. After reporting some of the data and the celebration of the report in *haredi* circles, the writer reports the responses of a number of Israelis (including a *haredi*) deemed knowledgeable about the nature of Jewishness in Israel. The journalist concluded by challenging the conclusion found in the press release and the *Highlights* about the absence of a split between the religious and the secular. He noted that according to the report itself, religious-secular relations were problematic.

Only a few journalists pointed to this apparent inconsistency, but the theme reappears among the academics discussed in the next chapter. As we noted, the press release and the cover page of *Highlights* stresses that: "the rhetoric of secular and religious polarization generally used to characterize Israeli society is highly misleading." A closer reading of *Highlights* itself, as seen in chapter 1, illuminates the meaning of this statement. What the authors mean is that the term *polarization* is inaccurate because, in the words of *Highlights*, "there is a continuum from the 'strictly observant' to the 'nonobservant,' rather than a great divide between a religious minority and a secular majority." Most Israeli Jews are not bunched at the two ends of the continuum, so, technically speaking, there is no polarization. If one reads the text of *Highlights* one understands this. But the statement as it appears in the press release and on the cover of *Highlights* is misleading for two reasons. First, many Israelis, including as we shall see not only journalists but academics as well, understood the assertion of an absence of polarization as denying the existence of deep divisions between Israeli Jews who are labeled "religious" and Israeli Jews who are labeled "secular." The categories "religious" and "secular" are meaningful categories to Israelis and, in fact, are terms that the Guttman Report itself utilizes. Had the authors of the report or the press release carried their argument about the absence of polarization or the existence of a continuum to its logical conclusion they could have argued that the very terms *religious* and *secular* are misleading. After all, if there is a real continuum of observance, where is one to draw the line? But such an argument would have been unrealistic given the widespread use of the terms in Israeli public life. So the authors continue to use the terms *secular* and *religious* but then deny that these terms are meaningful in distinguishing between levels of religious observance among the vast majority of Israelis. Second, contrary to the intention of the report, the assertion of an absence of "secular and religious polarization" was interpreted by many, I suspect by most journalists themselves, to mean that there is no polarization at the social or political as well as the religious level between those who are defined as religious and those who are defined as secular. Anyone who reads *Highlights* or even the press release carefully would realize that that is not what the report is affirming. But the fact is that even scholars who, one hopes, read texts carefully misinterpreted what was said. A lengthy *Jerusalem Post* story describing the Van Leer Institute conference was headlined: "Survey Says No Religious-Secular Gap; Academics Differ."

The deliberations of the December 26 Van Leer Institute conference are the subject of the next chapter. Besides the major story in the *Jerusalem Post* referred to here, the media ignored the substance of the conference. Perhaps there was no press release upon which they could rely.

ALTERNATE CONCEPTIONS

The media reports and feature stories that appeared before December 27, with the few exceptions already noted, accepted the Guttman conceptual framework, especially the notion that Israeli Jews were by and large united in their traditional beliefs and religious behavior. The major exceptions were the reports that selected out a few bits of data, especially the fact that 90 percent of the public favor drafting yeshiva students, ignored the conceptual framework of the press release, and allowed the selected data to speak for themselves. The *haredi* press offered its own interpretive or conceptual scheme, and whereas many of their stories also chose the data selectively, they built upon rather than rejected the Avi-Chai conceptual framework. The first explicit challenge to the report came on December 27, from the distinguished historian and Arabist, Emmanuel Sivan, writing in the pages of *Ha'Aretz* under the heading "The Gulf Will Widen." Sivan criticized the report at three levels. First, he noted, as the *Highlights* themselves indicated, most respondents were selective in their observance of religious ritual. This selectivity, Sivan pointed out, bore no connection to the centrality of the ritual, from a religious point of view, but rather to the frequency with which Jews were required to observe it and the difficulty or inconvenience involved in its performance. For three quarters of Israelis, Sivan concluded, observance was tied to Israel's national culture not to the Jewish religion.

Second, Sivan argued, in addition to the different meanings and levels associated with religious observance, the report itself indicated that deep divisions existed between religious and nonreligious at the social level. Israeli Jews, Sivan maintained in accordance with the report, do not interact with those whose religious lifestyles are different.

Sivan's third and final point was that the most serious and potentially threatening gulf between religious and secular was at the political rather than at the religious or even the social level. In a somewhat polemical tone, Sivan maintained, independently of the report, that the most serious division in Israeli society is between the West Bank settlers and their religious supporters and, by implication, all other Israelis. He identifies the former as those who place "one religious commandment–the commandment of settling the entire land"–as the supreme religious principle.

Sivan's points, as we will see in the chapter that follows, are repeated in the presentations of a number of academics. However, Orit Shochat, a columnist for *Ha'Aretz,* responded to Sivan the following day in an article that rephrased the Guttman conception in more dramatic and far-reaching terms than the authors themselves might have dared.

The article was subheaded:

> Most Jews living in Israel are religious in one way or another. Even if they would be allowed to marry in a civil ceremony they wouldn't want to. They only want the option to decide.

The first paragraph praised the report as a serious, in-depth study. The key lines read as follows:

> After one hundred years of secular zionism, after it appeared that Israeli culture was dominated by the ethos of the secular-sabra who negates diasporaness and celebrates the army . . . [and after it appeared that] the religious are only a small shrill minority, it now appears that the cutting off of *peot* [a reference to the anti-religious coercion of Yemenite immigrants in the first years of statehood] didn't succeed. The Jews living in Israel feel that the Jewish tradition is the force that united them and is responsible for the fact that they live in this land and not elsewhere.

Shochat then refers directly to Sivan's column of the previous day. Ignoring many of his points, she argued that his distinction between observing the tradition and observing a religious commandment is a philosophical question. Furthermore, she argued, Sivan's formulation suggested that religiosity was a matter of all or nothing, and this is contrary to the findings of the Guttman Report itself.

Another alternative conception, one far less sophisticated than Sivan's, emerged in an article in *Ma'Ariv* on the last day of the year. Under the heading "Since We Are Already Talking About Religion," the journalist, picking up on a minor thread in an article in the weekly *Shishi* referred to earlier, concluded that the upshot of the Guttman Report was that Israelis are Reform Jews. "We are Reform because we know that it is possible to be a Jew even without a *streimel* [a fur hat worn by a few though hardly all *haredim*]." The article seems too farfetched to merit further attention except for two facts. One, this is, as far as I can tell, the only mention of the Guttman Report in *Ma'Ariv,* the second-largest daily in Israel. Two, the story was picked up by a radio announcer who used it two days later as the focus of an interview with a Reform rabbi from Haifa who endorsed the journalist's conclusions.

One more alternative to the Guttman conception was offered by the media before the topic of the Guttman Report disappeared. It began with a column by the distinguished columnist from *Yediot Aharonot,* Nahum Barnea, in the January 9 edition. Barnea did not challenge the Guttman conception, indeed, unlike prior journalists he argued that the "general findings were to be expected, practically obvious." But, he argued, the details were wrong. His evidence to refute the details were based primarily on "common sense" and an appeal to the reader's own behavior. Barnea's second point, repeating in part what Sivan said and duplicating what many of the Van Leer participants felt, was that it was inappropriate to label the observance of practices embedded in Jewish history or Israeli society as the observance of religious norms. It was impossible, according to Barnea, to find an appropriate label for this behavior. "Anyone who tries to measure the religiosity of Israelis is destined to confound himself in a maze of internal contradictions."

The effort to belittle the report–the general conclusions are obvious and well known, the details are wrong–was followed, a few days later, by a more serious attack on both the report and the Guttman conception. The noted satirist B. Michael, in his January 14 column, slammed the Report under the heading "We are all 'Religious'." Michael used the derogatory term *dosim* instead of the Hebrew word *datiim* for "religious." (Dosim is the Ashkenazic pronunciation of the word, but its usage is heavy with pejorative overtones. It is, in many respects equivalent to the term *nigger* for an American black or *redneck* for a white southerner. It connotes, at its kindest, a caricature of a *haredi.*) The author is distressed by the fact that the Guttman Report "raised concern and depression in the heart of the secularists" and that "a number of respected journalists even relied, sadly, on the result of the research to bewail the death of secularism." Michael charged that the Avi-Chai Foundation, which commissioned the report, has a religious ax to grind and that the authors of the report formulated their conclusions to suit the Avi-Chai Foundation's religious agenda. Michael refrains from mentioning the fact that the report was produced by the Guttman Institute. Since the Guttman Institute's reputation for impartial survey research is unimpeachable, it seems likely that he chose to confine himself to the Avi-Chai Foundation for polemical purposes.

Michael cites Barnea and agrees that the accuracy of the report's figures are doubtful. He seeks to demonstrate that the questions were biased and therefore led to the findings of high levels of observance. The alternative conception was expressed in the concluding section under the subtitle "So what are we?" It read:

> We are just a plain nation. With one quarter religious and three-quarters non-religious. A nation that enjoys participating in its ethnic folklore, like every other nation, whether it is called Christmas or whether it is called *Hanukkah.* A nation, that like any other nation has its superstitions, whether it is a mezuza against traffic accidents or a cross against vampires.

THE END OF THE STORY

During the last week in December a few weeklies that had not carried the Guttman story before did so now. Most followed the outlines of the press release. Further mention of the report in the daily press or on television was generally a hook to a discussion of some other topic, such as the nature of secularism in Israeli life, civil marriage, or the issue of burying a non-Jewish army officer in the Jewish section of a military cemetery. This last issue aroused some excitement toward the end of the year. The *haredi* press defended the decision to bury the deceased in a plot distanced from Jews by referring to the Guttman Report finding that the majority of Israelis prefer to be buried in accordance with religious norms. Tom Segev, a well-known journalist, also made the connection in his weekly column in the December 31 issue of *Ha'Aretz.*

In January, *haredi* Knesset member Avraham Ravitz requested a discussion of the Guttman Report on the floor of the Knesset. He raised the issue, he claimed, so that in the future, Knesset members would no longer refer to the religious as a minority and to the secular as the majority. Only the *haredi* press reported that story.

The argument that religious Jews constitute a majority in Israeli society, which the *haredi* press, and Ravitz in its wake, reported, had additional consequences. If the religious are really a majority, then *haredi* leaders and the *haredi* press have a responsibility for Israeli society that they had, heretofore, eschewed. *Haredi* writer Moshe Grilack, writing a guest column in a secular weekly on December 30 and basing it on the Guttman Report, concluded that:

> As long as we [*haredim*] believed that the secular majority abhors the Torah of Israel and us, the small minority of religious, we despaired of any chance of a positive tie with them. We abandoned all our ties to that public [leaving these ties] to the politicians and functionaries. And they, quite properly, devoted all their efforts to obtaining benefits for the minority of religious, ignoring entirely the deep spiritual needs of the majority about whom we knew nothing. The survey requires us, therefore, to rethink our priorities. To recall that the general public is much closer to us than the noise of the politicians and newsmen had allowed us to imagine.

The same point, albeit more judiciously expressed, was made the following day in *Ha'Modia*. The author maintained that since the *haredi* press is now shown to represent the vast majority of society, its responsibility is a heavy one, demanding nothing less than "professional retraining" and a new attitude to public controversies.

Soul searching was not limited to the *haredim*. An article in the leftist daily *Al Hamishmar* on December 31 appeared under the heading "The Secular Minority." The writer noted that the religious are a minority, but, as the Guttman Report demonstrated, real secularists, like himself, are also a minority. A lengthy and thoughtful article in a local weekly, *Tzfon Ha'Ir*, under the heading "There Is A God" sought to understand, from a secular point of view, the need for religion that the Guttman Report demonstrated. The author concluded that secularists have no explanation for Jewish history or Jewish survival.

On March 6, *Ha'Aretz* published a review of the Guttman Report by Yitzhak Roeh, a journalist and faculty member of the Hebrew University's Department of Communications. The review was written in a polemical tone. Leaving that aside, and his charge that the survey's questions were biased, Roeh repeated the same arguments raised by some of the participants at the Van Leer conference of December 26. These are discussed in the next chapter.

NOTES

1. Barbie Zelizer, *Covering the Body: The Kennedy Assassination, the Media, and the Shaping of Collective Memory* (Chicago: University of Chicago Press, 1992), p.8.

2. This survey is based on material submitted to the Avi-Chai Foundation by a press clipping service commissioned for that purpose. My hunch is that almost but not quite everything was collected by the press clipping service. I have no doubt, however, that even if a few references to the report were overlooked, nothing of major importance was omitted.

3. An important exception to this rule was during Shulamit Aloni's tenure as minister of education and culture. Any statement, reference, or even innuendo by Aloni that might have been interpreted as challenging the Jewish tradition or the Jewish nature of Israeli society was seized upon by the press in full knowledge that this would be a matter of embarrassment to the minister.

4. For example, a story on February 10 in *Ha'Modia*, one of the *haredi* dailies, described in troubled tones the phenomenon of nonreligious and Jewishly ignorant Russian immigrants with calligraphic skills seeking to make a living by preparing parchments for *mezuzot*. A *mezuzah* is a parchment in which words from the Torah are inscribed. Jews are commanded to attach a *mezuzah* to each of the doorposts of their home. The journalist makes a passing reference to the Guttman Report, which reported that over 90 percent of Israeli Jews attach *mezuzot* to their door frames.

5. This phrase, a biblical adaptation, resonates among Israelis with good political memories. *Davar* readers, many if not most of whom were political functionaries of one kind or another, no doubt possessed good political memories. It recalls the 1982 postelection television broadcast. As the polls closed, the only Israeli television channel at that time announced that exit poll results forecast a Likud victory. The cameras then switched to Likud election headquarters where a Likud supporter shouted, "there is a God."

6. Each of the dailies is associated with a different *haredi* party. For purposes of this chapter, the differences among the *haredi* parties are of no substance. They all portrayed the Guttman Report in the same manner.

7. See Amnon Levy, "The Haredi Press and Secular Society," in Charles S. Liebman (ed.), *Secular and Religious: Conflict and Accommodation Between Jews in Israel* (Jerusalem: Keter, 1990), pp. 21–44.

8. Charles S. Liebman, "The Entry of Haredim into the Government Coalition in Light of their Responses to the Yom Kippur War," *Iyunim*, vol. 3 (in Hebrew), pp. 380–93, and in English "Paradigms Sometimes Fit: *Haredi* Responses to the Yom Kippur War," *Israel Affairs*, no. 3 (Spring, 1995), pp. 171–84. Reprinted in Robert Wistrich and David Ohana (eds.), *The Shaping of Israeli Identity: Memory, Myth and Trauma* (London: Frank Cass, 1995), pp. 171–84.

9. It is unlikely that the *haredi* journalists who reported the fact that the authors were all secularists actually bothered to check their facts. In

fact, it isn't true; certainly not by the Guttman Report's criteria. Rather than suggesting to me that the *haredi* journalists were careless, I suspect it is a sign of the compartmentalization that is so basic to the *haredi* mentality. Non-*haredi* Jews both are and are not part of an authentic Jewish world depending very much on the context. When individuals function in their capacity as academics, as social scientists in particular, they are assumed to be outside the "real" Jewish world unless they identify themselves as part of it. Curiously, however, it also shows how the *haredi* press didn't really internalize their own conception of the Guttman Report findings.

3

Academics and Other Intellectuals

CHARLES S. LIEBMAN

THE VAN LEER CONFERENCE

On December 26 the Avi-Chai Foundation convened a conference at the Van Leer Institute to discuss the Guttman Report. Thirty-two individuals were invited to prepare written responses to the report. Sixteen responded. Five additional individuals, most of them among the thirty-two invited to offer written responses, delivered oral presentations at the conference. In other words, twenty-one written and/or oral papers were presented at the conference.

Fifteen of the twenty-one authors are eminent scholars. Their fields of expertise include Jewish literature and history, Jewish thought and contemporary philosophy, and the social scientific study of religion. The remaining six include a community rabbi, two heads of organizations devoted to secular-religious relations, the former editor of *Davar*, the chancellor of Bar-Ilan University who has written widely in the field of Jewish law and theology, and a prominent leader of a religious-Zionist *yeshiva*.

Of the twenty-one individuals who presented papers, eleven could be classified as "religious," that is, fully or almost fully observant of Jewish law. The fact that more than half the papers were prepared by religious Jews appears to render the choice of academic respondents unrepresentative and the responses, taken as a whole, biased. In fact, of the sixteen academics who declined to prepare written papers only two are "religious." Had they all participated, the balance between religious and nonreligious would look considerably different though I do not believe it would have made any difference in the overall nature of the responses. With the exception of two papers, one by a "fully observant" Jew and the other by an ardent secularist, none of the papers expresses a distinctly religious or nonreligious point of view. These two papers aside, one cannot determine the religious orientation of an author from the content of the paper. What should also be clear, however, is that the academic authors who are religious (this is less true of the rabbis) are in no way representative of Israel's religious community. On the other hand, the greater willingness of religious intellectuals to respond suggests that the topic is of greater concern to them than to nonreligious intellectuals.

The written responses were circulated to roughly sixty additional individuals who accepted an invitation to attend the conference. There were questions and comments from the floor, generally by scholars of considerable reputation. It is unlikely that so distinguished a group of social scientists and Judaica scholars had ever before gathered to discuss one specific topic. Ten of the written papers are reprinted in the Appendix. The choice of papers was based on an effort to provide the reader with a range of responses to the Guttman Report, not on any judgment concerning the relative merits of the papers.

Whereas the media saw its primary role as presenting the *results* of the Guttman Report, the scholars and intellectuals who participated in the Van Leer conference were asked to discuss the *implications* of the Guttman Report and to offer any additional comments they wished to make. Hence the papers and the discussions at the conference itself often extended beyond the Guttman Report findings. The purpose of this chapter is to understand what twenty-one very distinguished Israeli intellectuals had to say about Jewishness in Israel as it was reflected in the Guttman Report. The discussion here is further informed by the comments and questions from the floor.

Most authors focused their attention on one or two Guttman Report findings that they perceived as central. First, the "traditional bent" of Israeli Jewish society, that is the high degree of religious observance and religious belief among Israeli Jews, and second, the absence of religious polarization among Israeli Jews.

THE TRADITIONALISM OF ISRAELI JEWS

Only one paper seriously questioned the reliability of the data rather than its interpretation. Shlomo Deshen, professor of anthropology and a foremost authority on contemporary Sephardic Jewry in Israel, noted the distortion that occurs in grouping respondents by four levels of observance. Deshen pointed out that respondents who grouped themselves in the category "observe nothing" may resemble, in all other respects, those located in the category "observe some of the commandments." On the other hand, respondents who grouped themselves into the same category, for example, into the category of those who observe all the commandments, may be very different from one another. Deshen cited as examples politically extreme ultra-Orthodox *haredim* who oppose the state of Israel but fall in the same category as the religious ultranationalists. In addition, different groups of Jews, for example, Ashkenazim and Sephardim, attribute very different meanings to the same rites of passage that all may observe. Deshen also pointed to an Ashkenazi bias in the formulations of the questions, that is, in considering what is or is not worthy of measurement. Finally, he wondered about the accuracy of some of the answers.

A few other respondents also noted that the categorization of the respondents by four levels of observance generated results that might have been different had the respondents been grouped differently. But most of the participants at the Van Leer conference, certainly the authors of most of the papers, accepted the Guttman Report data on patterns of observance as reliable. Some questions were raised about some of the specific findings, but, Deshen's paper aside, the discussions centered on what the results meant rather than on their accuracy.

There are two basic modes of interpreting the finding that a high percentage of Israeli Jews observe many religious commandments and affirm many basic religious beliefs. One might infer that Israelis are "religious" or inclined to religiousness. A second method of interpretation is to argue that whereas Israeli Jews may *appear* to be religiously observant, the behavior and belief of the majority or indeed of all the respondents is best understood in some other way. Only one author, Rabbi A. Yehoshua Zuckerman, adopted the first mode of interpretation. Most adopted the second mode or an intermediate position closer to the second mode.

Zuckerman is a figure of importance at Yeshivat Merkaz HaRav Kook, an institution for advanced Talmudic study that venerates the teachings of its founder, the country's first Ashkenazi chief rabbi, Abraham Isaac Hacohen Kook, and is associated with religious ultranationalist orientations. In addition to his position in the Yeshiva, Rav Zuckerman heads an organization dedicated to strengthening relations between secular and religious Jews by strengthening their Jewish commitments.

Zuckerman interpreted the Guttman Report as evidence that "Israeli society clearly tends toward the Torah's values and the observance of its *mitzvot*." According to Rav Zuckerman, "the country's youth thirsts for spiritual values, and their answer will come from our cultural origins," through the leadership of "great Torah scholars."

Zuckerman's interpretation resembles, in one respect, that offered by the *haredi* press. But Zuckerman disassociates himself from the *haredim*.

According to the author, *haredim* resemble the antireligious "because they see things in black and white terms, as a result of their individual[istic] demands." What Zuckerman means is that Judaism is a system of faith and belief appropriate for the "nation of Israel," that is, for the Jewish people living in their own land. The majority of Israeli Jews understand Judaism as the religion of the Jewish national collectivity. But the *haredim* understand religious belief and behavior as a set of obligations that are imposed upon them as individuals. In this respect they resemble the antireligious who also are concerned exclusively with themselves as individuals. Zuckerman, therefore, is encouraged by the study's finding of "the general public's distaste for these groups."

An example of an intermediate position was the one espoused by former *Davar* editor, Hannah Semer. She accepted the notion that Israeli Jews are essentially traditional without inferring that they are prepared to affirm Torah and *mitzvot*. She assumes that their traditionalist orientation stems from their need for an identity and for symbols of belonging. Their behavior proves that the "the nation of Israel lives . . . it is alive and well."

The authority on Jewish mysticism, Yosef Dan, also adopted this position, which is quite consistent with the Guttman conception described in the previous chapter. He went on to argue that the *haredim* are the Jewish model of Judaism and that Jewish society can be measured by their closeness or distance from *haredi* behavior. Dan attributed this to nostalgia for the pre-Holocaust world that was destroyed.

Other authors were more reluctant to accept this interpretation of the Guttman data. They questioned whether the behavior of most Israelis is best captured by the term *observance of commandments*, or even *tradition*. Many shared the belief that what the Guttman Report had tapped was the observance of cultural norms rather than distinctly religious behavior. Michael Rosenak, a philosopher of Jewish education, suggested that the Guttman data was misleading. The apparent affirmation of tradition by Israeli Jews, he suggested, may simply point to its trivial importance in the mind of many of the respondents. The high number of respondents affirming traditional theological beliefs led him to wonder whether Israeli Jews understand the implications of these beliefs in terms of their relationships with non-Jews as well as with Jews. This was an allusion to what Rosenak views as prejudiced treatment by Jews of Palestinians. Rosenak's point, which he shared with many other academics, was that those who were less than fully observant were not affirming the religious values of "holiness and comprehensive commitment."

The notion is elaborated upon in separate papers by political scientists Bernard Susser and Charles Liebman. While they did not reject the Guttman conception of the report, they suggested an additional possibility. They admitted that the Guttman results might be understood as demonstrating a pattern of observance, among Israeli Jews, ranging from total or nearly total observance to nonobservance; but the results could also be understood as denoting high levels of observance among roughly 20 to 25 percent of the population, as well as a pattern of folkways heavily derived from the Jewish tradition among the remaining Israeli Jews.

According to Liebman, individuals seek order in their lives and find it by adopting a variety of rituals. These rituals serve to mark their status and identity to themselves and others, to demonstrate their claim to rights and prerogatives that accrue to individuals of a certain status, to differentiate themselves from certain groups and to integrate themselves with other groups. Rituals are modes of delineating and thereby assigning meaning to transformations in one's own life as well as changes in the cycle of the year. Israelis, too, are ritually oriented. It is not surprising that a good portion of the rituals that they have adopted are derived from the Jewish tradition. This is a function of the richness of the tradition whose rituals lend themselves to adaptation and to the deep mark that the tradition has left upon Israeli Jews, on some, (Sephardim) more than on others (Ashkenazim).

In accordance with this mode of categorization, Israeli Jews are engaged in two related though theoretically distinct types of behavior. The smaller group is observing religious commandments, whereas the larger group is developing a ritual pattern of living that borrows heavily from the tradition but adapts that tradition and adds additional elements as well.

Israel is a family-oriented society. In many respects, its family orientation more closely resembles the Islamic world than that of Christian Europe. The overt signs are marriage and fertility rates. The pattern of ritual observance, both that revealed by the Guttman Report and some aspects that the report does not probe, functions to reinforce this family orientation. This includes the importance of family participation in a festive Shabbat meal; spending Friday evening at home in a family setting (where we may assume television plays an important role); building a *succah* regardless of whether it is built in accordance with *halakhic* standards; participating in a Passover *seder* regardless of whether the *hagada*, the ritual text accompanying the *seder*, is recited in full; lighting *Hanukkah* candles; masquerading on Purim; picnicking on Independence Day; visiting and caring for graves; and commemorating the death of family members, especially those who died in wars.

Yisrael Bartal, professor of modern Jewish history, interpreted the observance data from a different perspective. At one level, he accepted the Guttman conception. He found it perfectly natural that virtually all

Israeli Jews observed at least some aspects of the religious tradition. However, he went on to say, when this observance is coupled with the support expressed by 42 percent of the respondents for separating religion and state, we are confronted with a new historical reality—the separation of the political and religious dimensions of Judaism. Religion is no longer the total system it once was. Instead, Zionism has substituted a "national church" (including a chief rabbinate) with limited powers while leaving the individual Jew a wide margin of choice with regard to how the tradition is to be observed, including transforming some of its parts. One example he cited was lighting Sabbath candles without a blessing. Contrary to the Guttman conception, Bartal believed that selectivity in observance, the transformation of many commandments, and even the imputation of national, social, and peculiarly moral meaning to the commandments and customs of Judaism constitutes a *de facto* rebellion against the tradition. This, he pointed out, may be far more threatening to the Orthodox than total nonobservance.

The distinction between observance by the "observant" and observance by the "nonobservant" was raised, in different forms, by many authors. A few noted that from the perspective of religious law partial observance may be worse than none. For example, lighting Sabbath candles after the onset of the Sabbath entails a more serious violation of religious law than not lighting candles at all. Interestingly, however, the religiously observant participants did not raise the *halakhic* issue. One of them even alluded to its transformative potential in positive terms.

Gerald Blidstein, professor of Jewish thought, noted that whereas the Guttman Report measured behavior (and nominal belief), it offered no measure of commitment. In comments reminiscent of points raised by Emanuel Sivan in his *Ha'Aretz* article described in the previous chapter, Blidstein noted that the Guttman Report was unable to test what lay behind observance. The foundation of classical Jewish religiosity is commitment to *halakha*, that is, to Jewish law itself and to the Divine legislator who is the ultimate authority for the law. Presumably, the less than fully observant lack this foundation. But, Blidstein goes on to note, the findings of the Guttman Report suggest an alternative to the classical religious model—the emergence of a national-cultural and familial framework of loyalty that allows for *halakhic* selectivity. Blidstein offers no judgment about whether this phenomenon is welcome or not and whether it may even imply a model of behavior that is capable of incorporation within the *halakhic* system.

Many referred to this pattern of selective observance—the transformation of traditional commandments and customs and the imputation of new meaning to traditional observances—as "civil religion" or folkways. Rabbi

Steven Riskin, former leader of the Lincoln Square synagogue in New York City and at present the rabbi of the community of Efrat, a religious leader who has made a significant impact on religious life in Israel, adopted a sanguine view of this pattern. Embracing Mordechai Kaplan's definition of Judaism as a civilization, he interpreted the Guttman Report's findings to mean that virtually all Israeli Jews participate in that civilization. These Jews, in turn, are divided between those who "observe the commandments of Israel" (i.e., the Jewish religion) and those who "observe the culture of Israel."

Gershon Shaked, the esteemed literary critic, also referred to the emergence of two cultures. The correct interpretation of the Guttman Report, according to Shaked, is to acknowledge that there are two Jewish cultures–a culture based on faith and *mitzvah* observance and one "based on the [Jewish] tradition although . . . [it is] not a religious culture." This is the Zionist culture which secularized the sacred and by transforming the historical Jewish community that was a religious community into a nation, sanctified the profane. Shaked acknowledges that Zionist culture has lost much of its coherence in recent years. This accounts for the "crises of cultural and social identity in secular society." He expressed his anxiety lest the two cultures, the religious and the secular-Zionist, become alienated from one another.

In his written presentation, Eddy Zemach, professor of philosophy and linguistics, directed his attention to the majority of the population that is not fully observant. Like Riskin and Shaked, he also suggested that it is a culture rather than a religion that Israelis today affirm. But Zemach posed a sharper distinction between religion and culture than any of the participants. For the past thousand years, he claimed, Judaism was a religion. A religion is like a chain. To break any link means destroying the chain. But Israelis do not want a religion whose elements are inseparable. This is why, he claimed, they also reject Reform Judaism. They want "a living culture which has many related elements; people adopt items that are meaningful to them out of their cultural heritage, without deep commitment to the remaining ones."

A more radical interpretation was offered by the eminent Judaica scholar, Moshe Idel. Idel maintained that it was wrong to judge the behavior of the respondents according to the yardstick of Jewish law, that is, measuring how much or how little they deviated from the codified *halakha*. Instead, Idel maintained, the Guttman Institute researchers should have sought to ascertain what the respondents' pattern of observance meant to them. Idel seems to assume that behind the observance pattern of the respondents, or perhaps of groups of respondents, lies a coherent religion. In such a case it is unreasonable to label their behavior as "traditional." Zemach offered a similar argument in his oral presentation. He maintained that it was impossible to ascertain the essence of Judaism. Judaism is that which Jews do. "The Jewish people define what the Jewish religion is. . . . What people do and what people observe strictly will be important to religion and what people do not observe strictly and do not observe at all is eliminated from religion." But unlike Idel, Zemach accepts the notion of cultural patterns, a kind of ethno-religion that can be grasped without necessarily inquiring about the reasons that lie behind its acceptance for each individual.

Both Idel and Zemach (in his oral as distinct from his written presentation) seem to suggest that it is wrong to identify the partially observant as participating in a culture defined by the tradition. According to them, all are participating in different forms of the Jewish religion.

RELIGIOUS POLARIZATION IN ISRAELI SOCIETY

Virtually everyone addressed the Guttman Report conception concerning the absence of religious polarization among Israeli Jews. Some accepted it, others challenged it.

Most of the Van Leer participants understood the report to be saying that whereas relations between the observant and nonobservant are viewed by many Israelis as a cause for concern, there is no cause for concern; that the popular image of polarization, that is, the image of two extremes, religious and secular, poised at each others throat, is an inaccurate image. Whether this is or is not what the Guttman Report says is something that readers of chapter 1 may decide for themselves. In this chapter we are not concerned with defending or challenging the Guttman conception but rather with describing the responses of leading Israeli intellectuals.

Even those who agreed that the Guttman Report was correct—that the popular image of a rift is incorrect—believed that the peace between the sides was a fragile one or that it had another side.

Moshe Lissak, distinguished sociologist, one of the six recipients of the Israel prize who participated in the Van Leer discussions, explained the absence of polarization in sociological terms. His paper sought to answer why Israel has not experienced "some sort of all-out *kulturkampf*." His answer was the existence of many intermediate moderating groups with overlapping memberships. According to Lissak, among the fully observant, the less than fully observant, and the totally nonobservant one will find both Sephardim and Ashkenazim and individuals at a variety of age, educational, income, and occupational levels. In addition, he noted, the Guttman Report found that virtually all Israeli Jews feel a strong attachment to Diaspora Jewry. This is a shared value that generates solidarity and reduces tensions. Nevertheless, Lissak added, the public perception of a gap does reflect a reality and not simply a misrepresentation of reality. The majority of the public objects to being coerced by religious legislation and perceives the demands for public funds by *haredim*, demands that the government often meets, as lacking an objective basis. In addition, the public resents *haredi* denial of religious legitimacy or even religious significance to the state. The debate over territorial boundaries and the adoption by the religious public of *halakha* (Jewish law) as the guideline for resolving this key public issue is also a source of tension, according to Lissak. Finally, the existence of sociocultural enclaves of religious Jews based on closed educational and residential systems harbors the potential seeds of conflict. Lissak concluded that "mutual feelings of alienation and hostility will not disappear from the scene in the foreseeable future. . . ." and with the diminution of Israeli-Palestinian tensions, "the non-polarized rift between religious and secular may take on a more polarized character in the form of a more serious *kulturkampf*."

Lissak's mentor, the preeminent sociologist S. N. Eisenstadt, also pointed to secular fears of the religious as a potential source of conflict. It is the secular who fear the religious rather than religious the secular since the religious are perceived as a homogeneous and organized camp, threatening the rights of the secular. This condition is quite different from that which prevailed in the 1950s when it was the religious who feared the secular, according to Eisenstadt.

Emmanuel Rackman, chancellor of Bar-Ilan University and an active participant in issues of contemporary Jewish concern, concluded that "while in almost every area in which Israeli society requires integration progress is being made . . . almost no progress is being made in the relationship between the religious and the non-religious, and none also in the relationship between the so-called ultra-religious (a reference to *haredim*) and the less ostentatiously religious (an apparent reference to religious-Zionists)." He deplored the present condition whereby religion is a cause for separation and divisiveness. He called upon the Orthodox to reexamine their preference for "living in ethnic communities" and limiting admission of children from nonobservant homes or nonfully observant homes into religious schools. He also decried the extremism of the religious right who refuse to accept democratic ideals that Rackman asserts are at the heart of Judaism.

Rackman's essay, which took the form of a plea to the Orthodox to do something about relationships between the religious and the nonreligious, was unusual, but his concern about the nature of the relationships, as we have already seen, was not. Three other authors spoke to this same point. However, they understood the Guttman Report to be saying something different than the authors already discussed.

Menachem Friedman, the preeminent student of the modern *haredi* community accepted the Guttman Report findings on the absence of sharp separation between the religious and nonreligious. But, he added, the absence of polarization is confined to the realm of observance. Friedman acknowledged that the majority of Israeli Jews are not "secular" if "secular" is interpreted to mean the rejection of religion. But they and Israeli society are what Friedman called "secular by default." In a sense, Friedman is describing, in sociological terms, what a number of other writers described in theological terms. Whereas they contrasted the philosophy or theology that distinguishes observance by religious and nonreligious Jews, Friedman focuses on the extent to which religious observance is essential to one's lifestyle and the rhythms of one's life. Religion and observance of the religious commandments are basic components in the life of the religious Jew. By contrast, they represent an occasional, partial, and perhaps trivial aspect of the nonreligious Jew's life. The consequence, argues Friedman, is a social rift. The observant Jew does not necessarily welcome segregation from the nonreligious. It is the consequence of the different lifestyles and value systems that the religious and the nonreligious pursue and the effort of religious Jews to protect themselves and their families from the impact of the secular environment.

Friedman explains how the family car, the multistory apartment building, the supermarket with its variety of nonkosher goods all create a secular reality which excludes religious Jews and thereby prevents friendships or intimate relations with the nonreligious. But, says Friedman, this does not mean confrontation and violence. On the contrary, he argues, the level of conflict between religious and nonreligious is less today than in the past. The result of the segregation of religious Jews is to allow both the religious and the secular to find expression for their styles of life and their values in the public as well as the private realm.

This otherwise sanguine portrait of social peace, which is purchased at the price of social isolation, is marred, however, by the specter of political conflicts that now loom on the horizon. This specter, I would add, has become much more real since the 1993 Van Leer conference. Friedman called this the "existential political question that must now be resolved," in an obvious reference to the controversy over the peace agreements between Israel and the Palestinians and the Israeli government's willingness to surrender all or at least part of the Holy Land it captured in 1967.

Unlike Friedman, Aviezer Ravitzky, professor of medieval and modern Jewish thought, challenged the Guttman Report finding of an absence of polarization. Ravitzky interpreted the report to be saying that polarization could only be present if there were two extreme positions and no intermediary positions bridging them. But, claimed Ravitzky, polarization also refers to the distance between two extreme positions assuming these positions are upheld by significant cultural, social, and ideological groups. And, he added, this is the case in Israel even though one can point to a continuum of religious observance. One finds, at the extremes, individuals who are most influential in shaping public opinion. In addition, Ravitzky maintained, it is often minorities who determine historical processes. So the fact that most Israeli Jews can be ranged between the extremes is no proof that the society is not polarized.

Eliezer Schweid, recipient of the Israel prize in Jewish thought, carried Ravitzky's argument further. His disagreement with the Guttman Report's conclusions about polarization were the most emphatic. Polarization exists, he claimed, and "greater or lesser degrees of observance do not necessarily create a bridge." One can not simply dismiss the "rhetoric of polarization" since, this polarizing rhetoric reflected the positions of "political leaders, molders of public opinion in the media, the rabbinical elite [and] secular intellectuals." In other words, the rhetoric is part of the reality and therefore, contrary to the Guttman Report, is not "without foundation."

Schweid was unhappy with the Guttman conception for a number of reasons. One that merits special attention is Schweid's understanding of the different meanings, significance, scope, and authority that the fully observant and the less than fully observant ascribe to the tradition. The highest value for the nonreligious, according to Schweid, is "self realization." As recognition of this priority grows, Schweid says, "the less interest there is in the symbols of national identification, and . . . the less willingness to observe customs classified as 'commandments' or 'obligations'."

SOME SUMMARY REMARKS

Despite the authors' reservations about the blurred boundaries between the fully observant and the nonobservant in the report, despite differences in interpretation that are offered to explain the behavior of the nonfully observant (is it another variety of the Jewish religion, is it Jewish culture, is it national behavior, is it best described as folkways, is it simply a different and lesser degree of religious observance), one fact emerges clearly from the report and no one really took issue with this. As Gerald Blidstein put it, the Guttman Report deals with the power of religion to influence the nature of Israeli society. The report found that the Jewish religion retains an influence that many had heretofore refused to acknowledge. That influence does not necessarily reduce the levels of segregation between different circles or camps among Jews nor is there any assurance that this influence will continue unabated. In the last two chapters we return to a discussion of this final point.

4

Behavioral and Phenomenological Jewishness

ELIHU KATZ

Sociological surveys on sensitive issues cause their readers—enlightened ones as well—to ask, "Is this us?" and "Is this me?" "How do its findings compare with my own image of everybody else and of where I stand in relation to the rest?" The Guttman Report on "Observances and Beliefs" did exactly that. It evoked interest in every quarter—probably more than any previous empirical study of Israeli society—and challenged its readers to compare their images of the Jewishness of Israelis and of themselves against the findings obtained from a representative national sample. Confronted with such evidence, not everybody immediately suspends disbelief or abandons his/her prejudgments in favor of the evidence of the study. This is as it should be. Many people were surprised by the study's findings, others disputed its interpretations, while still others raised questions about its methodology. This book gives them voice; it also offers an opportunity to the authors of the report to respond.

This chapter, then, is an effort by one of the study's authors to contribute to a dialogue with its commentators and critics, friendly and unfriendly, understanding and misunderstanding. It expands and presents again elements of the study—going beyond specific findings—so as to make clear where contemplation of our findings has led us, what we have profited from our critics, and thus where we agree and disagree with them.[1] It also restates the design of the study, and several of its findings, in order to address certain questions that have arisen in the press and in public discussion.

In the course of responding to queries and criticisms, this chapter can also give insight into the attention, even the passion, that the study aroused. It will reveal, I believe, that some of the questions addressed to the study, and some of the unease that accompanies them, are not strictly about the study itself but are philosophical and personal questions about Judaism and Jewishness. Thus our study reawakened gnawing problems such as: Who is a Jew? Are ethnicity and religion disconnectable in Jewish identity? Is Judaism a religion of performance or belief, or both? What is a secular Jew? If one can be a nonreligious Jew, why is Jewishness incompatible with assuming another religion? Is Zionism—or living in Israel—a religious commandment? Is Judaism open to change? Is there room for selectivity in observance or should such "inconsistency" be condemned? Some of these questions were actually put to our sample of respondents, but, manifestly, public opinion need not be accepted as a normative guide.

The survey caused readers to ask themselves why they perform certain religious practices when they are avowed secularists, just as it caused persons who consider themselves observant to ask why they selectively perform some behaviors and not others. In short, the study aroused dissonance at a personal level, which is well portrayed in the angry outburst of a distinguished colleague, who said, "How dare you call me religious when all I do is not eat pork?" To which I replied, "We don't call you anything. You may define yourself as you please. All we have done is to note that, for some reason, you are observing an explicit commandment of the Torah." The professor thought for a while, plagued by the malaise of dissonance that we had brought upon him. "Okay," he muttered with annoyance, "from now on, I'm going to eat pork!"

WHAT THE STUDY DOES: THE RESEARCH DESIGN

The Guttman Institute was commissioned by the Avi Chai Foundation to map the extent of religious observance among Israeli Jews. The emphasis was on observance—that is, performance. We also examined some of the reasons for observing or not observing with respect to certain specific observances such as *kosher* food, but observance itself was its focus. Along with observance, we also surveyed various kinds of religious belief.

How was this done? To put the matter succinctly, one might say that we (1) "sampled" religious observances, that is, with the help of expert scholars, we chose a set of typical ritual behaviors that are prescribed or proscribed by the religious tradition and (2) asked a representative sample of adult Israeli Jews whether and to what extent they observed each of these behaviors and with what frequency. In addition, we (3) asked respondents to characterize themselves as "strictly observant," "observant to a great extent," "somewhat observant," and "not observant at all."

In these terms, the overall task of the study was to map the patterns, or profiles, of religious observance against the demographic groupings of which the population sample is composed, and the self-definitions of observance. This method allows the analyst to compare the patterns of observance of, say, different age groups or groups of different ethnic origin. By the same token, specific patterns of religious behavior can be assigned to each of the self-definitions of religiosity to explore what "strictly observant" or "not at all observant" look like in behavioral terms.

In appraising the implementation of the study design, the following points are noteworthy:

1. An unusually large sample of the population was drawn in order to permit in-depth analysis of subgroup behavior by age, ethnic origin, educational level, and self-definition by religiosity.

2. We are satisfied that the sample population is a good representation of the overall population both in demographic terms and in terms of less concrete categories, such as *haredi* (ultra-Orthodox). Six percent of our sample defined themselves as *haredi*, compared with the guesstimate that 10 percent of Israeli Jews may be *haredim*. Since this population is often uncooperative to interviewers, the study may be deemed particularly successful in this regard.

3. As for religious self-definition, several alternative measures were employed. One of these was a seven-point scale along which respondents could locate themselves on a continuum of religiosity (*dati*) from "very religious" to "antireligious." These measures are so highly intercorrelated, that we chose the four-point scale of observance ("strictly" to "not at all") mentioned earlier. We preferred this measure to the others because it is closest to the characterizations one overhears in everyday conversation.

4. Many of the specific questions about observance and belief employ precisely the same language used in other Guttman Institute surveys (and in a set of smaller-scale surveys conducted at Bar-Ilan University) in order to identify changes that have occurred over time.

WHAT THE STUDY SAYS (AND DOES NOT SAY): RESEARCH FINDINGS

From the report—the highlights of which appear as Chapter 1 in this volume—I want to single out several essential findings to illustrate what the study does and does not say. I will also show how these findings underpin our interpretations.

1. When respondents were asked to characterize the extent of their observance of Jewish religious tradition in the everyday language of conversation, 14 percent said they observed "strictly," 24 percent said

"mostly," 41 percent said "somewhat," and 21 percent said "not at all." It is noteworthy that these percentages are not substantially different from Guttman Institute studies over many years. This is striking in view of the major demographic changes that have taken place, particularly in the achievement of near-parity in the population of Jewish adults between those who trace their origin to Europe and the West and those who derive from the Eastern countries. Indeed, cross-tabulation of self-defined religiosity with ethnic origin shows that the stability in the distribution of religious observance can be traced to demographic change itself! It is *because* of the greater religiosity of the Eastern communities that nearly 40 percent of all Israeli Jews continue to characterize themselves as "strictly" and "mostly" observant. Only about 20 percent of Ashkenazim place themselves in these two categories compared with about 60 percent of Sepharadim. (No wonder the critics of the study–almost all Ashkenazim journalists and academics–often fail to recognize what we see.)[2] About 70 percent of the "mostly observant" are Sepharadim, while most of the "not at all observant" are educated Ashkenazim.

2. There are some signs of change. The second generation of Eastern Jews (born in Israel, father born abroad) is less observant than its parents. No such change is evident between the two generations of Western origin. Strikingly, the overall distribution of observance is not much affected by age, even if respondents think of themselves as less religious than their parents and less religious than they themselves used to be. As if in self-criticism, one third of respondents say they would like to be more observant than they are now, compared with only 5 percent who say they would prefer to be less observant. Half of the "not at all" observant wish their children to be somewhat observant.

3. The Jewishness of Israelis, behaviorally speaking, can be sketched as follows: (a) about 25 percent of the population carefully follow the rule-governed life of Judaism on a daily basis; in American terms, they are Orthodox Jews; (b) twice this number–that is, 50–60 percent of respondents–observe the dietary rules (*kashrut*); (c) this is also the proportion (50–60%) who do something special to mark the Sabbath eve–lighting candles, reciting the *kiddush*, serving a festive family meal; (d) 70 percent fast on Yom Kippur, 75 percent light the *Hanukkah* candles, 90 percent participate in a Passover *seder*; (e) the Jewish rites of passage are performed by almost everybody (80–90%): circumcision of males, *bar mitzvah*, religious marriage ceremony, religious ceremonies of death and remembrance; (f) almost everybody has a *mezuzah* on his/her door. In other words, there is near-universal observance of the life-cycle ceremonies and of the holidays of Passover, Yom Kippur, and *Hanukkah*. Well over half mark the Sabbath eve in a traditional manner and observe the

dietary laws. Note that in this ethnography, the Sabbath has shriveled to home rituals on Friday night, and that other major Jewish holidays have been eclipsed.

4. Many different practices and ceremonies were included in our sample of observances. Only 7 percent of the respondents told us they performed none of these. This is far lower than the percentage who characterized themselves as not observant "at all."

INTERPRETATION OF THE FINDINGS

Based on these findings, and on others to be reported later, we came to the conclusion that "Israeli society has a strong traditional bent, and, as far as religious practice is concerned . . . there is a continuum from the 'strictly observant' to the 'nonobservant' rather than a great divide between a religious minority and a secular majority." Throughout, we reasoned, our analysis was based on practice, and from the point of view of practice, it would be incorrect to speak of polarization. From the point of view of self-description as well, it can hardly be said that people who distribute themselves (14%-24%-41%-21%) over the range from "strictly" to "not at all observant" are polarized. That does not mean that there are no marked differences among the groups or that the two ends of the continuum feel comfortable with each other. What it does mean is that behaviorally speaking, at least, it is incorrect to imagine a religious minority doing "everything" and a secular majority doing "nothing." It is more accurate to say that a minority of about 15–20 percent are ideologically and behaviorally Orthodox, about 20 percent a self-defined secular minority (only very few of whom observe "nothing"), while two thirds of the population fall in-between.

WHAT THE STUDY MEANS: RESPONSE TO THE CRITICS

Many found this conclusion irritating. Some misunderstood its behavioral emphasis.

Some felt they knew better and looked for flaws in the research: the questions were biased, the sampling was inadequate, and so on. For example, some said that the wording was biased; using words like *tradition* or *mitzvot* ("commandments") positioned respondents as loyal or strayed Jews who dutifully supplied the responses "expected." While such arguments deserve attention, the fact is that these concepts are not much in evidence in the questionnaire that, on the whole, asks respondents whether or not, and how frequently, they observe one or another ritual or ceremonial behavior.

When we do use the word *mitzvah*—here and there in the questionnaire and much more in the report—we feel altogether justified in doing so. Without concerning ourselves with their historic origin, their functions, or their meanings, the practices we studied are part of a corpus of ritual behavior that is anchored in a rulebook called *halakha* (code of rabbinic law) and named *mitzvot*. Even if some have appropriated the word *mitzva* from this context and narrowed it to denote only universal good deeds, such as visiting the sick, that does not change the fact that the language, classically, uses the name *mitzva* for eating *matzot* on Passover or circumcising one's male child, *a fortiori* when the appropriate blessing is pronounced.

Going a step further, our nastiest critic asked, in effect, "how can anybody in his/her right mind answer "never" to the question 'do you refrain from driving on the Sabbath' when he/she would have to drive continuously for 25 hours each Sabbath in order to answer 'never'." This was proof positive, said the satirist, that the questions are meant to produce the results that were paid for by the foundation that sponsored the study. Had our critic read the respondents' *replies*—not just the questions put to them—he would have learned that 56 percent of respondents replied that they "never" refrain from driving in automobiles on the Sabbath! They understood the question perfectly, even if our critic refused to.

Others, who had no quarrel with the empirical findings, felt that our interpretation was wrong, arguing that observance itself is not an adequate indicator of religiosity. Whether or not this critique should be addressed to the authors of the Guttman Report—rather than to the rabbis and philosophers of Judaism—remains to be considered. For the moment, however, I want to spell out the several different ways in which this objection was formulated and to bring other aspects of the study to bear on the discussion. Briefly, these critiques say that the conclusions of the study are unwarranted because (a) Judaism is a *system* of practices, not the random selection of individual choices reported in the study; (b) Jewish practice requires *intent*, not just rote performance; (c) practice without *faith* in the divine is empty and Jewishly unacceptable; (d) practices must be accompanied by acceptance of the *halakha* as the source of authority for their performance; (e) observances are central to the life of a truly religious Jew, whereas observance in the style reported here does not seem central to the lives of their practitioners. Each of these arguments wishes to reinstate the idea that there is, indeed, a religious minority and a secular majority, and to 'disqualify' the observances of those who define themselves as less than "strictly" observant. We will consider each of these objections in turn, agreeing in part with some and altogether disagreeing with others.

1. *Judaism is a system of practices, not the random selection of individual choices reported in the study*. True, Judaism is an elaborate system of practices, governing every aspect of life. It is also true that, apart from the "strictly" observant and some part of the "mostly" observant (perhaps one third of the population), the others–especially the modal (41%) group of the "somewhat" observant–are highly selective in the practices they observe.

Of course, one may rule, a priori, that those who do less than "everything" (which would include just about everybody, including the "strictly" observant) do not qualify as practitioners of Judaism. Or, one may decide to exclude the observances of those who violate certain cardinal rules.[3] For example, perhaps eating *kosher* food should not "count" as a religious observance if that person also operates an automobile on the Sabbath. These questions are obviously not for the authors of this study to decide.

But we would not consider our job well done if we simply mapped the distribution of each of the observances separately. We looked for *patterns* of practice to characterize the respondents. And, while selectivity is rampant, what we found is that observances are not randomly selected. There is no free-for-all. There is, rather, (a) high consensus on what practices are and are not observed and (b) an underlying order that marks the path from more to less observant. This is a popular order, of course, that may or may not be articulated anywhere–not in the minds of the people and certainly not in the rule books. Thus, as already indicated, there is a high consensus in the population over the importance of religious performance of rites of passage, over how to observe the Sabbath, which holidays are more important, and so on. Moreover, we discern patterns in the process of declining observance: the observance that is "first to go"–that is, the first deviation from strict orthodoxy–is the injunction against activating electricity on the Sabbath, followed by Sabbath travel, followed by doing work on the Sabbath, separating meat and dairy dishes, reciting the Sabbath blessing over the wine, lighting Sabbath candles, fasting on Yom Kippur, participating in a Passover *seder*. These practices form a "scale" such that one can predict–with high certainty–that a person who lights candles on the Sabbath eve, for example, will also fast on Yom Kippur, but one cannot predict in the opposite direction, that is, a person who fasts on Yom Kippur may or may not light Sabbath candles. "Last to go" is attendance at a Passover *seder*.

2. *Jewish practice requires intent, not just rote performance*. Those who raise this objection imply that they *know* that behavior without explicit motivation is unacceptable in Judaism, and what the study reports as observance is "surely" devoid of such conscious intent. At best, they say, it is folklore and at worst ritualistic (not ritual) performance that has long since become disconnected from its source. Stated this way, the objection is incorrect.

These critics would be surprised to learn that observances are typically accompanied by pronouncement of the blessing that incorporates intent. Thus, of the approximately 60 percent who light candles regularly on Friday evening, fully 51 percent light the candles and say, "Blessed are thou, Lord, our God, King of the universe who has sanctified us with His blessings and commanded us to light the Sabbath candle."

But if this is not acceptable—because the blessing may also be rote—let us see what the respondents themselves say about why they perform the *mitzvot*. While the emphasis of the study was behavioral, as has been stated repeatedly, we did ask for "reasons" at several points. Thus the predominant reasons for observance of dietary laws are to "continue tradition," and "because that's what Jews do."[4] These may be considered wrong reasons by critics who refused to perceive a connection between sociology and theology, but one cannot say that observance is without intent. And, as Hanna Zemer emphasized in her remarks at the Van Leer symposium, observing for the sake of Jewish continuity is not trivial. Moreover, even the most observant (those who defined themselves as "strictly observant" and "mostly observant") include identification with the Jewish people as an important reason. Thus, Jewish identification as a reason for observance was given by 90 percent of the "strictly" and "mostly" groups, by 70 percent of the "somewhat observant," and by 35 percent of the "not at all observant." This is not the issue that splits the "strictly observant" from the others, although we shall soon see what does.[5]

"Just folklore," continue the critics, or "civil religion," alluding to the cooptation of religious ritual by secular nationalism. But before rejecting the continuity of Jewish peoplehood as a motive for traditional observance, let us ask ourselves whether we can be certain that our pious ancestors would have answered otherwise if they were asked about motivation. Perhaps reference to the concept "Jewish people" incorporates the normative injunctions of Jewish Law or the Jewish God, and perhaps it has always been so.

Others raise the question whether Jewish behavior in the Jewish State can be considered voluntary at all. Indeed, goes this argument, it is difficult to find meat that is not *kosher*, and which hospital would let a newborn male child go uncircumcised? Anticipating such objections, the study delves deeper into these areas, basing its conclusions not on whether respondents eat *kosher* meat, for example, but on whether they have separate dining utensils for meat and dairy dishes; not just on whether a male child is circumcised but whether he is ritually circumcised and whether he/she has had a *bar/bat mitzvah* ceremony.

3. *Practice without faith is empty and unacceptable.* Another set of critics disagree with the conclusion that observance, however selective, is

widespread by insisting that observance is hollow unless it is accompanied by belief in the divine. Their argument is not about the dedication that is supposed to accompany practice (as in the discussion of intent) but about the normative expectation that Jewish behavior is supposed to be accompanied by specifically Jewish beliefs in divinity.

Here, even more than before, the assumption that Jewish Israelis are nonbelievers is incorrect. A very large proportion of Israelis believe in God and that the Torah was given on Mount Sinai. Half believe that *mitzvot* are God's command and that there is divine reward for performing *mitzvot,* although only one quarter agree that one is punished for nonadherence.

There are major differences in the beliefs of those who are more and less observant. Thus, over 60 percent of Israelis "believe completely" that there is a God, but that includes only 20 percent of the self-proclaimed nonobservant. In other words, as one would expect, there is a correlation between believing and observing, when subjectively defined.

Again, we should note that Jewish experience–certainly modern experience–supplies us with examples of Jewish persons who believe but do not observe and others who observe without believing. Both of these syndromes are present in the study. Thus, 20 percent of those who call themselves nonobservant believe in God; 10 percent of the "mostly observant" (3% of the "strictly") do not.

4. *Practices must be accompanied by acceptance of the* halakha *as the source of authority for their performance.*

The system of Jewish observance is anchored in the code of rabbinic law known as *halakha.* It is the normative source of authority from which all observances–except for certain folkloristic customs–derive.

Do observers recognize the authority of the *halakha*? For a majority, the answer is obviously in the negative. We have already seen that, when asked why they observe practices such as dietary laws, the predominant reasons tend to be sociological or instrumental or sentimental in nature: this is what Jews do, this is the way it was done at my home, it is more hygienic. Even though the "strictly observant" are also more likely to give these sociological answers than those who observe, the "right" answer–"because it is a commandment"–is given almost exclusively by the "strictly" and "mostly" observant. Thus 86 percent of the "strictly observant" say they observe *Kashrut* because it is a commandment from the Torah compared with only 7 percent of those who keep the dietary laws among the "nonobservant." This coincides with responses of the four replies to the more general question, "To what extent do you believe or not believe that the Torah and *mitzvot* are God's command: 93 percent, 75 percent, 36 percent, and 6 percent, respectively, "believe completely."

Acceptance of the code of law as the source of authority for observance does, indeed, divide (but not polarize) the population. Among the "strictly" and "mostly" observant, almost all overwhelmingly say yes, among the "not at all" almost all say no. The "somewhat" observant are full of doubt.[6]

Nonacceptance of this authority also explains the selective character of observance among the majority. More than half doubt the divinity of the *halakha*–indeed, we know that most do not feel guilty about their failure to perform one or another of the mandated practices, and this is true even of those who would like to be "more" observant.[7] The very idea of picking and choosing is unacceptable to Orthodox Judaism but is widespread among Jewish Israelis. When we asked respondents to assess the importance of several reasons typically offered for nonobservance, "selective observance is sufficient" was accorded second place in a list of four reasons and particularly characterized those who are, indeed, "mostly" and "somewhat" observant.[8]

It appears, then, that what distinguishes the "strictly observant" is not only the extent of their observance but their loyalty to the source of authority that governs the practice and holds the practices together. The "not at all observant"–even though they do participate in certain observances–tend to reject the idea that observance is a mandated requirement; indeed, they associate religion with morality and ethics rather than with observance. Those who define themselves as less than strictly observant–more than half the population–are aware of their selective behavior, but rather than resort to the ideological "ethical people don't need *mitzvot*," they simply agree that "partial observance is sufficient," and, pragmatically that "it is difficult to observe the *mitzvot*." Not do they sound apologetic. It is true, then, that the two extreme groups are at polar extremes by the acceptance and rejection of the need for authority to govern their behavior, but the rest of the population appears to reject both doctrines. The majority do not explain their observances as mandated by authority nor do they argue that observance is detachable from Jewishness.

5. The data also offer support to those critics who argue that many of *the observances reported in the study are not central to the lives of their practitioners*. It seems reasonable to assume that observance was central to most Jews in the past; indeed, the *halakha* is a virtual agenda for lifelong behavior, on an hour-by-hour basis. That is not so today–at least not for the 60 percent who are neither "strictly" or "mostly" observant by their self-definition. We asked about the centrality of the Sabbath, for example, because the Sabbath rituals–the prescriptions and proscriptions–are so emblematic of the richness and complexity of Jewish tradition. Questions such as "How important is it to you to observe *mitzvot* as a guiding prin-

ciple of your life?" or "How important is it to you to observe the Sabbath in a traditional way as a guiding principle of your life?" are answered affirmatively by 97%-85%-35%-5%. About 25–30 percent of the population experience the Sabbath as "very" central, while the majority–in spite of their widespread, albeit selective, Sabbath observances–do not share this experience. They do not negate the experience–it is meaningful for most–but they do not affirm its centrality in the same way as what might properly be called the most "religious."

CONCLUSION

In summary, most criticism of the Guttman Report charges that the study has decontextualized ostensibly religious observance and reported only behavioral performance. This is true. The authors undertook to report on patterns of behavior. The study is a portrait of the extent to which a representative sample of Israeli Jews adhere to a sample of religious practices (*mitzvot*) ordained by the *halakha*.

Critics say, in effect, that these practices should not be characterized as religious nor even "observant" because their performance–so the critics assume–is unsystematic, without intent, devoid of belief, unaccepting of the legitimacy of *halakha* authority, and marginal to the lives of many of their practitioners.

To this we replied, first of all, that these questions are more properly addressed to Judaism than to the Guttman Institute. Somebody else–not us–should decide what "counts" and what does not, what is blasphemous and what is religious. We are not qualified to say whether partial performance is better than none, whether the 'people' have any say in what will be defined as traditional or religious, whether there are "right" and wrong" reasons for traditional behavior–or, indeed, any reasons at all.

Nevertheless, the study also explored self-definitions of religiosity and, to a limited extent, some of the reasons for observance and non-observance. On the basis of these data one can conclude that (a) observance, while partial and selective, is not random, individual, and unsystematic; there is a pattern of practice that describes the (religious) behavior of Jewish Israelis; (b) these observances are not without intent; they may lack "proper" intent but they are motivated by a conscious commitment to the continuity of the Jewish people; (c) moreover, those who observe them are not without belief; religious faith is widespread and there is a high correlation between ritual performance and belief; (d) the most observant groups (25–30%) and the rest differ at the level of acceptance of the authority that dictates practice; and a majority of those who practice are apparently aware of their "deviations" and are unperturbed by them, even if many would opt to be "more religious" than they are at present; and (e) the most observant groups also differ from the rest in the central place accorded to these practices in their lives.

Behaviorally speaking–and, perhaps, even from a Jewish philosophical perspective–certain traditional practices are widespread in Israel and extend far beyond the group that defines itself as "strictly observant." Phenomenologically speaking, the picture is more complex. Observance is selective (but patterned), voluntary (but not without a sense of obligation), and is accompanied by belief in God and in the divinity of the Torah. That it deviates from the system of which these practices are a part, from the centrality of these practices in personal life, and from the mandate of *halakha* is also evident.

Nevertheless, myths of the origin of the religious civilization that is Judaism still have force, as is evident in the beliefs of present-day Israeli Jews. Ironically, more recent history seems to be more easily forgotten. After all, the Zionist revolution was not only supposed to be political–the return of a dispersed people to its homeland–but cultural, as well. And, indeed, the Jewish State has tried cultural experiments, such as efforts to disconnect with the Diaspora and reconnect with a primordial Canaanism or efforts to create a suntanned socialism based on kibbutz agriculture, urban industry, and so on. These efforts, and others, emphasized discontinuity with the religious tradition. If the Guttman Report has a major message, it is that such experiments have yielded to an expressed commitment to traditional Jewish continuity.

That the expression of this continuity is experienced as voluntary and selective is therefore, paradoxically, also an expression of discontinuity with the traditional authority of the *halakha*. Israeli Jews reject the idea of religious imposition–whether of codified authority, or contemporary rabbis, or religious lobbyists. The report makes this amply clear.

NOTES

1. These ideas represent the thinking of all three authors–Dr. Shlomit Levy, Hanna Levinsohn, and myself–but their formulation here is my sole responsibility. Dr. Levy has also had occasion to elaborate on the study in an address to the faculty and students of the Jerusalem branch of the Jewish Theological Seminary at Neve Granot and at a seminar of the Education Branch of the Israel Defense Forces.

2. The study suggests that in spite of its professed pluralism, the educated nonobservant Ashkenazim group has the least day-to-day contact with others who are religiously unlike themselves.

3. The tradition is reluctant to be lenient even with respect to the lesser practices and thus resists justification of *mitzvot* in terms of relative importance.

4. Reasons of hygiene are almost as popular because the nonobservant give them greater weight.

5. It is worth noting that this distribution of replies to the general question, "Is identification with the Jewish people an important factor for you in observing Jewish tradition," coincides, almost exactly, with citing "home tradition" or "that's what Jews do" as reasons for eating *kosher* food.

6. The "somewhat" observant "believe completely" (36%), "believe with doubt" (43%) or "don't believe at all" (22%). Compare the nonobservant, 71 percent of whom "don't believe at all."

7. Among the "somewhat" observant, about two-thirds "seldom" or "never" feel uncomfortable doing something that violates the Sabbath.

8. The reason judged most important–in which even the "not at all observant" concurred–is "people lack proper education"; it is the reason cited by two-thirds of the population. Only the "not at all observant" gave equal weight to "ethical people don't need *mitzvot*," and of course the "strictly observant" judged this the least important reason. From this perspective, the group that is "not at all observant" stands out most sharply from the other three–who are not so very different from each other.

5

Religion and Modernity

The Special Case of Israel

CHARLES S. LIEBMAN

If we locate Israel on a global map of religious development, then the Guttman Report conclusions are puzzling. There is no evidence for a decline in traditional religious observance (i.e., the performance of ritual) or traditional religious belief that characterizes virtually all of Western Europe and that many observers find to be true of the United States as well. Opinions are divided about the changing status of religious practice and belief in the United States, but even those who argue that religious practice and belief have not declined, affirm the "growing secularization of a self-described religious people"[1] and "the changed perspective of many Americans that religious beliefs as such, especially insofar as they underpin moral certitudes, constitute a threat to freedom."[2] One may argue over whether or not church membership or church attendance has declined in the United States,[3] but there is no question about the decline of traditional Christian belief among mainline Protestants or the majority of Catholics. Nor, as we shall see, does religion appear to play the role in public life that it does in Israel with the concurrence, if not enthusiasm, of the vast majority of Israeli Jews.

But whereas there is no evidence for the decline of traditional religion in Israel comparable to a decline in the industrial West, there is also no evidence for a religious renascence, or a dramatic growth in the number of Orthodox and devout believers, as has occurred in Moslem societies, in the Middle East in particular. Israel has not experienced a rise of religious fundamentalism or an increase in the number or proportion of religious Jews, and there has been no aggressive effort to change the nature of Israeli society or transform the state into a theocratic one. On the contrary, the participation of religious groups in the political process appears to have moderated the nature of their public demands.[4] In order to explain the seemingly special case of Israel, I want to look once more at the Guttman Report. Any interpretation of that report requires a measure of selectivity. Most of the commentary, in the media but even among the academics, examined the report's findings from an Israeli perspective. Understandably, these were measured against what the critics knew or believed they knew about Israeli society. In this chapter I want to look at the report's findings in a historical and cross-cultural perspective rather than an entirely contemporary Israeli one. This necessarily means ignoring some of the nuances of the data. But it is my sense that by taking not one but two steps backward, we can raise important questions about Israeli society and shed a bit more light on its nature.

In this chapter I examine what I consider three of the four most striking findings of the Guttman Report–the traditionalism of Israeli Jews; the acquiescence if not endorsement of religion in Israeli public life; and the relative isolation, in terms of personal relationships and in terms of values, of the "totally nonobservant." In the following chapter I discuss the fourth significant finding, the absence, at least until the end of 1993 when the Guttman Report was published, of sharp cultural conflict between religious and nonreligious. These four findings, I believe, are all part of one package that enables us to explain the nature and role of the Jewish religious tradition in contemporary Israel and why Israel is a special case among advanced industrial democracies.

THE RELIGIOUS TRADITIONALISM OF ISRAELI JEWS

Two question marks about the Guttman sample paradoxically strengthen rather than weaken its conclusions. For one thing, the *haredi* segment of the population appears to be underrepresented, and respondents who identify themselves as *haredim* do not express the religious extremism that scholars associate with that segment of the population.[5] Such underrepresentation only serves to reinforce the general conclusion concerning the high levels of traditional observance in Israeli society. Secondly, if respondents exaggerated the levels of their observance and belief, as some academic and media critics have charged, it would suggest that the Jewish tradition is so pervasive as to require respondents to conform to some supposed societal norm.

In order to understand the nature of traditionalism among Israeli Jews we have to first clear away some conceptual and semantic underbrush. Among all but a few pedants, a small group of philosophers of religion, and perhaps some sociologists of religion, being religious in Israeli society connotes being "religiously observant," that is, observant of *halakha* (religious law). This notion is so commonplace that the astute sociologist Hanna Herzog, in explaining an aspect of Israeli politics, observed that, "Judaism is a pluralistic religion in which the various streams are differentiated by their degree of religiosity."[6] Now the distinguishing characteristic of the different streams in Judaism is their orientation to *halakha*, which means that Herzog, who is by no means religiously observant, was equating observance of *halakha* with religiosity. Similarly, the Guttman Institute chose to depict religious behavior as a continuum of *halakhic* observance along which almost any Israeli Jew could be located. This is a valid way of describing religious behavior and is essentially the way Israelis commonly classify themselves when they describe their religious orientations. They identify themselves as either "religious," meaning strictly observant of religious law, "traditional," meaning selectively observant, or "secular." The secular orientation is the most complex one as we shall see. What it probably means to those who define themselves in this way, as many of the Van Leer participants noted and as is elaborated upon later on, is that whereas the secular Jew may observe practices and rituals that religious and traditional Jews classify as *halakha*, from the secular Jews' perspective, they are observing folkways, national custom, family inherited rituals, and so on, which are not performed out of any sense of religious obligation.

Human nature being what it is, not all those who define themselves as religious are scrupulous in their observance of Jewish law. But religious Jews agree that Jewish law is a package of norms that obligate them as Jews, and if one does not observe Jewish law, one is not, at least in many respects, behaving as a good or proper Jew ought to behave. So while there is overlap in the observances of those who define themselves as religious and those who define themselves as traditional, Israelis can and do speak about the "religious" sector of the population or about the "religious" public with assurance that their listeners understand that the subject is strictness of observance. The religious public, in turn, expresses its own identity in a variety of ways—the most overt and obvious among males being the practice of wearing a yarmulke (head covering). Observance is also assumed to be associated with belief but is rarely invoked as a measure of religiosity.

If we translate the Guttman Report findings on religious observance into the categories of "religious," "traditional," and "secular"; no more than 23 percent of the (male) respondents can be identified as religious and since gender differences were negligible, the figure probably holds for all respondents. The percentage is based on the number of male respondents who report that they use (don) phylacteries regularly.[7] One might use phylacteries regularly and not define oneself or be perceived by others as "religious" (there are probably a number of older Jews, especially Sephardim, who fall into such a category). But since there is no common sense or credible definition of a religiously observant (male) Jew who does not use phylacteries regularly, 23 percent is the upper not the lower limit of "religious" Jews whom the Guttman Report located.[8] Consequently, the first important observation to be made here is that the vast majority of Israelis are indeed not "religious" by conventional Israeli standards of performing a prescribed body of practices.

I suspect that the hidden agenda of some critics of the Report, and the incredulousness with which it was greeted by others, derived from a misunderstanding of this aspect. One academic who read the *Highlights* remarked privately, "I don't care what the Guttman survey revealed, I know it can't be true." His mistake was to think that if most Israelis are observant in part then most Israelis are religious rather than traditional or secular. And this is what he quite properly refused to believe. Of course, this is not what the Guttman Report claimed. But the association in the public's mind between "observance" on the one hand and being part of the religious camp on the other hand is so strong, especially in the minds of the "totally nonobservant" who are overrepresented in the media and among intellectuals anyway, that it really did not matter that the Guttman Report warned readers against this facile generalization. What the report finds, therefore, is that whereas less than a quarter, and perhaps only a fifth, of Israeli Jews are "religious," close to four fifths testify to their observing at least some aspects of the tradition.

Even among the remaining fifth, among those who identify themselves as "totally nonobservant," a majority also observe some aspects of the tradition. For example only 6 percent of the total sample report that they seldom or never participate in a Passover *seder* and 12 percent that they seldom or never light *Hanukkah* candles. A good question to ask is why, therefore, did this one fifth or most of this one fifth identify itself as "totally nonobservant" when they do observe aspects of the tradition. Two possibilities, which are not mutually exclusive, suggest themselves. One is that the respondents do not interpret their participation in a Passover *seder* or lighting *Hanukkah* candles or other activity of such a nature as having anything to do with religious observance. They are simply participating in a national Jewish rite. A second possibility is that regardless of how they behave in their personal lives, some respondents are so antagonistic to the role of religion in public life that they refuse to identify themselves with anything that smacks to them of religion. I suspect this is true of many of the totally nonobservant who, as I suggest at the conclusion of this chapter, dissent from the consensual values of Israeli society in more profound ways.

The second observation to be made about Israeli observance is that despite the high levels of traditional observance, a point to which I will return, there is some question about the degree of importance that most Israelis attribute to it. Eighty-eight percent of the respondents–including about half of the strictly observant–agree that a person can be a good Jew even if he does not observe the religious tradition.

Finally, as I elaborate upon in the final chapter, levels of religious observance alone do not ensure that public life will be conducted in accordance with religious tradition or that those who observe have much understanding or even commitment to what they are observing.

All these caveats to the contrary notwithstanding, the fact remains that the basic level of traditional observance appears quite high.

High or low are relative terms; relative to other societies but also relative to the history of the society being examined. The founders of the state of Israel and the culture that dominated the Jewish settlement in Palestine preceding and immediately following the creation of the state was emphatically secular, antireligious and even antitraditional. The early Zionists and the generation who created the state viewed themselves in revolt against the Jewish tradition, and they sought to transmit these sentiments to their descendants.[9] Until the 1960s, the Jewish tradition, as distinct from national symbols and ceremonials that for the most part were derived from that tradition, was not held in high esteem by the political and cultural elites who determined the nature of public life. Israeli Jews seemed increasingly indifferent if not alienated from their Jewish past. We need only recall that the noted French sociologist George Friedman titled his 1960s study of Israeli society, *The End of the Jewish People?*[10] This may have been an artifact of the domination of Israeli society by Western (Ashkenazi) Jews and the muted voice of Eastern (Sephardi) Jews who were just beginning to make their presence felt in the public arena. The Sephardic Jews, who arrived at a later period, resented their treatment by the veteran Ashkenazi settlers. Indeed, one of the reasons they maintained their religious traditions may have been as an act of resistance to the cultural orientations of those whom they resented. David Martin, seeking to explain why some societies are more hospitable to religion than others, notes that "the key element seems to be the explicit implication of a given religious institution in the central nexus of power so that those outside that nexus are motivated to reject the whole religious package. . . ."[11] In Israel, not only was religion uninvolved in the nexus of power, the elite who held power was explicitly secular.

I have sought to describe the changes that overcame Israeli society elsewhere.[12] Since the 1960s "Tradition" has been publicly embraced by growing segments of Israeli society. In addition, probably related to this, the religious tradition is being nationalized through the selective interpretation of history and text. The early Zionist settlers celebrated their radi cal departure from the religious tradition. They identified their efforts to reclaim and settle the Land as taking charge of their own fate. Furthermore, settling the land and tilling its soil was viewed as an expressly secular activity in contrast to the "holy" activity of pious Jews who spent their days in the study of sacred text. Israelis now sacralize the land and point to its sacred nature in the tradition itself. What is all the more remarkable is that *eretz yisrael* (the Land of Israel) has come to symbolize both loyalty to the state of Israel as well as loyalty to the tradition. Indeed, as Baruch Kimmerling points out, the term *eretz yisrael* has increasingly replaced the term *state of Israel* in the pronouncements of national leaders on the political right[13] who describe their own camp as "loyalists to the Land of Israel."

Erik Cohen describes this trend as

> a reorientation of the basic principles of legitimation of Israel: a trend away from secular Zionism, especially its pioneering-socialist variety, towards a neo-traditionalist Jewish nationalism which, while it reinforces the primordial links among Jews both within Israel and the diaspora, de-emphasizes the modern, civil character of the state.[14]

The 1992 elections, which resulted in a narrow victory for the Labor party and its allies to the Left, marks a new direction in Israeli political culture with consequences for the understanding of the Jewish tradition, a point to which we return in the next chapter. The results of the 1966 election demonstrate that the majority of Israeli Jews are not ready to embrace this new direction. At least not yet.

The Jewish tradition has assumed a positive valence in Israeli society today. The initial rejection of tradition was probably inevitable. Even those Zionists who did not reject religion itself were conscious of the fact that their efforts stood in opposition to central values of the tradition as articulated and interpreted by its rabbinical custodians and as experienced by their Eastern European parents. In addition, the very excitement and hope, the revolutionary ardor that the Zionist enterprise generated among many of its followers, youth in particular, undermined a basic sympathy for tradition of any kind. "No more tradition's chains shall bind us . . . the earth shall rise on new foundations" was the anthem of the Worker's International and is a sentiment that revolutionaries of all stripes are likely to share.

However, after the establishment of Israel, the need to consolidate rather than innovate a national consciousness, the mass immigration of traditionally oriented Jews from Eastern Europe but especially from North Africa, the decline of secular Zionism, all help explain the reemergence of the Jewish tradition in religious form as an important component of Israeli culture, with all the caveats to be noted herein.

The levels of ritual observance or traditionalism among Israeli Jews serve to distinguish them from their American counterparts as well as that of early Israeli society. A recent study of religion in contemporary American society (conducted, coincidentally by two very knowledgeable observers of trends among American Jews) notes that "secularization has progressed furthest among Americans of Jewish ancestry."[15] In 1991, UJA-Federation, the organizational arm of the New York City Jewish community, conducted a survey of New York Jews. It reported much higher levels of Jewish commitment and identity than did the National Jewish Population survey of 1990. Its author attributes this to Jewish population density rather than to the higher proportion of Orthodox Jews in New York City compared to the rest of the United States.[16] Therefore, I chose to compare the results of the Guttman Institute survey with the New York survey rather than with the national one.

If we look only at entirely Jewish households in New York City (i.e., omit mixed Jewish-Gentile households and use only what the author calls "perfect cases," individuals who indicate that their religion of birth, religion of upbringing, and present religion are Jewish), we find the following. With respect to some practices there is little difference between the behavior of New York and Israeli Jews but there are large differences on some key practices. For example, 48 percent of the New York sample report they light *Shabbat* (Friday evening) candles, whereas 67 percent of the Israel sample say they do so always or often (an additional 7% report they do so sometimes). Twenty-eight percent of the New York sample report that they use separate dishes for milk and meat compared to 48 percent of Israelis.

The Guttman Report found little variation by age (contrary to other advanced industrial societies in Western Europe or the United States[17]) between men and women and between newcomers and oldtimers in ritual observance. Indeed, the levels of ritual observance that the Guttman Report found is almost identical to the patterns of observance that a sample survey of the Jewish population of Israel found almost twenty-five years earlier. Elihu Katz points out in the previous chapter that this is probably a consequence of the changing distribution of the ethnic composition of the population. Decreases in levels of observance, which may signal decreases in levels of commitment to tradition, are probably occurring in Israel. But this decrease is masked by the increased number of Jews of Sephardic origin. This tentative conclusion is reinforced by the correlation between lower levels of traditional behavior and higher levels of general education. According to the report, among those who completed their college studies, mostly Ashkenazim, 43 percent consider themselves "totally nonobservant," whereas, as we noted, only 20 percent of the total population are "totally nonobservant."

Age and gender show little correlation with traditionalism, education shows some, but it is ethnic origin (*eda* in Israeli parlance) that is most clearly correlated with traditionalism, a point to which we will return.

ATTITUDES TOWARD RELIGION AND STATE

The Israeli public is fairly evenly divided over many issues of religion and state. Fifty-six percent believe that it is not a government concern that public life be conducted in accordance with the Jewish religious tradition. Fifty-four percent believe that religion and state should be separate. However, "separation" in Israel has a different meaning than it does in the United States. When Israelis think about religion and state they think in terms of legislation that limits their individual liberties, such as the closing of movie theaters and public transportation on *Shabbat* (67% support opening of movie theaters and 64% favor public transportation on *Shabbat*), or the absence of civil marriage (51% favor instituting civil marriage in Israel). Separation of religion and state, however, does not conjure up a religiously neutral state or a state that refuses to accord special benefits to religion. For example, state support for religious schools (most religious schools in Israel are, in fact, state schools) is taken for granted. It has never been on the agenda for public debate.[18] Furthermore, phrasing the question in terms of government concern with the Jewish *religious* tradition skews the response. Religion, when raised in a political context, carries negative connotations for the vast majority of Israelis, including many observant Jews. The term *Jewish tradition*, on the other hand, carries positive connotations. Had the question been phrased without the word *religion*, had respondents been asked whether they felt that government should be concerned that public life be conducted in accordance with the *Jewish tradition* rather than the *Jewish religious tradition*, I suspect that a large majority would have responded positively. This suggests that one can give a different spin to the data on religion and state. I would argue that in view of the negative connotation that the term *religion* bears when it is applied to public life, it is surprising that so high a proportion of the public, 44 percent, are not only prepared to admit the possibility that public life be conducted in compliance with the Jewish religious tradition but that it is proper for the government to concern itself with this question. In addition, whereas

33 percent of the respondents felt that public life in Israel should be less religious than it is, 51 percent felt that it should be just as it is and 16 percent felt it should be more religious.

Even were one to concede that a minority and not a majority support the presence of religion in public life, the size of that minority, over 40 percent, is quite high by Western European, not to say American, standards. Although it is the United States rather than Europe, whose "political landscape [has] resonated with religious rhetoric,"[19] it is the United States "that prides itself on separating church and state."[20]

Assessing the impact of religion on American politics is not only complex but is a matter of controversy among scholars.[21] If we compare the Israeli landscape with the American one we can formulate some generalizations that most scholars would affirm. There is no question that the majority of Americans respond positively to the articulation of a national vision or national goals in nondenominational religious language. The vast majority of Americans reject what they perceive of as efforts by the New Christian Right to change the present system of the separation of religion and state. Separation of religion and state is so widely accepted by the American public that even those who seek major changes in the role of religion or the distribution of public funds for religious institutions do not challenge "separation" but rather base themselves on the language of minority rights and fairness.[22] Furthermore, among churchgoers themselves, among whom evangelicals, fundamentalists, and the New Christian Right is only one segment, the impact of religion is "concentrated heavily on questions of sexual and social morality, much less evident on other important issues on the national agenda."[23] This is not surprising, for as Steve Bruce observes:

> In cultures where all or almost all people share the same religious world view, then there is no problem in allowing religious beliefs and symbols to dominate the public arena, in having religious leaders occupy positions of political, economic or social power, of allowing religious values to inform the socialization of the next generation, or of having every aspect of life dominated by religious precepts. . . . Conditions of religious pluralism profoundly change that and create the possibility of considerable social conflict. What is characteristic of most modern societies is the development of a polity and a culture that minimizes those conflicts by requiring that considerable freedom (of religious preferences as much as other choices) in the private sphere be matched by restraints of particularism in the public sphere. . . .

> Our societies permit (and in some places even encourage) the maintenance of distinctive religious world views and thus encourage sociomoral contests, but they also create a structure . . . and a culture . . . which of necessity restrains such contests and requires that they be fought on general universalistic ethical and public-policy principles. In modern democratic culturally plural societies, no sociomoral interest group can plausibly promote its cases on the ground that "the Bible (or the Koran or the book of Mormon) says so." Instead, it must argue that equity or reason or the public good says so.[24]

Israel, then is the special case that Bruce's analysis excludes. It is a society where almost all members of the dominant majority (i.e., the Jews) share the same worldview, which if not specifically religious is nonetheless grounded in a religious tradition. There is no problem, therefore, "in allowing religious beliefs and symbols to dominate the public arena, in having religious leaders occupy positions of political, economic or social power, of allowing religious values to inform the socialization of the next generation, or of having many aspects of life dominated by religious precepts" or informed, as we shall see in the next chapter, by religious conceptions.

THE "TOTALLY NONOBSERVANT"

As noted earlier, the religious tradition, once rejected by Zionist leaders, has become an important component of Israeli life. In the process, the tradition itself underwent a measure of transformation and assumed a more nationalistic content. But not all Israelis have adapted themselves to the changed role of the Jewish tradition. There are those whose dissent is an extension of their religious extremism. They are the antimodernist and non-Zionist *haredim* who interpret the Jewish tradition in its prenationalist and premodernist form. At the opposite extreme are those who because they continue to affirm the legitimacy of secular Jewishness, or because they are indifferent to Jewish matters in their private lives, vigorously resist any substantial role for the Jewish religious tradition in public life. These are the totally nonobservant, those who report that they observe nothing of the Jewish religious tradition. They constitute 20 percent of the sample. Their attitudes and values are interesting and all the more important because of who they are. The Guttman Report tells us that this is the portion of the population that is best educated (in terms of general rather than religious education) and disproportionately Ashkenazi rather than Sephardi.

Respondents were asked to grade themselves on a scale from one (very religious) to seven (antireligious). The distribution of the total sample was a statistical dream; a perfect bell-shaped curve. Thirty-two percent of the respondents located themselves at point four, the midpoint on the scale. Nineteen percent located themselves at point three and 19 percent at point five. Nine percent located themselves at point two and 9 percent at point six. Seven percent located themselves at the religious extreme and 6 percent at the antireligious extreme. All together 34 percent located themselves on the less religious side of the scale (points 5–7) and 33 percent on the more religious side of the scale (points 1–3).

However, among those born in the West (in other words, Ashkenazi Jews), 45 percent were at the nonreligious end of the spectrum and 26 percent at the religious end of the spectrum. Among the Israeli-born whose fathers were born in the West, 48 percent were at the nonreligious end of the spectrum compared to 28 percent at the religious end of the spectrum. Among those born in the East (in other words Sephardi Jews), only 18 percent were at the nonreligious end of the spectrum and 46 percent at the religious end of the spectrum. Among Israeli-born of Eastern-born parents, 26 percent were at the nonreligious end of the continuum and 37 percent at the religious end. As already noted, Ashkenazim remain consistent over two generations in their predominantly nonreligious identity. Among Sephardim there is a decline in the second generation in the proportion defining themselves as religious. Nevertheless, differences by ethnicity, even among the second generation are still substantial, and this is consistent with other studies[25] as well as the replies of the respondents to dozens of questions about their levels of observance.

Among those with a full college education, over 40 percent describe themselves as "totally nonobservant." Although the evidence is anecdotal and impressionistic, I am confident that the "totally nonobservant" are considerably overrepresented within the Israeli media and among Israeli academics and intellectuals, that is, the key figures in the creation and presentation of Israeli high culture, and among business executives and high civil servants, that is, the key figures in the formation and execution of public policy. It is my conviction that whereas the "totally nonobservant" constitute only a small proportion of the total Jewish population they comprise close to if not a majority of the Israeli elite.

Respondents were asked a battery of questions about associations with other Israelis. Questions probed whether respondents' friends, neighbors, building residents, work associates, and so on differed from them in religious observance. The "totally nonobservant" were the most likely, in some cases by far, to report few if any associations with people who differ from them in terms of religious observance. This is apparently related to the fact that they have the least accurate image of the religious orientations of the Israeli population. Fifty percent of the "totally nonobservant" believe that almost all or a large majority of Israeli Jews observe the religious tradition the same way that they do (i.e., don't observe), and an additional 28 percent think that about half the Israelis do so.

This error may stem from two causes that are not mutually exclusive. The totally nonobservant may have an inaccurate image of Israeli society because they are isolated from those who behave differently from them in a religious sense. But it is also possible that their inaccurate image stems from mistaken impressions of those with whom they do come into contact. They may not realize that others, with whom they are interacting, are unlike themselves in religious observance. I suspect that both these possibilities are true. But if true, it does suggest that the religious behavior, that is, the partial observance of tradition among those Israelis with whom the totally nonobservant come into contact, may be of a trivial nature.

There is good reason for many Israelis, regardless of their degree of observance, to minimize the number of Jews who observe the tradition. It is facile to believe that this is entirely attributable to the manner in which the cultural elite shape perceptions of Israeli society. It is a fact, for example, that celebrations of Christmas (albeit in a nonreligious manner), have penetrated into parts of Jewish Israel.[26] Yair Sheleg, the religious journalist, speaks of the "alienation from Judaism" in Israeli society and notes that the cause of:

> . . . the low esteem of Jewish culture in Israeli society is not [the result of] religious coercion (of which there is less and less all the time), nor even the absence of religion-state separation, but the lack of relevance of what is identified as "the Jewish world" to that which engages the Israeli in his daily life.[27]

How is one to explain the paradox of high levels of traditional observance, public support for tradition, the perceived symmetry between national and traditional values, and what Sheleg refers to as the "low esteem of Jewish culture"? The answer is that both tendencies seem to exist simultaneously. There is increasing tension today between two opposing segments of the Israeli public, a point to which we return in the next chapter. But Israel is still not experiencing a culture war between opposing factions of the population–the fully observant and the totally nonobservant. What it is experiencing is a tension that affects almost all Israelis. The tension is between ethnic loyalties and security fears that push most Israelis toward greater particularism and pressures of modern culture that undermine the significance of any religious tradition. The latter pressures expose Israelis to an eclectic culture of Western consumerism and the affirmation of individual autonomy rather than collective responsibility.

Having conceded this much to the pervasiveness of secularism, it is also apparent that the totally nonobservant not only deviate in their behavior but in their attitudes and values. For example, when respondents are grouped by their levels of observance we find distinctions between their identification with the Jewish people and with Zionism. Among the "strictly observant" and those who are "observant to a great extent," over 80 percent answer definitely yes to the question of whether they feel part of the Jewish people throughout the world. Sixty-one percent of the "somewhat observant" feel that way but only 46 percent of the "totally nonobservant" give that response. Sixty and 61 percent of the "totally observant" and the "observant to a great extent" answer that they definitely consider themselves Zionists. This is true of 45 percent of those who are "somewhat observant" and only 40 percent of those who are "totally nonobservant." In this case the dividing line is sharpest between the "observant to a great extent" and the "somewhat observant" groups. But on many other value and attitudinal questions, differences between the "totally nonobservant" and everybody else seem so pronounced that one is inclined to think of them as even more deviant than the *haredim*. For example, respondents were asked whether they felt that their way of life is in the spirit of Jewish values. Among the "totally nonobservant" 72 percent answered "no." Only 2 to 32 percent of the other three groups replied in that manner.

Another set of questions also demonstrated the dissent of the "totally nonobservant" from values that other Israelis share. Respondents were presented with a list of values and asked which if any of them they find to be very important or important as guiding principles in their lives. As we would expect, the "totally nonobservant" attributed little or no importance to values of Jewish observance. Secondly, in accordance with the findings in the previous paragraph, they attributed less importance than other Jews to the value of living in Israel or feeling part of the Jewish people. But they also deviated from the remainder of the sample on a set of general values, and it is this deviation that strikes me as being of major significance.

The deviation corresponds to what Ronald Inglehart terms the differences between *materialists* and *postmaterialists*.[28] In his analysis of survey data gathered in twenty-five industrial societies, primarily in Western Europe and the United States, between 1970 and 1986, Inglehart argues that "economic, technological, and sociopolitical changes have been transforming the cultures of advanced industrial societies in profoundly important ways."[29] Following A. H. Maslow's theory of "higher" and "lower" needs, he maintains that individuals are most concerned with the satisfaction of material needs and threats to their physical security. But once they have satisfied their basic material needs and guaranteed their physical safety they will look to the satisfaction of more remote needs—in the spiritual, aesthetic, and interpersonal realms. They will think in terms of self-fulfillment and personal autonomy rather than identifying themselves with their families, localities, ethnic groups, or even nations. An earlier generation came of age, that is, was socialized, in a period where their immediate material and physical needs were unmet, and they therefore concerned themselves with and forged societies structured to meet these needs. But among those who have been socialized in the present, when material and security needs are met, there is a search for the satisfaction of the more remote needs. There is also a shift from what Inglehart terms central authority to individual autonomy and from what I would term collective to individual concerns. Those who adopt this new set of values are what Inglehart terms postmaterialists in contrast to the materialists who remain wedded to the older set of values.

In the following chapter I will seek to apply Inglehart's analysis to Israeli society. For now, I am only concerned with demonstrating that the less observant one is, especially if one is part of the "totally nonobservant," the more likely one is to conform to Inglehart's definition of a postmaterialist. But the majority of Israelis remain, to borrow Inglehart's term, materialists.[30]

We will compare Israelis in terms of values that they consider "very important" as guiding principles in their life. We will not look at specifically religious values, such as observing *Shabbat*, where declines in levels of observance are obviously correlated with declines in the importance attributed to the value. We will only consider those values that are not expressly associated with religious-ritual behavior.

Let us look initially at those values that exhibit linear or virtual linear correlations between level of observance and the importance of the value as a guiding principle in one's life. I only consider values where differences between the two extremes are ten percentage points or more. For ease of comparison, the two middle groups, those who "observe to a great extent" and those who "observe somewhat," were collapsed, so that only three groups of Jewish respondents are compared. Those who are "strictly observant" constitute one group, those who "observe to a great extent" or are "somewhat observant" constitute the second group, and those who are "totally nonobservant" constitute the third group.

There are two values that become more important as respondents become less observant. Both are postmaterialist values: "enjoying beauty in one's life" and "behaving according to one's feelings." The values that are negatively correlated with religious observance are all materialist values. They are telling the truth (which the postmaterialist is less likely to affirm since he/she would regard moral imperatives as contextual and would abjure absolute values such as telling the truth), contributing to charity, raising a family, honoring one's parents, engaging in voluntary community work, feeling part of the Jewish people, and living in Israel.

Let us look more closely at the distance between the groups on these values. With regard to some, the distance between the two extreme groups and the middle group are quite large. In other cases, only one of the two extreme groups can be considered deviant. Thus with regard to the two postmaterialist values, "enjoying beauty in one's life" and "behaving in accordance with one's feelings," both extremes deviate considerably (ten percentage points or more) from the middle group. In other words, relative to the majority of Israelis, few of the "strictly observant" consider these values important and many of the "totally nonobservant" do so. With regard to the explicitly materialist values of living in Israel, raising a family, and honoring one's parents, the nonobservant deviate substantially from the remainder of the sample.

There is one value, not mentioned yet, in which the two extreme groups deviate in the same direction from the majority of Israelis. Both the "totally nonobservant" and the "strictly observant" are far less likely to view army service as a very important principle in their lives. The reason I suggest is that the *haredim* among the "strictly observant" abjure army service, whereas the "totally nonobservant" are more concerned with self and less committed to the collective national value. Finally, there is one value in which the "strictly observant" alone deviate. They are far less likely to list "having a good time" as a guiding principle in their lives.

A 10 percent difference, which in some cases is all that separates the extremes, may not seem to be very much. What I would emphasize here is that all the differences are consistent with Inglehart's categories. In addition, they suggest that if we compare the values that the "strictly observant" and the "totally nonobservant" affirm as guiding principles in their lives we find that the "strictly observant" deviate less than the "totally nonobservant" from the rest of Israeli society.

NOTES

1. Barry Kosmin and Seymour Lachman, *One Nation Under God: Religion in Contemporary American Society* (New York: Random House, 1993), p. 279.

2. Paul Johnson, "God and the Americans," *Commentary*, 99 (January 1995), p. 40.

3. Ibid.

4. Charles Liebman, "Jewish Fundamentalism and the Israeli Polity," Martin E. Marty and R. Scott Appleby (eds.), *Fundamentalisms and the State* (Chicago: University of Chicago Press, 1992), pp. 68–87.

5. Menachem Friedman is Israel's leading student of *haredi* society. The *haredim* in the Guttman sample would hardly be recognizable to readers of his *The Haredi (Ultra-Orthodox) Society: Sources, Trends and Processes* (Jerusalem: Jerusalem Institute for Israel Studies, in Hebrew, 1991) or his important article, "Haredim Confront the Modern City," in *Studies in Contemporary Jewry*, II (Bloomington: Indiana University Press, 1986) or to readers of Amnon Levy, *HaHaredim* (Jerusalem: Keter, in Hebrew, 1988).

6. Hanna Herzog, "Was It on the Agenda? The Hidden Agenda of the 1988 Campaign," Asher Arian and Michal Shamir (eds.), *The Elections in Israel–1988* (Boulder, CO: Westview, 1990), p. 55.

7. Except on the Sabbath and holidays, Jews are commanded to tie *t'fillin* (phylacteries) around their arm and forehead when they recite their morning prayers.

8. Twenty-two percent of the males report that they always cover their heads. This too is an important measure for identifying religious Jews in Israeli society and, as we suggested, one form of head covering, the skullcap, is a basic marker of religious identity.

9. Anita Shapira, *Land and Power* (New York: Oxford University Press, 1992), for the early period of Jewish settlement and Charles Liebman and Eliezer Don-Yehiya, *The Civil Religion in Israel: Traditional Judaism and Political Culture in the Jewish State* (Berkeley: University of California Press, 1983), for the later period.

10. George Friedmann, *The End of the Jewish People?* (New York: Doubleday, 1967). The book was originally published in France in 1965.

11. David Martin,"Is Europe Exceptional in Its Secularity?" p. 2. paper presented to the Conference on the Europe of Religions at the Institut fur die Wissenschaften vom Menschen, November 1994. Martin elaborates his theory of secularization in his *Toward a General Theory of Secularization* (New York: Harper & Row, 1978).

12. Charles Liebman, "Tradition, Judaism, and the Jewish Religion in Contemporary Israeli Society," Jack Wertheimer (ed.), *The Uses of Tradition* (Cambridge, MA: Harvard University Press, 1992), pp. 411–28. See also Charles Liebman and Steven Cohen, *Two Worlds of Judaism: The Jewish Experience in Israel and the United States* (New Haven, CT: Yale University Press, 1991).

13. Baruch Kimmerling, "Between the Primordial and the Civil Definition of the Collective Identity: *Eretz Israel* or the State of Israel?," Erik Cohen, Moshe Lissak and Uri Almagor (eds.), *Comparative Social Dynamics: Essays in Honor of S. N. Eisenstadt* (Boulder, CO: Westview, 1985), pp. 262–83.

14. Erik Cohen, "Citizenship, Nationality and Religion in Israel and Thailand," in Baruch Kimmerling, p. 70.

15. Kosmin and Lachman, p. 121.

16. Bethamie Horowitz, "Jewishness in New York: Exception or Rule?" Paper delivered at the conference on National and Cultural Variations in Jewish Identity and their Implications for Jewish Education," Jerusalem, January 1994. The Orthodox represent 15 percent of the New York sample, roughly equivalent to the 14 percent of the Guttman Institute sample who report that they are strictly observant of Jewish ritual though less than the maximum 23 percent of the sample we suggested are "religious." However, if we add Conservative Jews who more or less adhere to religious law (about a quarter of the Conservative Jews of New York), we arrive at a comparable figure. The New York report was published under the title *The 1991 New York Jewish Population Study* by Bethamie Horowitz (New York: United Jewish Appeal–New York Federation of Jewish Philanthropies of New York, Inc., 1993).

17. Ronald Inglehart, *Culture Shifts in Advanced Industrial Society* (Princeton, NJ: Princeton University Press, 1990), p. 187.

18. The point is elaborated upon in Charles Liebman and Eliezer Don-Yehiya, *Religion and Politics in Israel* (Bloomington: Indiana University Press, 1984), pp. 15–30.

19. Kosmin and Lachman, p. 157.

20. Ibid.

21. See, for example, the Fall 1944 issue of *Sociology of Religion*, vol. 55 devoted to the Christian Right in the United States.

22. Steve Bruce, "The Inevitable Failure of the New Christian Right," *Sociological Analysis*, 55 (Fall 1994), pp. 223–41. He cites John Garvey's observation that the new Christian Right has had some success in its "defensive agenda" but very little in its "offensive agenda." See John Garvey, "Fundamentalism and American Law," Marty and Appleby, pp. 13–27.

23. Kenneth Wald, Lyman Kellstedt, and David Leege, "Church Involvement and Political Behavior," David Leege and Lyman Kellstedt (eds.), *Rediscovering the Religious Factor in American Politics* (Armonk, NY: M.E. Sharpe, 1993), p. 132.

24. Bruce, p. 240.

25. Eliezer Ben-Rafael and Stephen Sharot, *Ethnicity, Religion, and Class in Israeli Society* (Cambridge: Cambridge University Press, 1991.

26. See the article "It's Beginning to Look a Lot Like . . ." in the *Jerusalem Post Magazine*, December 23, 1994, pp. 12–15.

27. Yair Sheleg, "Flesh and Blood Judaism," *Ha'Aretz* (December 12, 1994), p. 1B.

28. Inglehart, pp. 133ff.

29. Ibid., p. 3.

30. I have no brief for the labels *materialist* and *postmaterialist*, which I find misleading. But these are Inglehart's terms, and since I rely heavily upon his analysis I feel constrained to use them.

6

Cultural Conflict in Israeli Society

CHARLES S. LIEBMAN

The Guttman Report's statements about the "rhetoric of polarization" between religious and nonreligious in Israel, occasioned a great deal of comment and some criticism in both the media and among participants at the Van Leer Institute conference. Some of commentary stemmed from confusion about what the report meant by the term *polarization*. I treat the term *polarization* in this chapter as synonymous with cultural cleavage. The question is not whether there are differences in practices and beliefs concerning traditional Judaism among Israeli Jews. Of course there are. The important question is why differences between segments of the population that have been alluded to in the previous chapter, that is, differences in religious behavior, different attitudes toward religion and state, and differences in values, have not resulted, at least until the present, in serious cultural conflict, or more dramatically in a *kultur kampf*, a culture war.[1] The answers that sociologists favor–that the religious cleavage is moderated by cross-cutting cleavages based on income and age, and to a lesser extent education and ethnicity–are not entirely adequate, in my opinion. Predictions about the imminent appearance of a culture war in Israel have been prevalent since the establishment of the state. Indeed, some observers argue that Israelis are already engaged in such a war and then predict that it will only deepen. "The culture war in Israel has still not reached its peak," writes the journalist and author Tom Segev.[2] Assessments of whether Israeli Jews are engaged in a culture war and predictions about its likelihood depends on how we understand the term. A recent analysis of American society is instructive in this regard.

American sociologist James Hunter, who has written a number of widely acclaimed studies on the topic, argues that Americans are engaged in a serious cultural conflict that he sometimes refers to as a culture war.[3] He defines cultural conflict as

> political and social hostility rooted in different systems of moral understanding. The end to which these hostilities tend is the domination of one cultural and moral ethos over all others. Let it be clear, the principles and ideals that mark these competing systems of moral understanding are by no means trifling but always have a character of ultimacy to them. They are not merely attitudes that can change on a whim but basic commitments and beliefs that provide a source of identity, purpose, and togetherness for the people who live by them. It is for precisely this reason that political action rooted in these principles and ideals tends to be so passionate."[4]

Hunter argues that the cultural conflict or culture war that America is experiencing is new. Disagreements existed in the past as well, but they took place within the boundaries of a larger biblical culture. Underlying the disagreements was a basic consensus about "the order of life in community and nation" forged "by biblical symbols and imagery." Today's disagreements are "around our most fundamental and cherished assumptions about how to order our lives—our own lives and our lives together in this society"[5] and there is no common set of symbols or imagery to provide the basis for common discourse.

According to Hunter, the underlying issue is moral authority, "the basis by which people determine whether something is good or bad, right or wrong, acceptable or unacceptable, and so on."[6] The two impulses that divide the American people are what Hunter labels, "the impulse toward orthodoxy and the impulse toward progressivism." Orthodoxy is distinguished by its belief in the existence of an "external, definable, and transcendent authority," whereas progressivism defines moral authority "by the spirit of the modern age, a spirit of rationalism and subjectivism."[7] To summarize Hunter's thesis, the basis for culture war arises when the sides to the controversy disagree about the basis upon which good or bad, right or wrong, acceptable and nonacceptable is to be decided and have no common authority to which they can appeal.

My argument is that, following Hunter's definition, Israel is not experiencing a culture war, at least not until the last year or so, and this experience is too recent to properly evaluate. Israeli Jews do share a common set of symbols or imagery that provide the basis for common discourse. And whereas there is a sharp tension between the Jewish tradition and many of the characteristic values of modern society, between what Hunter calls the impulse toward orthodoxy and the impulse toward progressivism, both these impulses are shared by almost all Israeli Jews. As suggested in the previous chapter, the tensions that divide orthodoxy and progressivism are present within most Israelis Jews rather than dividing one large set of Jews from another. The sociologist Baruch Kimmerling describes this condition in the following manner.

> There are secular individuals, groups and even sub-cultures in Israel. Their daily behavior and their own identity is secular. There are even those who wage a cultural or religious war against this or that aspect of state efforts to impose this or that religious practice or *halakhic* norm on the general public or on one segment of that public. But when the vast majority of Israeli Jews refer to their collective national identity, that identity is defined for the most part by concepts, values, symbols and collective memory that is anchored primarily in the Jewish religion. In other words, there are secular Jews in the world and in Israel, but there is grave doubt if there is such a thing as secular Judaism. But at the same time the state functions in accordance with universalist secular codes drawn from what is called "western culture." Without them it is impossible to conduct a modern state and maintain its military power, its relatively developed economy and all the rest of its apparatus. These values don't necessarily stand in contradiction to the "Jewishness" of the state despite the permanent tension between them.[8]

Bearing all this in mind, let us look more carefully at Israeli society.

Israelis, as the Guttman Report and other studies note, perceive secular-religious cleavages as a problem of a serious nature and of greater magnitude than, for example, ethnic cleavages (Ashkenazi-Sephardi cleavages).[9] Seventy-one percent of the Guttman Report sample consider relations between religious and nonreligious people in Israel to be "not so good" or "not at all good." But there are two elements to the cleavage and they merit distinction. In a book that has assumed classic dimensions in its description of Israeli society, the late Dan Horowitz and Moshe Lissak point out that nonreligious Israelis distinguish between efforts to impose religious observance on the nonreligious–efforts that invariably lead to a backlash–and efforts to interpret Israeli life in religious terms, that is, to impose a religious worldview and religious meaning on reality. Horowitz and Lissak call this latter effort, "religious embellishments to the secular-nationalist ethos."[10] Efforts to impose religious observance are deemed improper. They not only violate individual liberties but cannot be justified, according to the vast majority of Israelis, in terms of the very point about which most Israelis emphatically agree, the Jewishness of Israeli society. As noted in the previous chapter, 88 percent of Israeli Jews believe that one can be "a good Jew" without "observing Jewish tradition."

On the other hand, because Israelis view their society and their state as Jewish, and wish it to remain Jewish, and because efforts to formulate secular Judaism in conceptual, not to mention ritual, terms no longer attracts more than a small number of Israelis, the vast majority resonate to the conceptualization of their condition, their problems, and their future in the rhetoric and symbols of the religious tradition. As Hanna Herzog writes in her description of a recent political campaign in Israel:

> The more Jewish terms the secular people could use to define and perceive themselves, the less alienated they felt from the Orthodox. Jewish tradition became a source of legitimization for the political claims of all the parties—each of which endowed it with its own meaning.[11]

My argument is that two central values or beliefs have, at least until the present moment, provided a basis for the broad consensus that exists among Israeli Jews. They offer a common set of symbols, a common language of public discourse, and the sense of an integrated social order. These are the values of Jewish peoplehood and what Asher Arian, Ilan Talmud, and Tamar Hermann call "the religion of security."[12]

According to these authors there is a symbolic and psychological dimension to the security threat that Israel faces. Israel's security is such a pervasive issue in the country, and the resources that it demands are so large, it is not surprising that the Israeli public has developed unique ways to deal with it. "At the symbolic and psychological levels [it is through belief in] the Almighty and the Jewish people."[13]

Basing their conclusions on questionnaire responses from a representative sample of Israeli Jewish adults conducted in 1986, the authors demonstrate the interrelationship between the values of Jewish peoplehood and security. "Just as Israeli Jews identified with Judaism . . . so too did Israelis concur about the centrality of security. . . ."[14]

The notion of a hostile world is deeply embedded in the Jewish tradition and the "impression that the world was basically hostile and often anti-semitic . . . characterized the way the Israeli public viewed national security policy."[15] According to the authors, even mainstream Zionist parties analyze the conflict between Israel and Arabs "in the spirit and often in the lexicon of the persecution suffered by Jews in most European countries and some of the countries of the Muslim world."[16]

Accompanying the sense of security threat is a high level of certainty that Israel will prevail despite Gentile hostility and antisemitism. "Israel must trust in the guardian of Israel,"[17] and "the guardian of Israel will prevail," Israelis affirm. This core value, the authors note:

> is related to religious belief, but the religious have no monopoly on it. It is to be found more often among those who support the right but supporters of the left also share the belief. . . . It permeates the society and legitimates behavior and policy.[18]

Israelis disagree as to who or what is represented in the referent "guardian." Most Israelis think it refers to the Israeli army, some to God, some to the people of Israel, and some to the state of Israel. It is not only the language of this core belief that is religious (the term *Guardian* is a synonym for God in the tradition), but as Arian and his associates point out, the conviction that some entity must be trusted and will prevail is at its core an extra-rational belief. Hence, disagreement over the referent to the term "guardian" does not prevent the development of broad consensus and a common language of discourse.

Israeli concerns over security are related to Israeli commitment to the Jewish tradition. By tradition I refer to the sense of Jewish continuity, Jewish history, and the central myths of Judaism that evoke a sense of identity and commitment among the vast majority of Israelis. This is a broader definition of tradition than that which the Guttman Report tapped and which is discussed in the preceding chapters. But it does subsume the rituals, beliefs, and attitudes that the Guttman survey found.

Tradition, understood in this broader sense, reinforces concerns over security, and concerns over security reinforces commitment to tradition. This, in turn, supports the pattern of ritual behavior and traditional belief among Israeli Jews. For the majority of Israeli Jews, those from Sephardic background in particular, the tradition's conception of the Jewish condition in the world (the classical metaphor, "a lamb among seventy wolves" suggests the flavor of the conception) provides some explanation for Arab enmity toward Israel.[19] The classical Zionist expectation of normal relationships between Jews and non-Jews once Jews have obtained independent statehood, appears to lack a foundation in reality. The normalization of relations between Israel and some Arab countries and negotiations with Palestinians may raise reservations in the minds of many Israeli Jews about the traditional religious paradigm of Jewish-Gentile relations and that may be crucial in predicting future developments. But it has certainly seemed credible up until the present.

The tradition socializes the Jew to the expectation of security threats, but security threats also serve to strengthen the Jews' commitment to the tradition. It is helpful, in this regard, to recall Inglehart's analysis. "Vulnerability," to use Inglehart's term, promotes the "need for a sense of security, which religion and absolute cultural norms have traditionally provided."[20] Inglehart attributes the decline of traditional religious social and sexual norms in advanced industrial society to the increasing sense of security that the population enjoys. One does not need, he says, the security of the absolute, rigid rules that religious sanctions can provide. The belief that Israeli Jews share—that their physical security is threatened—would strengthen rather than weaken their need for absolute cultural norms.

The second reason, according to Inglehart, that societal and religious norms are more important to those who feel vulnerable has to do with the function these norms perform. Without such norms, Inglehart observes, "a society would tend to tear itself apart."[21] Religious norms such as "honor thy father and mother," he says, are linked to maintaining the family unity, which, he believes, is less crucial than it once was with the rise of the welfare state. But it remains crucial, I would add, when one feels a sense of physical vulnerability. Family, as the Israeli army itself believes, is absolutely critical in maintaining the morale of the soldier and in providing him, and virtually all Israeli Jews, with a support system for their fears.[22]

This sense of the importance of the immediate family and then, by extension, the broader community of Israeli Jews (that is, the extended family), is further strengthened by the nature of the threat that Israelis face. The threat to their survival stems from the fact of their Jewishness and can only be met through the collective effort of Jews. An individual may be able to overcome the threat to his material welfare through his own initiative; indeed, he may be better able to do so by acting alone. An individual may also feel that challenges to his mental or physical health can only be met through his own initiative. But threats to the physical safety of Israeli Jews can only be confronted through collective activity. The strength, security, and well-being of the individual Jew in Israel rests primarily on the strength, security, and well-being of the larger community.

Inglehart points out that the norms and values that reflect this need may not be perceived by the individual members of society as a direct reflection of their needs. Norms are not established through a process of rational calculation. They are, instead, internalized at an early age and reinforced by prerational sanctions. Hence, they do not disappear as soon as their functional need vanishes. In the case of security threats of the kind Israel faces, particularly in times of relative peace, perception is no less important than reality. Indeed, perception, to a great extent (though not entirely) dictates policy that, in turn, interacts with reality. As the political anthropologist Myron Aronoff notes, that which fundamentally divides Israeli Jews is "their evaluation of whether or not the Jewish people and its state are capable of being 'normal' and whether or not such a condition (if it is possible) is one that should be sought."[23] He goes on to observe that "these orientations are related to different perceptions of security, perceptions of 'the other' and temporal perception of myth and history."[24] It is a small minority who is likely to perceive the Israeli condition as secure, to identify "the other" as benign, and to see history as linear.

Aronoff, like Inglehart, tends to phrase his analysis in value-laden terms. The language of these authors expresses the bias of each in favor of what Aronoff calls "humanist Zionists" as opposed to "nationalists," and what Inglehart calls the "postmaterialists" as opposed to the "materialists." But despite their biases, each, I believe, is very helpful in understanding the findings of the Guttman Report, even if the survey did not explicitly ask respondents about their attitudes toward and sense of security.

The "humanists" and the "postmaterialists" are disproportionately represented among the Guttman Report's "totally nonobservant." They fit Inglehart's value pattern, as was seen in the previous chapter. In addition, as Aronoff predicted, they are the least nationalistic—both in terms of their sense of Jewish peoplehood and their Zionism. As noted in the previous chapter, only 40 percent of the totally nonobservant answered "definitely yes" to the question of whether they considered themselves Zionists compared to 61 and 60 percent, respectively, of the two more observant groups. Forty-three percent of the totally nonobservant said that feeling part of the Jewish people was very important as a guiding principle in their lives compared to 86 and 82 percent of the more observant groups; 46 percent of the totally nonobservant felt that they were definitely part of the Jewish people throughout the world whereas this was true of 83 and 80 percent of the more observant groups; and 52 percent of the totally nonobservant felt that living in Israel was very important as a guiding principle in their lives compared to 84 and 85 percent of the more observant groups. On the other hand, 55 percent of the totally nonobservant described their attitudes toward Arabs as positive compared to 26 and 32 percent of the more observant groups.

The pervasive nature of secular, postmaterialist values in Western society suggests that all Israelis, even the more observant will have internalized some of them to some degree. On the other hand the pervasive sense of threat to security, which Arian, Talmud, and Hermann document, helps us understand why there are so few totally nonobservant Israeli Jews or why, to use Inglehart's terms, the vast majority of Israelis have internalized materialist rather than postmaterialist values. Indeed, the pervasiveness of the "religion of security" suggests that it is probably only a minority of the totally nonobservant who are extreme postmaterialists. But it is my impression, to repeat a point raised earlier, that this minority is an especially influential one—that it comprises the cultural elite of Israeli society, the journalists and political commentators; a disproportionate share of the academic community, social scientists in particular; and the top echelon of the governmental and business bureaucracy. This is the "new class," as social scientists increasingly refer to them. This "new class" is distinguished from the older middle and upper-middle class by their professional expertise, their creation of social symbols, and their control of information rather than their ownership of property.

The totally nonobservant, I believe, compromise that segment of the Israeli public who are least attracted by and most disdainful of the Jewish concepts, symbols, values, norms, and collective memory of Judaism and the Jewish people. It is not surprising if we were to find that they are the very segment of the public most engaged in occupations (the media, academics, senior bureaucrats, industrial leaders) whose very foundation is universalist in orientation and that relies most heavily upon universalist rather than Jewishly particularist associations. These are the same groups that offer the strongest support to the peace process. It was from within their ranks that the technocrats who drafted the first Israeli-PLO accords were drawn. They are the individuals, whom political scientist Michael Keren characterizes as "a knowledge-power nexus, dominated by [foreign minister] Peres and his allies among Israel's professionals, who had little concern for cognitive changes."[25]

In an article, no less tendentious in one direction than Inglehart and Aronoff are in the other, but no less instructive, the late Christopher Lasch describes this same type of elite in the United States and its attitudes toward America.[26] Members of the elite, he says, "have lost faith in the values, or what remains of them, of the West."[27] They have mounted a crusade, he goes on to say, "to extend the range of personal choice in matters where most people feel the need for solid moral guidelines."[28] The majority of society appears

> to the makers of educated opinion [as] hopelessly dowdy, unfashionable, and provincial. They are at once absurd and vaguely menacing–not because they wish to overthrow the old order but precisely because their defense of it appears so deeply irrational that it expresses itself, at the higher reaches of its intensity, in fanatical religiosity, in a repressive sexuality that occasionally erupts into violence against women and gays, and in a patriotism that supports imperialist wars and a national ethic of aggressive masculinity. Simultaneously arrogant and insecure, the new elites regard the masses with mingled scorn and apprehension.[29]

In an observation that seems especially relevant to Israel and the family values that most Israelis espouse, Lasch notes that:

> . . . the new class has to maintain the fiction that its power rests on intelligence alone. Hence it has little sense of ancestral

> gratitude or of an obligation to live up to responsibilities inherited from the past. It thinks of itself as a self-made elite owing its privileges exclusively to its own efforts.[30]

Lasch argues that the loyalties of this elite are international rather than national.[31] What is true of the Israeli elite, especially the academics and intellectuals whom I know, is that their significant reference groups are colleagues and peers in the West. It is the intellectual elite of the West who shape the worldviews and value preferences of Israeli intellectuals. Their political loyalties may be Israeli but their cultural affinities are not Israeli and least of all, Jewish.

We can return now to the question that was introduced earlier in this chapter. Why has Israel not experienced a culture war, at least not until the present? I suggest the following admittedly speculative answers.

First, the religion of security is pervasive. The media that, I suspect, is controlled by that very segment of the totally nonobservant least in touch with the sentiments of the majority of Israelis, is, with the exception of the influential daily *Ha'Aretz*, a critical agent in projecting this religion. For example, an interesting study of the use of the Holocaust paradigm in Israeli society suggests that it is the media itself that translate problems of security into Holocaust metaphors and thereby evoke echoes of Jewish history, Jewish destiny, and Jewish tradition.[32] In this respect recent charges by Israeli intellectuals who have labeled themselves post-Zionists and whom their opponents call anti-Zionists, a group anxious to denude the state of its Jewish character,[33] are of interest. They have mounted an attack on the Zionist establishment for its insufficient concern with the fate of European Jewry during the Nazi period and for exploiting the Holocaust to further their own political agendas.[34] I am not concerned with the justice of their charges. What I find most interesting is that the post-Zionists, who recoil from terms such as *aliya* rather than immigration because, they claim, *aliya* is value laden, the very same post-Zionists who argue that the state of Israel was born in a sin committed against the local Palestinians, now evoke the Holocaust to parade their concern with the Jewish people and utilize the Holocaust to delegitimate the Zionist establishment. In other words, even among the most radical Israeli Jews, one finds a shared rhetoric of discourse, a common set of symbols, and, up to a point, a common sense of history and destiny.

A second reason no culture war exists is that it takes two sides to wage a war. The side diametrically opposed to the "totally nonobservant," or to that minority among the totally nonobservant who do not share the consensual values of the society, are, at the present time, the *haredim*.[35] And while the rhetoric of their spokespeople is one of culture war, as seen in the chapter on the media response, the *haredi* community is too weak and too alienated from the rest of society to wage such a war. Nor is it in their interest to do so. Nothing in *haredi* ideology suggests the importance of imposing *their* culture on Israeli life. Their effort is basically a defensive one; ensuring their own survival by insulating themselves from the forces of modernity and secularism. They project and nourish their image as a beleaguered and oppressed minority and operate in the interstices of politics at the national level. Their achievements at that level stem from their capacity to negotiate arrangements with a variety of nonreligious parties. A culture war, which they know they would lose anyway, would be counterproductive in obtaining further public benefits and even in defending that which they have already obtained. It is well to recall that, according to the Guttman Report, the majority of Israelis are only antagonistic to the two "extreme" groups in the society–to the "antireligious" and to the "*haredim*." Although some individuals are antagonistic to one rather than the other, the total level of antagonism toward these two groups is the same.

LOOKING AHEAD

As I wrote elsewhere,[36] one must not exaggerate the compelling quality of the Jewish tradition in contemporary Israeli society. Clifford Geertz distinguishes between affirming religious convictions, which he calls "religiousness," and affirming the value and the importance of these convictions, which he calls "religious-mindedness."[37] I suspect that tradition, in Israeli society, is analogous to religious-mindedness. And regardless of their religious beliefs and their favorable attitudes toward tradition only a minority of Israelis are prepared to submit themselves to religious imperatives. Tradition in the modern world–because it is self-conscious; because it exists, even in the mind of its adherents as something apart from them; because one can imagine nontradition–means that one must make choices with respect to it. The necessity to choose tradition rather than simply live one's life in accordance with its norms and values inspires fanatical devotion among some but leads others to adopt a more permissive, latitudinarian, and less submissive orientation. It is this orientation that characterizes the vast majority of Israelis.

Furthermore, despite the deference that Jewish society in Israel accords the Jewish tradition, it is my impression that many Israelis are ignorant of (not simply mistaken about) its basic tenets. Ritual and ceremony is certainly a source of knowledge about tradition and a mechanism for socializing its adherents to its norms, especially in Judaism. The fact that at most, slightly over 20 percent of the Israeli Jewish population defines itself as *dati* suggests that the position of Jewish tradition within

Israeli society is not as secure as one might otherwise believe. If the compelling quality of the Jewish tradition is so limited with respect to ritual and matters of religious law, then how compelling can it be in matters of values and general social norms where it confronts a world of competing and alternative values and norms? Individualism is becoming far more commonplace in Israel. The demand for self-fulfillment and personal gratification is growing. The mass media, foreign travel, and the structure of the economy are enough to ensure that. And those who dissent from the tradition, even if they constitute a small minority, occupy key positions among the economic, political, and cultural elite.

Among such people, generally the better educated and more "enlightened," to use Shils's term, there is a prevailing notion that

> a great many of the beliefs, practices, and institutions . . . [need] to be changed, replaced, or discarded in favor of new ones which would invariably be better ones . . . the accent of intellectual and political discourse still remains on a movement forward from the recent and remote past. The emphasis is on improvement.[38]

It is difficult to sustain tradition in a social milieu antagonistic to the norms of the past. We have only to remember that the opposite of utilizing tradition as a basis for decision making is utilizing reason, and we are reminded of tradition's inherent weakness. The fact is that the Israeli street, as noted in the previous chapter, is penetrated increasingly by concepts, symbols, and values of a cultural nature that are not Jewish. Popular Israeli culture is increasingly universalist and Jewishly neutral. A culture of "McDonald's and Madonna" is a phrase which Israel politicians and cultural critics evoke.

Coupled with the discussion in the last two chapters, one might infer that the future for both traditionalism and social peace within Jewish society is a dim one. If, as was argued here, the "religion of security" is tied to Jewish traditionalism then a decline in one must lead to a decline in the other. The "demographics" seem to be against Jewish traditionalism. The sharpest generational decline in religious observance is taking place among the descendants of Sephardi parents, and this is the population group that is increasing. In addition, religious observance is negatively correlated with general education, and the education level of the population is increasing and will continue to increase dramatically in the coming decades as the number of local colleges expands. This too may contribute to declines in religious observance.

Lower levels of traditionalism may, in turn, contribute to diminished perceptions of security threats. Security threats are less likely to be perceived through the lenses of Jewish destiny and fate and thereby appear less ominous. Alternately, loss of traditional faith may mean loss of optimism about the capacity of Israel to survive the threats that it faces and, hence, a greater willingness to compromise and surrender.

The other side of the coin is that if security threats diminish, or if the perception of such threats diminish, the kind of postmaterialist rise that Inglehart predicts may overwhelm Israeli traditionalism. If Israeli Jews no longer perceive their collective security as tenuous, if they believe that their society no longer exists under siege, then many of the values that currently characterize Israeli society–tradition as the cement for national consensus and order, the primacy of collective as opposed to individual welfare, self-identification with the Jewish people, family as the core institution that protects as well as comforts the individual–are bound to dissipate.

Should all this occur, it would provoke grave resistance among a substantial segment of Israeli society. This resistance is likely to be sharpened by a conviction that security threats only appear to have dissipated or that those who refuse to express their political convictions in the language of Jewish traditionalism are disloyal and even threatening to the social order. In other words, the kind of culture war that does not at present exist will then be waged with intensity. And one does not have to look very far to find its signs on the contemporary horizon.

The 1996 Israeli election campaign and the elections results can be understood in this context. Shimon Peres, candidate of the left for the post of prime minister campaigned on the slogan "peace and security." He virtually suspended all talks with the Palestinians during the campaign and he closed off the west bank and Gaza to prevent terrorist acts and to demonstrate how tough he was. Two months before the election, *Hizbollah*, the Syrian supported terrorist organization in south Lebanon, shelled a town in northern Israel. Peres' opponents immediately charged that he was soft on terrorism and lacked the courage to take dramatic military steps. Under political as well as some army pressure Peres authorized the bombardment of villages in south Lebanon over a two week period leaving hundreds of thousands of Lebanese homeless and causing the deaths of hundreds of civilians. Peres' efforts to demonstrate his own commitment to Israel's security were insufficient. His opponent, Benjamin (Bibi) Netanyahu, the right wing candidate for the post of prime minister, won 55 percent of the Jewish vote. Netanyahu's campaign theme was that his opponent, Shimon Peres, had sacrificed the security of the country in the effort to reach a peace agreement with Yassir Arafat and the Palestinian National Authority. Netanyahu promised to continue the peace process but at a slower pace conditioned upon guarantees for Israel's safety. A campaign slogan which appeared two days before the election, "Only Netanyahu is good for the Jews" captured the flavor of the campaign. It was paid for and distributed by an ultra-Orthodox group but it evoked enthusiasm among almost all of Netanyahu's supporters and revulsion among his opponents. A bumper sticker circulated earlier in the campaign carried a similar message. It read, "Bibi or Tibi." (Ahmed Tibi, adviser to Yassir Arafat, had formed an independent Arab party to run for the Knesset. He actually withdrew from the race before the elections were held.)

In addition to voting for prime minister, Israelis also voted for parties to represent them in the Knesset. The religious parties increased their representation from 16 to 23 seats. My own estimate is that around a quarter of a million non-religious voters, some nine percent of the Jewish electorate, voted for the religious parties. The campaign material of these parties stressed the need for more Judaism and more Jewishness in Israeli society. There were no promises or threats of religious legislation but rather a promise to strengthen the Jewish climate of the country. The two religious parties that improved their own position most dramatically stressed the fact that non-religious as well as religious Jews supported them.

The previous discussion, however, suggests that the victory for Jewish tradition in the 1996 election is unlikely to be a lasting victory; especially if the religious parties who have become such important players in domestic affairs, overplay their hand. But the threat to Jewish traditionalism and the rise of postmaterialist values will undermine the social order in Israel just as it is threatening to do in the United States. A weakened social order, weakened consensus, weakened willingness to defer personal needs for collective purposes will prove dangerous to Israel's survival given that the "peace" process is likely to remain a tenuous one for many years. This will continue to evoke some kind of counter-cultural affirmation of tradition. Whether Humpty Dumpty can be put back together again remains to be seen.

NOTES

1. There are many observers who believe that the present conflict in Israeli society over the question of surrendering territory in return for peace, a conflict that pits the vast majority of religiously observant Jews against what is probably a majority of the remaining Jews, represents the opening battle in a culture war. I believe that the conflict is still primarily political and that key voices on both sides, each for their own reasons, have heretofore, avoided transforming their political differences into a culture war.

2. Tom Segev, "The New Professionals," *Ha'Aretz* (May 12, 1994), p. 1B.

3. James Hunter, *Culture Wars: The Struggle to Define America* (New York: Basic Books, 1991). The citations in this chapter are from this book. Hunter has sought to be more prescriptive in his later study, *Before the Shooting Begins: Searching for Democracy in America's Culture War* (New York: The Free Press, 1994).

4. Ibid., p. 42.

5. Ibid.

6. Ibid.

7. Ibid., p. 44.

8. Baruch Kimmerling, "Religion, Nationalism and Democracy in Israel," *Zmanim*, nos. 50–51, 13 (Winter 1994, in Hebrew), p. 129.

9. See chapter 1, which reproduces the *Highlights* of the Guttman Report. See also Eliezer Ben-Rafael and Stephen Sharot, *Ethnicity, Religion and Class in Israeli Society* (New York: Cambridge University Press, 1991), p. 161; Dan Horowitz and Moshe Lissak, *Trouble in Utopia* (Albany: SUNY Press, 1989), p. 63; and Charles Liebman (ed.), *Religious and Secular: Conflict and Accommodation Between Jews in Israel* (Jerusalem: Keter Books, 1990), p. 215 for a report of similar results from another survey.

10. Horowitz and Lissak, ibid.

11. Hanna Herzog, "Was It On The Agenda: The Hidden Agenda of the 1988 Campaign," Asher Arian and Michal Shamir (eds.), *The Elections in Israel, 1988* (Boulder, CO: Westview Press, 1990), p. 58.

12. Asher Arian, Ilan Talmud, and Tamar Hermann, *National Security and Public Opinion in Israel* (Boulder, CO: Westview Press, published for the Jaffee Center for Strategic Studies, Tel-Aviv University, 1988).

13. Ibid., p. 48.

14. Ibid., p. 4.

15. Ibid., p. 80.

16. Ibid., p. 46.

17. Ibid., p. 84.

18. Ibid. See also Asher Arian, *Security Threatened: Surveying Israel: Opinion in Peace and War* (New York: Cambridge University Press, 1996).

19. Charles Liebman, *Attitudes Toward Jewish-Gentile Relations in the Jewish Tradition and Contemporary Israel* (Kaplan Centre, University of Cape Town, Occasional Papers, 1984).

20. Ronald Inglehart, *Culture Shifts in Advanced Industrial Society* (Princeton, NJ: Princeton University Press, 1990), p. 177.

21. Ibid., p. 178.

22. Elihu Katz, Yaacov Trope, and Hadassah Hass, "Integration in Army and Nation: An Essay in Institutional Permeability," Erik Cohen,

Moshe Lissak, and Uri Almagor (eds.), *Comparative Social Dynamics: Essays in Honor of S. N. Eisenstadt* (Boulder, CO: Westview Press, 1985), pp. 315–33.

23. Myron Aronoff, "The Origins of Israeli Political Culture," Ehud Sprinzak and Larry Diamond (eds.), *Israeli Democracy Under Stress* (Boulder, CO: Lynne Rienner, 1993), p. 58.

24. Ibid.

25. Michael Keren, "Israeli Professionals and the Peace Process," *Israel Affairs*, 1 (Autumn 1994), p. 150.

26. Christopher Lasch, "The Revolt of the Elites: Have they canceled their allegiance to America?," *Harper's*, 289 (November 1974), pp. 39–49. The essay is adapted from a posthumous book *The Revolt of the Elites and the Betrayal of Democracy* (N.Y.: Norton, 1995).

27. Ibid., p. 39.

28. Ibid., p. 40.

29. Ibid., p. 41.

30. Ibid., p. 46.

31. Ibid., p. 47.

32. Hillel Nossek, "The Narrative Role of the Holocaust and the State of Israel in the Coverage of Salient Terrorist Events in the Israeli Press," *Journal of Narrative and Life History* 4 (1994), pp. 119–29.

33. There is, as of this writing, no scholarly book or article that treats post-Zionism and its critics in any systematic manner although a number of such studies are being prepared. The discussion of post-Zionism assumed popular dimensions in the summer of 1994 with the publication of an article by the well-known Israeli writer Aharon Meged, "The Suicide Wish of the Israeli," *Ha'Aretz* (June 10, 1994). The article under the title "Self-Hatred in the Jewish State," is found in English in *Avar veAtid: A Journal of Jewish Education, Culture and Discourse*, 2 (September 1995), pp. 36–40. Post-Zionists replied with vigor in the weeks that followed (one of the articles also translated into English, is by Benny Morris, "My Response to Aharon Megged," pp. 41–44 of the same issue), and they were answered, no less vigorously, by their critics. The sense that denuding Israel of its Jewish character is the primary item on the post-Zionist agenda was articulated by the distinguished historian of modern Israel Anita Shapiro in an interview with her in *Yediot Aharonot*'s literary supplement, (December 23, 1994). Post-Zionist thought is to be found on the pages of two Hebrew-language journals, *Teoria U'Bikoret* (Theory and Criticism), published by the Van Leer Institute and more selectively in the pages of *Zmanim* (Times), a publication of Tel-Aviv University's School of History. Most of the editorial and feature writers of *Ha'Aretz*, Israel's most prestigious daily newspaper, espouse post-Zionism. See, most recently, Orit Schochat, "Who is a Post-Zionist," *Ha'Aretz*, (September 1, 1995).

Post-Zionists scholars are best known as historical revisionists—the phrase that best catches their mood is the one attributed to Benny Morris proclaiming that "the State of Israel was born in sin." Many though not all of the contributors to a volume by Uri Ram (ed.), *Israeli Society: Critical Perspectives* (Tel-Aviv: Breirot, in Hebrew 1993) are post-Zionists. For a critical evaluation of their effort in sociology see Moshe Lissak, "Notes on the Debate Between 'Critical' and 'Establishment' Sociology in Israel," *Israel Studies Bulletin* 11, No. 1 (Fall 1995). A good proportion if not most of the articles on politics that appear in the annual *Critical Essays on Israeli Social Issues and Scholarship: Books on Israel*, published by SUNY Press (three volumes have appeared as of this writing), are written from a post-Zionist perspective. For example, an essay in the third volume holds Israel responsible for the Six Day War, which it initiated in order to resolve internal political problems.

34. Hillel Halkin, for example, characterizes Tom Segev's book *The Seventh Million* as an accusation against "Zionist and Israeli leaders [for] unscrupulously exploiting and distorting the history of the Holocaust for political ends." Hillel Halkin,"Israel Against Itself," *Commentary*, 85 (November 1994), p. 36.

35. What we are already seeing, as I suggest in the final section of this chapter, is that the major religious protagonists in the culture war will come from the ranks of the religious-Zionists, and this will change the rules of the game.

36. Charles Liebman, "Tradition, Judaism, and the Jewish Religion in Contemporary Israeli Society," Jack Wertheimer (ed.), *The Uses of Tradition* (Cambridge, MA: Harvard University Press, 1992), pp. 411–28.

37. Clifford Geertz, *Islam Observed: Religious Development in Morocco and Indonesia* (New Haven, CT: Yale University Press, 1968).

38. Edward Shils, *Tradition* (Chicago: The University of Chicago Press, 1981), p. 2.

Appendix

Selected Papers from the Van Leer Conference

The selections that follow are edited versions of ten papers prepared for the Van Leer Conference. The papers reprinted here were chosen because they represent the range of opinions offered to the participants, not because in our opinion these papers were more meritorious than those not selected for inclusion. References in these papers to the Guttman Institute study refer to the *Highlights*. That booklet is reprinted in slightly amended form as Chapter 1.

The Closeness which Alienates or the Alienation which Brings Closer?

Jewish Religion and Israeli Culture

ISRAEL BARTAL

Professor of Jewish History, Hebrew University, Jerusalem

The data presented by the Guttman Institute study, "Beliefs, Observances, and Social Interactions among Israeli Jews" do not surprise an Israeli "sabra," born in 1946, who grew up in an urban environment in the center of the country. For one for whom the neighborhood synagogue in "Giv'at Rambam" was a few hundred steps away from his home, I spent my childhood days among many similar to myself, for whom "religious culture" and blunt secularism mingled into one pageant. Among my classmates there were those who fasted on Yom Kippur, in whose homes a festive Sabbath family dinner was held, and who read from the Torah when they had their *bar mitzvah*, but who also participated in the evening activities of the youth movement, where boys and girls danced together to the music of the accordion immediately after the Sabbath dinner and rode to the beach on the Sabbath. I never accepted the simplistic differentiation of Israeli society into two camps. My childhood experiences in the Israel of the fifties, which included a most interesting mixture of remnants of religious customs and influences of radical secularist nationalism, did not permit this. And indeed, the results of the survey clearly demonstrate the gap between the image of Israeli society in the eyes of the spokespeople of the extreme flanks (complete "religionists" on the one hand, and distinct "secularists" on the other), and a cultural reality in which religious precepts, secular national symbols, mysticism, and rationalism are all mixed together. In other words, according to the responses given, a person in Israel could wholeheartedly believe in the existence of the deity and yet desecrate the Sabbath; have intercourse with a woman during her menses and yet define himself as "traditional"; fast on Yom Kippur in order to atone for his sins against the Lord and light *Hanukkah* candles as a symbol of the heroism of those who did not expect a miracle from Heaven. It goes without saying that those with the religionist-nationalist outlook and disciples of Rabbi A. Y. Kook will see in this reality a distinct sign of the people of Israel's constant coming closer to their God, and a step on the way to accepting fully the yoke of the Torah and commandments. The "Orthodox" will see this exact same reality as a clear sign of dissolution of the Jewish society outside the guarded walls of Orthodoxy and a step on the road to complete assimilation, whereas the radical secularists (who are a minority in Israeli society, according to the findings of the study) will see this reality as a sign of loss of the modern character of the Israelis and a step on the way to the downfall of secularist nationalism, which is the heritage of the generation of the state's founding fathers. It therefore appears that despite the images existing in the consciousness of ideologically cohesive groups, which also influence patterns of political behavior with respect to religion and culture, the country has quite a wide stratum of people with behavior patterns of its own. These patterns in the meantime contradict the precepts generally accepted by religious leaders and politicians. Moreover, according to the study, those with such behavior patterns find no fault with the current cultural situation, that is, 51 percent of the respondents find that "public life in Israel should remain the way it is." This means that this sector of the population does not share the predictions for the future mentioned previously and does not make the improvement of the nation's condition or the salvation of mankind and universal reform conditional upon habits of eating and drinking or upon family rituals celebrated in their homes. This is so, even though these customs and ceremonies are an inseparable part of their identity as members of the Jewish people.

The results of the study may teach us an important lesson concerning the relation between stated ideologies of movements and political parties, and cultural patterns. Culture is always more complex and less one-dimensional. A considerable portion of the society that was investigated very clearly expressed the feeling that there is a gap between culture and the legislative position of religion in the state: 42 percent support separation of state from religion. But, first and foremost in my opinion, the study shows that in the state of Israel a new phenomenon is being created in the history of the Jewish people (and also in the short history of the "Settlement" [Yishuv] in Israel), as a society that is no longer the traditional Jewish entity of the Middle Ages nor part of an Orthodoxy that organically integrates religious patterns with a clearly secularist heritage. In this society there is a clear tendency to separate the political dimension from that of the religious one. True, some of the *haredi* public lean in that direction because they are not interested in integrating religion with the Zionist state of nonbelievers, not because of their acceptance of the ideology of the Enlightenment (Haskala) Movement. But this is not the only case in which–for completely different reasons–anti-Zionist Orthodoxy and radical secularism are partners in the demands to sever the connection between the state and religion. What happened to the Jewish society in the state of Israel is that the totality of religion, in the style of the premodern community, was replaced by a state in which there is a sort of "national church." The Zionist Orthodoxy accepted this "national church," and there is even a state establishment–the "Chief Rabbinate"–which is one of the innovations of the absolutist states of the eighteenth century, that is supposed to provide for the religious needs in a society in which religion was relegated to a very secondary place. And indeed, the power of this church is limited, and alongside it a variety of completely non-Orthodox combinations of religious behavior exist. Paradoxically, the state of Israel realized the vision of the Enlightenment Movement. It limited the power of religious coercion to an establishment under the supervision of the state and left a wide margin for different degrees of "religiosity" determined by the faith and inclination of the individual. What was completely impossible in the religious community, that is, selective observance of commandments and a mixture of commandments and transgressions became the normative behavior of a considerable portion of Jewish society in Israel. Furthermore, the transgressions are justified as being part of observing tradition (such as lighting *Shabbat* candles without a blessing).

"Traditionalism" in Israeli society is not necessarily compatible with the accepted religious norms of Orthodoxy. Indeed, on the one hand, partial observance of commandments and religious customs is a bridging factor between different strata of society. But, on the other hand, the "partial" observance of the commandments and customs is a divisive factor creating tension and opposition. Thus, for example, an Orthodox Jew who believes in "all or nothing" will say that it is preferable not to light the Sabbath candles than to light them a minute after the Sabbath begins. Certainly "partial *kashrut*" is a complete abomination in the eyes of those who are meticulously observant. More serious are the elements of faith and ideology by which the non-Orthodox justify observance of customs and commandments. Here there is a tremendous charge of religious explosives that might blast away coexistence if not treated with extreme caution. Modern

Jewish nationalism in the secularist formula created a complete system of nontraditional explanations to religious customs, part of which originated in Europe. Passover as a symbol of social freedom, *Shavuot* as a festival of harvest in which the first produce is presented to the "Jewish National Fund," and *Hanukkah* as a festival of political activism are only three examples of the strong affinity between Orthodoxy and the secularist-nationalist culture. This affinity contains a demand for the use of similar symbols and terms, but there is a complete lack of agreement as to their significance. Those sections of Israeli society that succeeded (perhaps for only a short time, perhaps from not understanding the tremendous religious power hidden behind what is called "tradition"?) in settling the open contradictions between the religious source and its Orthodox realization, and the use they make of values and symbols, perhaps unwittingly perform a unique pioneering cultural act of challenging the religious establishment and the ruling Orthodox version. The selectivity in observing tradition is, even if unintentional, an open and blunt contradiction. Attributing national, social, and moral (nontraditional) content to customs and commandments is, even if not so intended, a rebellion against tradition. This means that what unifies the Israeli culture, in all its widely different components, is also the cause for the continual rift. This is so because as long as the Orthodox version exists as the only normative plane of reference for maintaining Jewish tradition, all other courses will be considered to be an intermediary stage, without their own value, or terrible mistakes that are worse than total nonbelief. And since I do not foresee in the near future any relaxation of the Orthodox monopoly that exists in the state of Israel over who determines who is "God-fearing" and ways of worship, I am afraid that great aversion is hidden behind any "openmindedness" on the part of the Orthodox toward the "traditionalists" of various types. This aversion is real from the aspect of the internalized set of values of those who so feel, and it is necessary because Orthodoxy, as such, is based on fear and aversion from the great external and internal threats.

The study of the Jewishness of the Israelis reveals that "Israeli society has a strong tendency toward tradition," and that "there is no sharp delineation between a religious minority and the secular majority." The tendency toward tradition is revealed in the same gradual continuum of partial observance of tradition and commandments. Will those at the very ends of this continuum recognize this tendency, which characterizes a large segment of the Jewish society in Israel, as a legitimate phenomenon that has a right to existence and has value in itself or will they try to drag it toward the extremes?

The Guttman Report–
The End of Commitment?

GERALD J. BLIDSTEIN

Professor of Jewish Thought, Ben-Gurion University of the Negev

What I have in front of me is the report, not reality. The report shapes and directs reality, beginning with the formation of the triangle, "Beliefs, Observances and Social Interaction" as integrated foci of reference and research, and ending with the graphic techniques through which the report presents its results. While "observances" and "beliefs" are clearly and essentially interrelated, this is not the case with "social interaction." I believe that I am not far wrong in assuming that taking this topic as a central focus of attention suggests that the topic itself and its relationship to other topics constitutes one of the main objectives of the report. To put it more precisely: the research does not deal with the degree of religiosity of the Israeli public per se, but rather with its power to influence the nature of this society, and especially its power as a socially unifying or segregating factor. Moreover, the report indicates that religiosity is not such a divisive factor as is generally thought ("there is no basis for the rhetoric of secular and religious polarization of Israeli society"); it may even be regarded as a unifying factor.

As a matter of fact, I am not so certain that the data do not point to fairly large divisions among different sectors of the population. Even if, from a sociological, objective-comparative point of view, we do seem to be a "society that has a traditional bent," it may be that such a definition will not be acceptable to members of our society who are sensitive to the divisions and actually experience them. Also, it should be borne in mind that "polarization" is not necessarily the main factor in segregation; indeed, those who are similar in their opinions are the ones who are usually in bitter dispute with each other, as we can learn from the history of religions and cults. In any event, the publication of the data presented in this report can alter the (mistaken) self-image of this society as a religiously divided society, and thus con tribute toward the basic purpose of the project.

In view of the aforementioned, it is rather a pity that the report (or the abstract I have) neglected to present concrete data on social interaction among the various population sectors. For example, it is difficult to determine when the findings refer to encounters at the place of work and when they refer to encounters "after five o'clock," as the Americans say, and this distinction is not to be taken lightly. Hints are made regarding "segregation of the Israeli-born of Western origin," but they are not sufficiently clear. In any event, I am not sure that the picture is so rosy. Although the report says that 76 percent are "ready" or "definitely ready" for their children to marry someone of a different degree of religiosity, these vague terms become clearer when we learn that only 16 percent are "definitely ready." This is, perhaps, the bottom line. (Incidentally, with regard to the similarity of the groups in question, it would be interesting to learn how similar are the percentages of marriage-readiness of secular–Orthodox vs. secular–"somewhat observant," and so on.)

I cannot refrain from a remark that I probably share with others: the report almost totally ignores differences between the sexes. Aside from one finding–that is, that 10 percent of Israeli women pray every day, a percentage that I find surprising and not sufficiently defined–I have not found reference to any other area of observance that is common to men and women. Can we conclude from this that there is no difference in the extent of religiosity between men and women? If so, it is a shame that this was not stated explicitly.

A conclusion–perhaps the main conclusion–is that "there is no basis for the rhetoric of secular and religious polarization of Israeli society." Indeed, this conclusion is not only stated verbally; it is also the conclusion that emerges from the graphic sketches–both from the data presented, their form of presentation, and even the nature of the use of colors. In other words (borrowing the known terminology from the writings of Rabbi Soloveitchik), we can talk about "common fate" and "common destiny" as types of Jewish identity, but we may not claim–as perhaps is convenient to do–that Israeli society is indeed divided into "people of a common fate" and "people of a common destiny."

However, it seems that this conclusion is based mainly on behavioral data alone, unaccompanied by the interpretative, internal, emotional correlate of these data. This lack of interest in the ideological dimension (as we shall identify it generally for the time being) is expressed, as I have already mentioned, in the central place given to the behavioral aspects in the research and in the detailed analyses they are given. The question of "beliefs," on the other hand, receives a more modest handling. (It may be that it is easier for sociology to deal with behavioral questions; or perhaps it holds that the essence of things is in fact thus revealed.) In any event, the neglect of the ideological aspect and the presentation of observance in terms of "more" or less" do not reflect the whole truth–neither the religious truth nor the secular truth.

Thus, the respondents were asked for the reason for their nonobservance: 67 percent agree that it stems from lack of "proper education." This finding seems very surprising to me. If cross-reference is made between this finding and one that 63 percent reported that "they have not acquired religious education" (a very unclear finding, in my opinion), then the implication is that most Israelis think that more education will result in more observance. However, I think that these data omit or ignore the respondents' emotional-spiritual reasons. Perhaps people did not and do not acquire more religious education because they do not think it contributes to their spiritual life. Or, to refer to the previous investigation of nonobservance, we cannot be restricted to options such as: "People did not get proper education," "Are content with partial observance" (an argument, by the way, that seems neither more nor less than a repetition of the examined behavior itself!), "It is hard to observe *mitzvot*." We cannot but include an emotional-cultural response, that is, that the person feels that he does not need what the *mitzvah* provides and that the extent of his current religiosity is quite sufficient for his needs in this respect.

Let me put this differently. The pupils of Rav J.B. Soloveitchik often heard him use the word *commitment*. He meant that observance of *mitzvot* is expressed (and even controlled) by a volitional and emotional relationship that is crystallized in a commitment, a granting of priority to what lies behind those *mitzvot*. This has been defined in purely religious terms, namely, *halacha*. And this, the Rav claimed, is a basic component of "Jewish religiosity." The main thing–and I admit that I greatly simplify the implication–is that it is impossible to detach the differences in the levels of observance from the ideological and/or emotional aspects they express. On the contrary, the question of commitment should be treated as a cardinal and shaping component. It is not only an interpretation of the behavior (its semantic alternative); it is a basic fundamental.

There is no doubt that including the component of commitment creates not a little complexity. It may create statistical contradictions to the data on observance and indicate hypocrisy, failure, feelings of guilt. It certainly raises the question–perhaps already answered by sociologists–whether there is a difference between an act of commitment and an act that stems from aesthetic or other reasons. It may point to divisions between groups in the population, not to a continuum; but it may also point to an unexpected continuum. Another complexity is introduced when we realize that religious commitment is not the only factor to be considered. I refer, for example, to the empathy that observant academics feel toward their nonobservant colleagues, an empathy that exceeds that which they might feel toward the Orthodox world with whom they share the metaphysical/national commitment; the same applies to religious kibbutz members and their feeling toward people from nonreligious kibbutzim (and, conversely, the empathy that people with deep religious consciousness sometimes feel toward deeply religious people from other religions, a closeness that may surpass [so I am told] the closeness they feel toward fellowmen of the same religion who are not observant); and there are other examples. It has already been said: "I cannot talk with those with whom I pray, and I cannot pray with those with whom I talk."

The behavioral situation described in the report presents a picture that is perhaps an alternative to that of classic normative Judaism, that is, Jewishness based on total commitment, which I have just described. The classic situation acknowledges observance of the *mitzvot* and/or total rejection of them altogether, and it has created a terminology of its own and has determined normative frameworks: the "apostate," the "ignorant," and so on. In general, such terms are applied to people who deny or neglect to observe a *mitzvah* and indicate a definite type of behavior. It was always known that there are Jews who neglect observance of *mitzvot* because of the laziness or the difficulty involved in the observance, and it was always also known that there are Jews who reject observance altogether from ideological or emotional reasons. But it seems to me that there is now another aspect of nonobservance–apart from that of choosing among the *mitzvot* what to observe and what not to observe, or "observing somewhat," both with respect to the timing and the frequency–which is different from that which was known to classic Judaism.

The new reality denies *halachic* authority as such. Yet, there is no doubt that the *halacha* still functions–if nonauthoritatively–in that new reality, and even in terms of observance. Is there, then, another type of commitment? Perhaps we now have a different sort of internalization, another framework of loyalty? Perhaps we should rather talk about national-cultural loyalty or familial loyalty, albeit out of conscious awareness. Of course, Jews have behaved throughout history out of national, social, and familial incentives and not only from purely religious motives. "Ask your father and he will tell you" does not suggest solely a source of information but also an essential connection. But all these were channeled into the basic religious loyalty and served it, at least on the conscious level. Nowadays, among the observant themselves, we can talk about different types of loyalties.

No doubt there are people who would claim that this ideological sensitivity is in itself a modern phenomenon and reflects the threatened situation of modern Orthodoxy. And, generally speaking, why should we probe into the complexity of motives and emotional states; Judaism, as is well known, has always given priority to deeds rather than to thoughts. Moreover, *halachic* Judaism recognizes the legitimacy of the position that "observing mitzvot needs no intention," although this position has certainly not gained general consensus. But let us not linger on trivialities: the idea of commitment–mainly the emotional but also the ideological–is fundamental. It is expressed in the original covenant pledged between the Jewish people and their God, in the oath sworn at Sinai and the deserts of Moab. Of course, there is nothing to oblige a modern person or Jew to keep that ancient pledge or even acknowledge its existence. I only mean to emphasize the fundamentality of the concept in the history of Jewish thought.

This discussion also brings to mind the problem raised by Rabbi Jacob Ettlinger at the beginning of the nineteenth century: what to think of those Jews who attend synagogue on Sabbath morning but open their businesses in the afternoon? There is definitely a desecration of the Sabbath here, he said. On the other hand, desecration of the Sabbath stems from the denial of the concept of the Creation and the existence of the Creator. Those Jews who attend synagogue do believe in the Creation and the Creator. What, then, is the weight of the behavioral aspect under such circumstances? We, too, considered this question, though from different points of view.

The State of the Religious Rift Among Jewish Israelis

The 1993 Guttman Institute Study

SHLOMO DESHEN

Professor of Anthropology, Tel Aviv University

Many years ago, I published an essay under a title that asked whether ethnic politics had disappeared from the Israeli scene (Deshen 1972). Raising the possibility at that time seemed far-fetched to many, and the paper was greeted with skepticism. But since the 1980s, there is no doubt that ethnicity has become less salient than in the past. In place of the ethnic rift, both journalists and social scientists now stress a different rift, that between religious and secular, and present it as a most serious internal problem. There are those who even talk of a "kulturkampf." The importance of the Guttman Institute study lies in its central thesis, which casts doubt on the thesis of the dominance of the religious rift.

The study does not refute the fact that, indeed, public positions on religious issues are often extreme and expressed stridently; but the study also presents findings about a very large percentage of the population that is characterized by moderate behavior, which bridges and mediates in religious matters. This behavior, the study demonstrates, pertains also to a certain extent to those who define themselves as nonreligious. The study reveals that the large majority of Israeli citizens practice many religious customs. No less than 90 percent of the general public follow at least some of the traditional practices regarding dietary laws (*kashrut*) in their homes. A similar number mark the Passover *seder* in some minimal manner. More than 50 percent perform the traditional life-cycle ceremonies of *bar mitzvah* and marriage, not to mention the universal practice of circumcision. An astonishing percentage, no less than 60 percent of the respondents, expressed firm ("wholehearted") belief in the existence of G-d.

The most interesting findings of the study deal with the category termed by the authors "nonobservant," or in common terms "secular" or "nonreligious." The survey reveals that 20 percent of the population identify themselves as belonging to the category of "completely nonobservant." But actually only about one third of this number, approximately 7 percent of the total population, are indeed such. Most of the "nonobservant" category do in fact observe some traditions. The large majority of that category regard themselves as more secular than is reflected in their actual behavior. Thus, in terms of specific practice, 20 percent of the nonobservant refrain from eating leavened bread [*hametz*] during Passover. No less than 40 percent of them mark the Sabbath in some manner, and the number of nonobservant who affix a *mezuzah* to their doorpost skyrockets to the figure of 92 percent. No less than 20 percent of the nonobservant believe "wholeheartedly" in G-d. Thus, only a proportion of the nonobservant are unequivocal atheists.

In an analysis of the values and positions of the nonobservant, it is not surprising that the study discovers that values of individualism and self-realization figure prominently. It must, however, be stressed that among the nonobservant (as well, of course, as among the religious categories), the traditional values of establishing a family and respect for parents are salient. Thus there are traditional values and behavioral characteristics that are the norm, both in the religious groups of the Israeli population and among many of the nonobservant.

Another striking finding of the study must be added to this: half of the nonobservant are of the opinion that the reason for their nonobservance is merely because they were not educated in their youth to be observant. The nonobservant thus do not indicate positive ideological reasons for their lifestyle. Only a small number cite a humanistic explanation, such as ritualistic actions being unnecessary for people who behave morally. This finding makes the paucity of an ideological dimension for the absence of observance even more salient. Many years ago the philosopher Natan Rotenstreich (1965: pp. 325–29) pointed to the incipient emergence of this important phenomenon and aptly termed it "secularism by default" (*hiloniyut she'mimeyla*).[1]

There is a well-sustained thesis in Jewish social history that under conditions of modernization in Western countries, Jewish women adhered to tradition more than men (Kaplan 1991, chapters 1–2). The rate of intermarriage of Jewish men in the modern West is consistently higher than that of women. With this in mind, the finding in the Guttman study of the absence of a significant correlation in Israel between observance and the variable of sex (or even of age or number of years in Israel) is notable. The authors note only a small trend toward less religiosity on the inter-generational plane. But the findings of a study by Avraham Leslau and the late Mordechai Bar-Lev (1994) about the graduates of the religious-Zionist educational system attributes more weight to the age-generation factor. These researchers found a significant abandonment of ritual observance by many of the graduates of the Torah high schools (*yeshivot tichoniot*).

Along with the assertion as to the minor influence of the generational factor on the abandonment of tradition, the Guttman study claims that there is no marked trend toward becoming ultra-observant among those who were raised in completely secular families. According to this, the phenomenon of becoming newly observant relates mainly to those who are at an intermediate point on the continuum between the poles of extreme religiosity and secularism. This is significant: the study implies that religious change is most common among those who are at an intermediate point along the continuum. Therefore, those belonging to the religious and secular categories at the opposing poles are not those most threatened by the possibility of changing their religious habits. There is evidence in the study that this is indeed the subjective feeling of the general populace, because the summary of the study shows that everyone exaggerates the number of people in their own category, both the observant and the nonobservant. People are self-assured and confident. Such a social reality is theoretically a base for easing tension. it is a plausible basis for the conclusion of the researchers that religious rift in Israel gives rise to less severe social tension than is ordinarily imagined.

The principal categories of the study are defined quantitatively: "strictly observant," "mostly observant," "nonobservant." The limitation of the study's insights stem from this quantification. The quantifying method makes a distinction between people who are close culturally, only because of the quantified factors in which they differ. For example, many secular people may be rather similar to moderate, modern religious people (who are integrated into secular society, into its customs and leisure patterns). Much of the behavior of the people in these two categories may be similar, such as performing religious rituals and going to the synagogue, and their reasons for doing so may also be similar, primarily family loyalty. Among both these categories of people the theological content is apt to be tepid and minimal. Many are married couples who are heterogenous regarding observance, one spouse being observant and the other not (Weller & Topper-Weller 1990). Indeed, the thesis of the Guttman study is the delineation of the trend of integration and interweaving that is common to sections of the populations that are considered different. This thesis might have been further supported (and the paradigm that stresses the principle of differences between religious and secular might have been weakened) had the consistent quantification not blurred the perception of the common factors.

The study before us also thrusts into the same category various types of people whom it would have been more reasonable, on the basis of consideration of cultural variables, to separate. For example, the ultra-Orthodox-nationalists of *Gush Emunim,* and the ultra-Orthodox *hassidim* of the Satmar sect imbue many of their actions with very different meanings, even if these actions are formally and quantitatively the same. In addition, it might in some cases be worthwhile to separate people of different ethnic backgrounds who appear in the same quantitative category in this study, for this same reason–that they instill different meaning into similar actions. For example, attending synagogue among people in the "strictly observant" category may be different among the Ashkenazi Orthodox, compared to their counterparts of Moroccan or Yemenite descent. Among Middle Eastern Jews, motives of family loyalty for attending synagogue might be more important than for Ashkenazim. On the other hand, among newly ultra-Orthodox Middle Eastern Jews of the *Shas* political party variety, a new religious selectivity might develop with respect to synagogue selection. The new sensitivity can clash with, and contradict, old familial-community loyalties, similar to the pattern among many Ashkenazi ultra-Orthodox families. Pinpointing such differences might lead to a deeper understanding of customs observed and quantified, namely the level of significance and of cultural content.[2]

Consideration of the nature and weight of the family, with respect to religiosity, raises questions that deserve further study. For example, when examining the customs of Passover eve in different circles, attention should be given to an hypothesis that this event is particularly an extended family one among the nonobservant. There is reason to hypothesize that among the strictly observant, the Passover *seder* would paradoxically tend to be smaller and less familial in comparison because of the practical problem of avoiding motorized travel on the holiday.[3] The investigation of such differences in the organization of Passover eve festivities and other such events may lead to the discovery of various significant cultural patterns.

Some of the data in the Guttman study almost beg for a detailed cultural analysis of this sort. How can the astonishing figure of over 80 percent of the population, who are interested in traditional rites of passage, be understood, despite the lack of popularity of the rabbinical establishment that manages them? It would appear that people of different circles imbue the rites of passage with entirely different meanings. The study reports that of the many who say that they affix a *mezuzah* to the doorpost (over 90 percent of the population), 74 percent are of the opinion that it is effective in protecting the home. It is reasonable to assume that there are different nuances to this explanation, its weight, and its meaning among people of different circles in Israeli society. In regard to the popular rites of passage, we do not have a clue to understanding their significances, other than general anthropological theory concerning symbolic action.

The paucity of cultural analysis, juxtaposed with the emphasis on quantitative analysis, appears to me to be a fault in the study. This is especially evident in the section dealing with Jewish identity. That discussion completely ignores the fact that observance of religious custom may be linked with both extreme nationalistic values, and with values completely the opposite, such as those of the Satmar *hassidim.* As a result of this, those who observe religious practices may develop varied and differing images of the Jewish people, not to mention very different images of the state of Israel and consequent attitudes toward it.

The reader at times gets the impression that the researchers viewed the observant, and especially the Ashkenazi ultra-Orthodox and Middle Eastern Israelis, from an external observation point. Thus, for example, the subject of Torah studies takes up little space in the variables of the study, whereas in fact the subject of adult Torah studies among ultra-Orthodox people is central and prominent. Also among the other religious groups, Torah study has more importance than is manifest in this study. Other subjects as well that, according to ethnographic reports, have special importance among Middle Easterners, such as participation in pilgrimages to holy places, as well as mourning customs, do not figure much in the study.[4] On the other hand, reciting the "Prayer for the State" appears in the study incongruously as a measure for Sabbath observance. Reciting the *Yizkor* (memorial prayer) appears in the study incongruously as a measure of Jewish identification, whereas this prayer does not figure at all in the Sephardic liturgy. Similarly, the custom of eating dairy dishes and participating in the night vigil appear as measures of the *Shavuot* observance. These customs are secondary, and one of them (eating dairy dishes) is considered even less than that in Middle Eastern and *hassidic* circles. It may well be that the nontraditional and alien perspective of the researchers lead them to emphasize a domestic custom over and above its importance in many religious circles.

The presumed alien perspective of the researchers perhaps explains some puzzling details in the study. One of them is the finding about the small percentage of women who use the ritual bath (*mikve*) regularly–only 16 percent. It is astonishing that this particular custom of purification, deeply rooted in traditional female Jewish identity, should not encompass more than that low percentage. In contrast to other basic religious practices, such as the dietary laws and the Sabbath, the figure regarding the use of the ritual bath means that only the most punctilious observe this tradition. If indeed the datum is precise, it requires an explanation. But maybe the low figure is not reliable and is again linked to the particular perspective of the researchers: the lives of many traditional and ultra-Orthodox women follow a continual cycle of pregnancy, childbirth, lactation, and pregnancy again. The natural course of life seldom requires these women to visit the ritual bath, aside from occasional immersions after childbirth and after weaning. Modern religious women who control their pregnancies are the ones who require the *mikve* at the high frequency of once a month. It may be that the questionnaire was specifically formulated for this type of woman. Therefore, it may also be that a great number of Orthodox women are excluded from the category of women who make frequent usage of the *mikve*, despite the fact that the issue of purification is obviously very important to them.

Compared to the figure of the use of the ritual bath, which seems low to me, some other figures that appear in the study seem to me unreasonably high. No less than 10 percent of all women, according to the study, are said to pray every day. Considering the low importance given to women's prayers in traditional Judaism, this percentage seems to me exaggerated. Also, data indicating extreme liberalism in accepting religiously heterogeneous marriages are not very credible (70% are said to be willing to marry a partner differing in degree of observance, and 65% are supposedly even ready for a spouse who is a new immigrant from Ethiopia). Similarly, it is difficult to accept the figure that 27 percent of the population regularly visit hospitalized patients who are not close relatives or friends. And finally, the determination that no less than 80 percent of the men in the population have phylacteries (*tefillin*) in their homes is astonishing. It is possible that all these optimistic figures result from particular formulation of the questions and from idiosyncratic work by the interviewers.

Beyond the main argument of the study about the current prevalence of religious customs in the population as a whole, some of the details of the data indicate directions in which Israeli society is going. According to the study, one of the prominent causes for tension between religious and secular Israelis is the issue of inequality in military service based on religiosity. With the discussion, currently underway, of reducing the duration of compulsory military service, it is to be assumed that this cause of tension will decrease. Another point touches upon the principal cause for the moderate picture of the religious rift that the study paints: it would appear that the main stratum that is characterized by the prevalence of moderation is that of Israeli Middle Easterners. Few of them, relative to Ashkenazi Israelis, appear at either the extreme religious or the extreme secular pole of society. The significance of this is that the Middle Eastern Israelis fill an important role in bridging the religious rift between those who are at the opposite poles of Israeli society. This reality may have far-reaching political implications as to the question of the leadership of the country in the future. The future may lie with the Middle Easterners.

Finally, the study indicates Americanization of Israeli society. In utter contrast to the situation in the country during the 1950s, when there was a clear dichotomy between those who were believers and observant and those who were nonbelievers and socialist, Israel today is characterized by a large bloc of people who are lukewarm and moderate in religious practice. These people are comfortable with basic beliefs and occasionally attend a synagogue but are not insistent in their orthodoxy. The people at the extremes, while strident, are few. This picture is similar to the portrait of the mainstreams of religion in America today (Berger 1992).[5] The Guttman study thus indicates that there is more similarity between Israeli and American religion than we commonly realize.

NOTES

1. However, a note of reservation is called for: the sample of the research did not include kibbutzim, and the exclusion of that population, which is mostly secular, biases the findings in the direction I have highlighted. On the other hand, the kibbutz population overall is not of great weight, and so one might reasonably argue that the bias is not that great.

2. For a development of this discussion regarding a cultural approach to the study of religiosity in Israel, see Deshen (1990; 1994).

3. For a discussion of the weight of the family and home in modern nontraditional and Orthodox Jewry, see Deshen (1987) and Friedman (1991).

4. Such as, wearing a skullcap by one otherwise not accustomed to doing so and not shaving even when the deceased is not a close relation.

5. There is even a parallel for the relatively recent prominence, revealed by the study, of marking Sabbath, even among the Israeli secular, with practices in the American Jewish Reform movement.

REFERENCES

Hebrew

Deshen, S., "The Religiosity of Israeli Middle-Easterners: Lay People, Rabbis, and Faith." *Alpayim* 9, 1994: 44–58.

Friedman, M., *Ultra-Orthodox Society: Sources, Trends, and Processes*, Jerusalem: Research Institute, 1991.

Rotenstreich, N., *The People and State*, Tel Aviv: Ha'Kibbutz Ha'Meuhad, 1965.

English

Berger, P. L., *A Far Glory: The Question for Faith in an Age of Credulity*, New York: Free Press, 1992.

Deshen, S., "The Business of Ethnicity is Finished!? The Ethnic Factor in a Local Election Campaign." In *The Elections in Israel, 1969* (A. Arian, ed.), Jerusalem: Academic Press, 1972, pp. 278–304.

———. "Domestic Observances: Jewish Practices." *Encyclopedia of Religion*, vol. 4, 1987, pp. 400–2.

———. "The Social Foundation of Israeli Judaism." In *Social Foundations of Judaism* (C. Goldscheider and J. Neuser, eds.), Englewood Cliffs, NJ: Prentice Hall, 1990, pp. 212–39.

Kaplan, M. A., *The Making of the Jewish Middle Class: Women, Family, and Identity in Imperial Germany*. New York: Oxford University Press, 1991.

Leslau, A., and M. Ber-Lev, "Religiosity among Oriental Youth in Israel." *Sociological Papers* (Bar-Ilan) 3, no. 5, 1994.

Weller, L., and S. Topper-Weller, "Strange Bedfellows: A Study of Mixed Religious Marriages." In *Religious and Secular: Conflict and Accommodation between Jews in Israel* (C. S. Liebman, ed.). Jerusalem: Keter, 1990, pp. 173–92.

Comments on the Guttman Report

MENACHEM FRIEDMAN
Professor of Sociology, Bar-Ilan University

The study carried out by Dr. Shlomit Levy, Hanna Levinsohn, and Professor Elihu Katz makes a very important contribution to the understanding of how the Jewish society in Israel relates to the Jewish religion and tradition. While the study carried out by Dr. Y. Ben-Me'ir and Dr. P. Kedem, *Index of Religiosity for the Jewish Population of Israel (Megamot,* 24(3), 1979, pp. 353–62), already found that there is no basis in reality for the common belief that, alongside a religious minority, the majority of the Jewish population of Israel is secular in the full meaning of the term, the present study determines unequivocally that "as far as religious practice is concerned . . . there is a continuum from the "strictly observant" to "nonobservant," **rather than a great divide between a religous minority and a secular majority** (author's emphasis). Only about 20 percent of the respondents stated that they do not observe religious tradition at all, while 25 percent stated that they observe religious tradition to a large degree, and about 40 percent stated that they are "partially observant." Two thirds of the Jewish public mark *Shabbat* by observing a number of traditions, such as lighting candles or participating in a special meal. About half make *kiddush* over wine on Friday night. The data regarding the observance of *kashrut* are more impressive. Two thirds of the respondents said that they "always" eat *kosher* food at home, and about half of the respondents said that they have separate utensils for dairy and meat. Moving to the area of beliefs and values, the findings are even more surprising. More than 60 percent of the respondents believe "wholeheartedly" that the Torah was given to Moshe on Mount Sinai. To sum up, the study indicates that only a minority of Jewish society in Israel is clearly secular. On the basis of these data and other data that are no less impressive, the authors of the study come to the conclusion that "there is no basis for the rhetoric of secular and religious polarization generally used to characterize Israeli society."

This conclusion is, in my opinion, unwarranted. The majority of the Jewish citizens of Israel do feel some sort of commitment to the Jewish tradition. Furthermore, most Israeli Jews who do not define themselves as "religious" see Orthodox religiosity as the legitimate expression of Jewish religion and tradition, and they reject other expressions of Jewish religiosity that are widely accepted among American Jewry (Reform Judaism and Conservative Judaism). Nevertheless, in important social areas (which we will discuss later), the rift between religious and nonreligious, that is, between those who define themselves as committed to the *halacha* as understood by the Orthodox and those who define themselves as nonreligious, is not only substantial but has assumed serious implications for our daily lives. This statement would appear to contradict the findings of the study; however, deeper analysis reveals that this is not the case.

It seems to me that the contradiction between my conclusion and the conclusion of the study stems from different points of departure. The authors of the study looked primarily at the "religiosity" of the Israeli Jew who is not "religious," and they reached the justified conclusion that he is not "secular," although this does not mean that he is "religious" in the same sense that the Orthodox-religious Jew defines himself as "religious." My point of departure, though, is completely different. I am interested in examining the social implications of the religiously Orthodox identity within the framework of Israeli society. My assertion, which I will present at greater length later, is that the Israeli "secular" reality "forces" the Orthodox-religious Jew to live in neighborhoods in which religious people who are similar to him or her constitute at least a substantial minority, if not in "ghettos" that have a more prominent Orthodox-religious character; it does not allow him to maintain primary social relationships with those who are not Orthodox-religious like himself. I will present my assertion bluntly: It is difficult for the Orthodox Jew, today more than in the past, to maintain friendships that include frequent mutual visits and joint recreation with those who are not as completely committed to the religion and tradition as he/she is.

For the purpose of presenting my thesis, I would like to use a concept that I have used a number of times in the past for other purposes—"secularism by default." Originally, I used this concept to try to clarify the difference between what I referred to as "militant secularism" (which primarily characterized the approach of the socialistic-pioneering movements to the Jewish religion and tradition, until after the establishment of the state) and the attitude toward religion and tradition in the Israeli society of today. "Militant secularism" considers Jewish religion and tradition as it crystallized primarily in the Eastern European Diaspora, as a negative phenomenon that must be fought against. In contrast, "secularism by default" does not categorically reject religion and the right of religious Jews to live according to their beliefs. Today's secular lifestyle does not necessarily stem from an ideology that denies the legitimacy of Jewish religion and tradition. With the passage of time, I found that the concept of "secularism by default" could include additional social phenomena that have a far-reaching influence on the daily existence of Orthodox Jews. Thus, for example, I define the family car as "secular by default." This is because the family car played a decisive role in changing the individual's perception of time and distance in modern society. The family car changes to a large degree not only the recreational patterns of the modern family on the day of rest (Saturday in Israel) but also the geographic reach of the primary social network. The social network of the modern family is no longer restricted to the immediate neighborhood but is spread out across a relatively large radius from the family's place of residence. The Orthodox Jew, however, does not have one time-distance definition. The fact that the Orthodox Jew cannot use a car on *Shabbat* requires him to live in two different time-distance dimensions. He must live within a reasonable walking distance of a synagogue that is suited to his religious lifestyle, and he must also make sure that there are other religious families in the immediate area with whom he can maintain social-communal relations. This reality, in itself, makes difficult, if not impossible, the existence of mixed primary social networks, consisting of both those who are religious and those who are "secular." A primary social network, some of whose members cannot take part in these events, will have difficulty holding up over time.

From this perspective, one can also define the multistory apartment building that is typical of the modern metropolis as "secular by default." There is usually no place to build a *succah* (in such a building), it is difficult to manage without using the elevator, and there is usually a front door that is locked with an electric lock requiring visitors to use the intercom and have the resident open the door electrically. If an Orthodox Jew wants to live in a multistory building, then, he must buy an apartment on one of the lower floors (the operation of a *Shabbat* elevator is quite costly and depends upon the consent of the neighbors) and plan visits by friends and relatives on *Shabbat* (in advance) so that he can wait downstairs and open the front door for them.

I will be bold and also define the supermarket as "secular by default." The commercial basis of the supermarket is shelf consumption and as wide a variety as possible of similar products. This fact has serious implications in terms of *kashrut*, particularly the *kashrut* of snack foods and preserved goods—preserved fish and meat products. Some of these consumer goods are imported, and not all of them are necessarily *kosher*, or their level of *kashrut* is not always accepted by the majority of Orthodox consumers. The Orthodox Jew is aware of this problematic situation. He is aware of this not only because he himself wants to be careful to consume only *kosher* products but also because most of his friends do so and they may make a comment to him if he is not as observant. Thus, consumption by the Orthodox Jew is based on criteria that are determined by the primary religious group and not by the individual. However, those who do not define themselves as "religious," even if they have separate utensils at home for dairy and meat, are less aware, if at all, of the *kashrut* problems in the modern consumer society. As a result, it is usually difficult for the Orthodox Jew to have a "common table" (which is the basis for significant social relations) with those who are not religious, even those that say that they observe *kashrut* in their homes.

By the way, in this context, the findings of the study raise a number of problems. For example, two thirds of the respondents state that they "always" eat *kosher* food at home, yet only about half of the respondents have separate utensils for dairy and meat. If only half have separate utensils for meat and dairy, how can two thirds of the respondents "always" eat *kosher* food at home? It seems to me that many of the respondents are not familiar with the laws of *kashrut*, and, therefore, the validity of the responses in this area is questionable.

I could continue and define other social and economic characteristics as "secular by default," but time considerations do not allow it. To sum up, it does not matter if the overwhelming majority of the Jews in Israel believe in God or light candles with a blessing on Friday night or even if half of them keep separate utensils for dairy and meat. Orthodox society, including all of its various shades, maintains primary social frameworks that are separate from those of the nonreligious. I do not have to mention here the separate educational frameworks and the increasing tendency among all types of religious people, including the modern-religious, to block entry to religious schools to students from families that do not completely observe *Shabbat*, the laws of *kashrut*, or even laws concerning the external appearance of the parents (primarily a head covering for the head of the family). Furthermore, the findings of the study support the phenomenon, with which we are familiar from other studies, that nonreligious Jews of Eastern descent are more traditional and more observant of the *mitzvot* [than other nonreligious Jews]. The data also indicate that commitment to religion and tradition decreases as the level of general education increases. Thus, the expansion of the educated circles in Israeli society will lead to a reduction in the commitment to the religion and tradition among the Jews of Eastern descent as well. On the other hand, the activity of the *Shas* political party among the strata characterized by lower income and lower levels of education among the Jews of Eastern descent, and the expansion of the *Shas* educational system (*El Ha'ma'ayan*) will result in increasing polarization between the Eastern Jews who are religious and those who are not.

However, when I contend that today, against the background of "secularism by default" that characterizes life in the modern city, it is even more difficult for Orthodox Jews to maintain friendships with those who are not like them, I am not necessarily saying that there is no contact and dialogue between them. To a certain degree, the opposite is true. Anyone who has reviewed the history of the relations between religious and "secular" in Israeli society can see that in the past—the 1950s and the 1960s—the level of conflict between these two groups was much higher than it is today. A few examples: The public areas of the big cities in Israel are today much more secular than in the past. Many more food stores blatantly sell products that are not *kosher*. Most of the first-class restaurants are not *kosher*. Entertainment and recreation centers are open on Friday nights. Could anyone in the 1960s have predicted that movie theaters, restaurants, and pubs would operate undisturbed in downtown Jerusalem on Friday nights?

We are also witness to fewer and fewer conflicts stemming from marriage and divorce laws. And it is not because there are no longer *kohanim* (men of Priestly descent) who want to marry divorced women, or alternatively, that the rabbinate has begun allowing *kohanim* to marry divorcees. It is not that there are no longer *mamzerim* (bastards) in Israel, or alternatively, that the rabbinate has stopped keeping lists of *psulei hitun* (those forbidden to marry by religious law). The explanation for the secularization of the public areas of the large cities is connected to, among other things, the process by which the religious have geographically separated themselves. The move of the religious, and particularly the *haredim*, from the centers of the cities to separate residential areas ("ghettos") allows the religious and the *haredim* to give expression to their religious culture in the public areas of their own neighborhoods and, at the same time, allows the nonreligious to express the secular culture in the city centers. The explanation for the relative tranquility with regard to conflicts stemming from the marriage and divorce laws is that alternatives have been created that allow marital or pseudo-marital ("life partner") relationships without requiring the Orthodox Rabbinate. To sum up, it is precisely the cutting off of the religious from the nonreligious that allows a relatively tranquil existence, side by side.

This is not the place nor the time to expand this discussion into the political-national-religious area. However, today, more than ever, we cannot disregard the fact that the relations between the religious and nonreligious are not only reflected by different lifestyles but are also related to existential political questions that must now be resolved–the question of the territories and the rights to Judea, Samaria, and Gaza. There is no doubt that the question of the "occupied territories" is no longer just a political question but also a religious question of the highest level. The positions of rabbis, based on *halachic* rulings, have become an important component of this existential-political debate, and the aggressive activity on the part of national-religious circles to undermine the Agreement of Principles with the PLO is today at the center of Israeli politics. I have no doubt that this reality will influence the relations between the religious and nonreligious in Israeli society. It is, therefore, difficult for me to share fully in the "optimistic" tone that characterizes this study.

Jew or Israeli—Who or What Are Citizens of Our State?

RABBI SHLOMO RISKIN
Chief Rabbi, Efrat

Conventional wisdom would maintain that the citizens of Israel are polarized, divided between a great majority of secularists (*hilonim*) and a small minority of religionists (*datiim*), with the latter endeavoring to force their views on the former. The religionists speak in the name of G-d, and a fundamentalist interpretation of the Bible. The secularists insist that religion is outmoded, and while it may be necessary for maintaining Jewish identity in the Diaspora, it serves no positive purpose in Israel. The situation can best be described by a "blow-up" on a bus ride I took down King George Street a number of summers ago. The bus was crowded, and as I was longingly making my way to a single empty seat next to a *hassid*, a sleeveless young woman slid into it instead. I was again disappointed when the *hassid* remained in his seat, but the "action" that ensued helped me overcome my tiredness. "Would you please close the window," demurely requested the young woman, her hair all blown from the wind. Responded the *hassid*, in a quiet and respectful voice: "And would you please lengthen your sleeves?"

"Sir," the young woman said, her voice rising to match her indignation," the open window is bothering me!"

"Madame," replied the nonplussed *hassid*, in tones of matching volume, "your bare arms are bothering me!"

And, as is to be expected on an Israeli bus, almost everyone took sides. "Of course, the woman is right. The *hassid* didn't even give her a sewing kit." "What do you mean?" shouted someone from the back. "If she had longer sleeves, the wind wouldn't disturb her." At this point, it was time for me to leave the bus but not before overhearing an elderly gentleman say to his wife: "Now do you understand why our children wish to leave this country? When they are in control, they'll tell us how to dress, where to get off, and when to breathe!" The religionists, from their perspective, claim that they arrived in Jerusalem from Europe in large numbers before the secularist Zionists did (the students of the Vilna Gaon and the Hatam Sofer began coming in the eighteenth century), that the Labor government forced many religious immigrants–especially the Yemenite children–to live and study in nonreligious settings, and that the media constantly distort their position and rail out against them. Given two such extreme and antithetical camps, one must sometimes only be grateful for the common Arab threat, which seems to be the only prevention of an internecine war. And if, as seems inevitable, the secular camp wins, what kind of relationship will remain between a Canaanite Israel and past Jewish history, between a Canaanite Israel and world Jewry?

But the situation just characterized is far from the truth. The present political reality in Israel, where an extremist minority can earn the swing-vote right to determine which party has hegemony, creates the illusion that our nation is indeed divided between the two extreme positions of secularist versus religionist. However, the fact is that there exists not a religious polarity but rather a religious continuum in Israel, whereby the overwhelming majority of Israelis enjoy a positive relationship to the Jewish tradition that they regularly express in their ongoing personal behavior. This has been proven by a fascinating study initiated by the Avi Chai Foundation and carried out by the Louis Guttman Israel Institute of Applied Social Research. This study has many ramifications, especially for the future program and agenda of priorities for the religious community in Israel.

First, what are the facts about Israeli society? Fourteen percent observe the commandments completely, 24 percent observe to a great extent, 41 percent observe to a small extent, and only 21 percent observe not at all. What we have here is indeed a continuum of observance, with only a small minority at the edges of a rather broad spectrum. Moreover, when viewed from the perspective of observance, Israel emerges not as a Canaanite society with a Hebrew language, but rather as a remarkably Jewish society after all: 98 percent have a *mezuzah* at least on the front door of their homes (a great majority on all doorposts); approximately 90 percent engage in such life-cycle religious rituals as circumcision, marriage, and *kaddish* after a departed parent; 90 percent usually and close to 88 percent always participate in a Passover *seder*, with 80 percent generally not and 62 percent never eating *hametz* in Passover week; 72 percent light *Hanukkah* candles (and that is without the competition of Christmas), 71 percent fast on Yom Kippur; 66 percent always eat *kosher* at home, with 50 percent separating between meat and milk dishes; and 66 percent establish the uniqueness of the Sabbath by means of candle-lighting and special foods, with 50 percent making *kiddush*. As far as belief and opinions are concerned, 98 percent feel part of world Jewry, 84 percent visit the Western Wall; 60 percent believe with a full heart (*lev shalem*) in G-d who created and directs the world; 50 percent believe that the Torah was given to Moses on Mount Sinai and was ordained by G-d. The study indicates that there is even a positive pull toward Jewish tradition, with the overwhelming majority of Israelis caring desperately about Jewish continuity—70 percent of those who characterize themselves as not observing commandments at all base their desire to be part of the Jewish people upon their participation in Passover *sedarim* and their marking of Jewish festivals and the Jewish life cycle; one third want to keep more ritual observances than their parents (only 5% want to keep less!), and 50 percent of those who claim no observance whatsoever want their children to keep at least some rituals.

With statistics such as these, one can hardly characterize the majority of the Israeli population as denying their Jewish tradition or describe them as *hiloni* (secularists). But neither can we call them religious, at least not in our Western culture usage of the term. The perspicacious reader will note that although the participation in festivals and life-cycle rituals is quite high, there was no mention of prayer and synagogue (church) attendance, activities that Christian America almost exclusively identifies with religion. According to the Guttman Institute study, only 8 percent of Israelis attend synagogue daily, only 16 percent attend synagogue every Sabbath and festival, and only 22 percent of the men and 10 percent of the women pray daily in any venue at all.

Our inescapable conclusion must be that Judaism and the unique Jewish tradition that is expressed in Israel is far more than a religion with its church-prayer centered focus by which Western culture generally understands religion. Judaism is rather, as Mordechai Kaplan so aptly defined it in the title of his major theological work, a civilization, with a land, language, literature, history, life-cycle rituals, festival celebrations, eating habits, and overriding values that are uniquely its own.

While such a definition may well place a much more difficult burden on Diaspora Jewry, it is insufficient to merely espouse a "believing or belonging" relationship to a Judaism in translation, but there must be a commitment to a "behaving" relationship, a profound involvement with an additional civilization to that of one's host country that causes the *galut* Jew to live in a state-within-a-state, to be a perennial resident alien no matter how accepted he may feel in his adopted country. Nevertheless, it is a far more accurate description of the Jewish condition; it also provides a far more honest picture and assessment of what Judaism throughout the ages has really been. The Guttman Institute study demonstrates that an overwhelming majority of Israelis do participate in—and have a positive feeling for—the experience of our Jewish civilization, even while they generally eschew the specifically religious aspects of the tradition. From this perspective, our vocabulary requires a significant change: Israeli society (and world Jewish society) ought to be divided not between *dati* and *hiloni*, which if anything represent the extreme ends of the spectrum, but rather between those who observe the commandments of Israel and those who observe the culture of Israel. The former feel duty bound to a legal system whose authority comes from a divine source, the latter choose to align themselves in varying degrees to the unique culture of their forebears. Although there are fundamental theological and behavioral differences between these two groups, there are far more points of contact between them, with shared practices, vocabulary, and values that can and must serve as a basis for a united people.

And although the picture painted by the study is a rather positive one in terms of Israel's present religio-cultural continuum, unless fundamental changes are made, the situation may take a radical turn for the worse in the next generation. We must remember that according to the Union of Orthodox Jewish Congregations (the largest and most well-known *kashrut* certifying agency in the United States), 73 percent of American Jews bought *kosher* meat in 1949 and only 16 percent did so in 1979. Such changes can occur precipitously; moreover, the influx of Jews from the Soviet Union in the hundreds of thousands without any Jewish religio-cultural background and the peace prospect that can become a very mixed blessing indeed if it leads to economic and social interaction between Israelis and Palestinians, can dramatically alter the present statistics. The study itself points out the danger signals, if we read between the lines. The *dati-hiloni* descriptive term for Israeli society is not only incorrect; it is destructive. The Israeli mentality generally confuses Jewish culture with Jewish religion and is increasingly apt to reject both together, throwing out the baby with the bath water.

The majority of Israelis not only reject "religious" practices; they are uncomfortable with, and often harbor resentment against, those whom they perceive as religionists. Fifty-one percent would like to maintain public life in Israel the way it is religiously (with 94% agreeing that army and public institutions ought to be *kosher*), but 60 to 75 percent are dissatisfied with the religious status quo agreement, apparently suspicious of further encroachment by the religious establishment on what they perceive as their civil rights. Ninety percent of the population believe that there ought not to be wholesale exemption of Yeshiva boys from the IDF, and whereas two thirds believe there is no societal problem between Sephardim and Ashkenazim, Jews from Ethiopia integrating with Jews from other countries, two thirds likewise believe that religionists (*datiim*) are insensitive. Seventy percent believe that the Chief Rabbinate fails in its attempt to deal with problems facing our nation, and 75 percent never consult with a rabbi—neither concerning personal problems nor even concerning problems relating to religious observance. Not atypical is the sincere dilemma of Zvi Zameret, director of the Ben Zvi Institute, regarding his inability to properly observe *Tisha B'Av*, the anniversary of the destruction of both Temples. Zvi is an intellectual idealist-Zionist, profoundly committed to our Jewish civilization but equally turned-off by the religious establishment. (Remember Mark Twain's cynical comment that organized religion was born when the first scoundrel met the first fool.) Since *Tisha B'Av* is fundamentally marked by a synagogue ritual, he is at a loss as to how to incorporate this observance within his family context. To the degree that Jewish cultural involvement is identified with establishment religion, succeeding generations may well come to reject more and more of their heritage. From this perspective, it becomes significant to note that the Sephardi population of Israel is generally more observant of Jewish tradition than the Ashkenazim, with fully 70 percent observing the commandments completely or to a large extent; their children however, are significantly less observant (see p. 2 and p. 8 of the Guttman study), and there is a close correlation between the quality of religious education and the extent of religious observance: 37 percent of the respondents give their children religious education, and 38 percent are completely or largely observant. And when the respondents of the Guttman study were asked why they thought people do not observe commandments, 67 percent responded because of inadequate education as opposed to 38 percent who said that religion was unnecessary (p.11 of the study). Even more to the point, over 50 percent of those who characterized themselves as not observing at all agreed with the 67 percent as to the reason why.

The Israeli school system is divided between secular institutions (*Mamlakhti*) and religious institutions (*Mamlakhti Dati*). Whereas the religious school system is becoming more and more intensive (the extremist minority swing-vote again, forcing funds for a separate *Shas* stream), the secular school system not only excludes prayer from the curriculum but also provides less and less time (if any at all) for Bible, significance of Jewish ritual, and even Jewish history. Indeed, it has been suggested that the first and last be excluded from the newly established *bagrut* (nationally accepted graduate examinations) requirements, and the middle subject was never included in the first place. Apparently the curriculum-makers in the

Educational Ministry are confusing–and fusing–Jewish culture with Jewish religion, a situation that increasingly leads to the deletion of Jewish civilization from our educational requirements and clears the path for a national malady of Alzheimer's. Yaakov Hazan, one of the ideologues of the *Shomer HaZair* movement, put it very well: we may have wanted to create a generation of *apekorsim* (knowledgeable heretics), but we are producing instead a generation of *am ha'aretzim* (Jewish cultural ignoramuses). No wonder Michael Jackson and Madonna have replaced Maimonides and Bruria as national heroes for a not-insignificant portion of our youth.

And if this confusion–and rejection–contributes to something, and if our sought-after peace with the Palestinians population becomes a reality, we may well find the scourge of assimilation and intermarriage affecting Israeli society no less than the Diaspora.

The Guttman study also provides the basis for a solution. We need not create a new Israeli secular culture; we need only recognize the fact that our Jewish civilization–the culture of Israel as distinct from the religion of the rabbinic establishment–is precious to the majority of our citizenry and is a healthy foundation on which to build for the future. The model of the TALI schools, which conveys the significance of Jewish culture–literature, ritual and values within the context of the Israeli secular school system (*mamlakhti*), must become the rule rather than the exception, a curriculum that must be the educational heritage of every Israeli student. And most importantly, a cadre of suitable teachers–knowledgeable of and committed to our Jewish civilization without proselytizing to divine commandment–must be devoted to impart this curriculum effectively.

Furthermore, if we are serious in our desire to begin to heal the rift between the extremist *dati-hiloni* strains in our population and to help guarantee the perpetration of the broad-based center, we must produce a new modern Orthodox rabbinical stream in Israel, one that can effectively relate to that center. We need rabbis who are expert in the texts and traditions of our Jewish civilization but who are also committed to the modern state of Israel and the Israeli Defense Forces; rabbis who are conversant in the Talmud and the codes but who are knowledgeable in philosophy and science; rabbis who can answer religio-legal questions but who can also relate Jewish rituals to the existential problems of modern-day living; and rabbis rooted in our tradition who can also respect those who are ignorant or critical of that tradition. Such rabbis can facilitate dialogue between the contemporary Israeli and his ancient civilization and can serve as a bridge between those who observe the commandments of Israel and those who are identifying in varying degrees with the culture of Israel. The rabbi's orientation must be ethical-spiritual rather than legal or political, educational rather than coercive. He must reestablish the Israeli synagogue as a House of Study and a House of Cultural Assembly in addition to the House of Prayer it almost exclusively is today, and he must demonstrate the abiding relevance of the ritual for the Jew struggling to make meaning of his or her life in a complex and often tragic world. The Western European model of Hildesheimer's Rabbinical Seminary must become a valid option alongside of Ponevezh, Ariel, and Merkaz HaRav as a crucible for religio-cultural leadership, and Rav Kook's doctrine of "the old must be renewed, and the new must be sanctified" must assume equal legitimacy to the Hatam Sofer's doctrine that "the new is Biblically forbidden."

The Guttman study demonstrates that—at least for the present—Israel is indeed a Jewish society with shared values and rituals emanating from our traditions; our challenge is to lay the groundwork for a future in which our heritage will not only survive but will prevail.

Is There Really No Alienation and Polarization?

ELIEZER SCHWEID
Professor of Jewish Thought, The Hebrew University

The report summarizing the findings of the Guttman Institute study states categorically that there is no basis "to the rhetoric of secular and religious polarization generally used to characterize Israeli society." It would be more accurate to say that "Israeli society has a strong traditional bent; and, as far as religious practice is concerned . . . that there is a continuum from the 'stricly religious' to the 'nonobservant,' rather than a great divide between a religious minority and a secular majority." I will try to show below that, regretfully, this conclusion is not sufficiently substantiated. A different analysis of the study's findings demonstrates that, although most Jews in Israel have a stronger affinity to Jewish tradition than is publicly perceived, the "polarizing rhetoric" is not only well-founded in the social reality of Israel but is quite representative. Neither a bridge nor an approach to dialogue is necessarily created by the mere existence of people who are "observant to a great extent" or "somewhat observant," on a continuum whose extreme poles are "strictly observant" and "totally nonobservant." The difference between "strictly observant" and "observant to a great extent" is not only quantitative but also qualitative. This difference becomes greater and more pronounced as one proceeds from one group to the next and is reflected by cultural estrangement. The further one moves away from the basic position that could properly be defined as the "Orthodox establishment" and approaches the ideologically secularist pole, the greater the cultural and emotional alienation toward religion. Greater or lesser degrees of observance do not necessarily create a bridge.

It seems to me, therefore, that there is a problematic tension, even in the methodology, between the findings of the survey and the evaluation of the researchers. They themselves clearly state that more than two thirds of Israeli Jewish society express great dissatisfaction with the status quo regarding the relationship between religion and state and would like to see a change toward "separation of religion and state." One might say that the "polarizing rhetoric" represents this situation exactly. Moreover, such "polarizing rhetoric" does not represent the position of other researchers, with whom it would be appropriate for the present researchers to consult about the basis of their findings; rather, it reflects the varied positions of political leaders, molders of public opinion in the media, the rabbinical elite, and secular intellectuals. In other words, such rhetoric is part of the reality studied; therefore, instead of debating about it and declaring it to be "without foundation," the researchers would have done better to study and determine its source in their findings.

I think that, in retrospect, the "unknown" source of the polarizing rhetoric can be discovered in the findings of the survey. I am not challenging the credibility of the findings in themselves but the way in which they were analyzed and interpreted and perhaps the terminology used to define the questions and the positions as well.

The findings of the study indeed necessitate a revision of the prevailing public impression, as a result of the "polarizing rhetoric." This revised impression relates to the question of the attitudes of Jews from all sectors in Israeli Jewish society toward tradition and faith (but not necessarily toward religion in its institutionalized sense) and toward their Jewish identity in the sense of their belonging to the Jewish people. Moreover, this revised impression is encouraging from the perspective of those leaders who are worried by the alienation and the polarization and who would like to institute changes leading to more tolerance and dialogue between religious and secular.

The results of the study demonstrate convincingly that the desire to belong to the Jewish people and to maintain a certain level of Jewish identity is widespread, except for a small and extremist group who are content to be identitfied as "Israeli" only. Nevertheless, it must be noted that according to these findings, this group is growing as well.

The study shows that the nonreligious in the Jewish-Israeli society display greater readiness to understand the position of the religious than the reverse. There is also a greater readiness to accept those changes that will legitimize the pluralism prevalent in Jewish public life without completely giving up the traditional Jewish characteristics common to all Jews. This is not reflected in political party platforms nor in the rhetoric that the leading political groups use in their confrontations.

The desire to remain part of the Jewish people should be measured by the selection that nonreligious Jews make in choosing to observe or not to observe the commandments; or, alternately, the "rating" method by which those moving toward secularization gradually reach the minimum they wish to observe and pass it on to their children. The emerging picture shows that the last commandments that are abandoned on the road to complete secularization and that continue to be observed by most of the nonreligious who maintain some measure of tradition are those customs and ceremonies that reflect or prominently demonstrate a belonging to the Jewish people. On the other hand, they do not require too great an investment of time and effort and are not observed at the expense of other values, which are regarded as more important than expressing a sense of belonging to the Jewish people. It should be emphasized here that the use of the term *commandments* with respect to the "nonobservant" imposes a religious point of view to characterize the behavior of the nonreligious. After all, they do not feel that they are observing commandments in the religious sense but are merely performing traditional customs and ceremonies that they have in common with the Jewish community to which they belong. I refer to the circumcision ceremony, traditional weddings, *bar mitzvah*, mourning customs, affixing *mezuzot* to doorposts, wearing a skullcap on certain occasions, attending High Holiday services, lighting Sabbath candles, avoiding work in public places on the Sabbath, conducting a *seder* on Passover, building a *succah* on *Succot*, and so on. Findings that touch upon attitudes toward the Jewish Diaspora, absorption of immigrants, maintaining the family framework, and active contribution to society also reflect the desire to feel a sense of Jewish belonging. All these testify to the high value placed upon the individual's feeling of belonging to an organic society, which in this instance is the Jewish people.

A willingness to understand the religious position better is expressed in the attitude toward religious beliefs (the existence of God as Divine Providence, the divine origin of the Torah), which are held by an apparently larger number of the nonreligious than has heretofore been assumed, in nondogmatic and noninstitutionalized ways (we shall return to this matter and its significance presently). This is expressed by the willingness of many "religious" and most of the "nonreligious" to change the existing Jewish "status quo" in the public sector, so as to reduce the legal coercion upon those who reject it, while preserving the principle of publicly maintaining certain elements of the tradition, especially without infringing on Sabbath and holiday observance and *kosher* food in the Israel Defense Forces. But one may ask whether this readiness for tolerance is an expression of mutual understanding, mutual respect, and dialogue or whether it expresses, rather, weariness, disappointment, frustration, and a growing feeling on both sides that neither benefits from mutual coercion. Moreover, is this not in itself an indication of alienation and indifference toward the behavior, beliefs, and feelings of those who do not think and behave "as we do," so that it would be better to isolate and distance oneself as much as possible to avoid friction?

There are clear hints that the latter interpretation is correct if we look at the research findings relating to the image prevalent among those belonging to different groups, about the status of their group in Israeli society relative to that of other groups, as well as the findings relating to the aspiration of those in different groups to create a separate social environment that will reduce contact and conflict with other groups to the absolute minimum required for political and economic intercourse.

Even if a different dynamic would lead to some hope for a positive change in the polarized and alienated network of relationships, such change does not appear to be as easy and as simple as would be implied from the researchers' position. The problem that requires deeper examination is, therefore: Does the fact that relationships between the religious and the nonreligious groups can be described as a continuum, graded from those who "strictly observe tradition" to those who "do not at all observe," justify the claim that there is no alienation and polarization between these two positions? In addition, the methodological problem, in the use of terms that emphasize the continuum and minimize the confrontation, arises again and again. It is clear that if one examines the attitude of the religious, in terms of "observing tradition," and then examines the observance of tradition among the nonreligious in terms of "observance of commandments," a continuum will be formed. However, does the use of identical terms for all the groups present us with the correct picture?

In either case, what is worth examining is not only the theoretical significance of the difference between a religious and a traditional approach vis à vis a traditional and a national-cultural, customs-oriented approach to the same "commandments," attention should also be given to the qualitative differences reflected by the need for different terms to impart the degree of importance (partial or total) and to the significance that different groups assign to what the study defines as "commandments" or "religious tradition." After all, the difference between the attitudes of those groups toward tradition is not defined by the quantity of commandments observed but by the significance, importance, authority, and scope that individuals in each group assign to such commandments as a way of shaping their outlook and way of life and in terms of the priorities and values that determine their aspirations for themselves and their children, as well as their cultural and political inclinations. It would seem that as soon as the questions are formulated this way, the source of the "polarizing rhetoric" is sharply delineated. It is found in the stark contrast between those for whom religious commandments represent an absolute, supreme, and established authority, which determines their entire world outlook and way of life in a total and definitive manner, as against those who feel it is important to express a sense of belonging to their people through a social and cultural way of life containing elements of tradition but who do not imbue such traditions with authority. Hence, this group firmly resists being coerced into observing even those customs that they may in fact wish to maintain. They certainly do not imbue them with values that are unique, or even preferable, to other values in determining their world outlook. In shaping their way of life, in the intensity with which they belong to a community, or even in identifying and belonging to the Jewish "collective," they may at the same time belong to, and identify with, other groups, for example, "Israelis" (who are a group consiting of citizens of the state of Israel, and not only Jews). The modern individual may carry several cultural identities of varying degrees of intensity.

In order to test and substantiate these previously mentioned conclusions, the following findings must be considered:

1. The explanation by the nonreligious for observing commandments and customs in terms of belonging, and the explanation for not observing the commandments or other customs in terms of lack of knowledge or inadequate education–in other words, in terms of lack of interest or lack of a sociocultural context that would imbue them with significance. (It is very simple to acquire the missing knowledge or to give children the proper education when one is interested in so doing!)
2. The clear correlation between nonobservance of the commandments with a broader general education, coupled with the lack of, or reduced, Jewish education, as well as the obvious correlation between observing the commandments and less general education and a relatively higher level of Jewish education.
3. The correlation between a decline in observing the commandments and the degree of socialization of the individuals into the cultural ambience of general Israeli society, as witnessed by the fact that Israeli-born children of immigrants observe fewer commandments and consider them to be less important than do their parents.
4. The correlation between nonobservance of the commandments and the degree of importance ascribed to the value of individual self-relization as an indicator of identification with modern secularism.
5. The gap created, according to the findings, between the extent to which respondents wish to live in the cultural environment of their own peer group and the many encounters that they maintain with

> other groups in their day-to-day life. This is a highly significant indication not only of what is considered to be the ideal (although not yet fully realized) but also of the fact that an encounter with the group that represents one's own sense of belonging is deemed to be culturally and spiritually significant. On the other hand, an encounter with other groups is insignificant in these terms and hence is not valued as an interpersonal encounter that is real and influential but is merely utilitarian and functionally necessary.

It seems that the picture that emerges from these findings confirms my previous statements. For the nonreligious group, the definitive value is "self-realization." General education serves this value, whereas Jewish education does not seem to serve it nor promote social success. Belonging to the Jewish people is important (most probably because of existential-nationalistic reasons originating from an appreciation of the political situation of the state of Israel), but, from the personal point of view, it is at the same level of importance as the value of self-realization. Hence, as the importance of this value declines, there will be less interest in the symbols of national identification and, especially, less willingness to observe customs classified as "commandments" or "obligations." Traditional customs will be observed only if defined as customs that are not compulsory and only if they serve to express identification with the nation, without limiting or oppressing the value of self-realization. The interest in Jewish education for the individual or his children becomes marginal, with a measurable and considerable downward trend. This fact renders the encounters between the religious and the nonreligious as lacking real dialogue, and as culturally and spiritually insignificant, although they still have national significance related mainly to security (e.g., the consensus with regard to the army) and to politics (e.g., coalition considerations!)

The findings, furthermore, most clearly confirm that there is a growing trend in Israeli society toward separate living and educational environments for religious and nonreligious. The tendency is to minimize the encounters between the various groups, especially those that might have cultural and spiritual significance during the years of schooling–the period when personality and world outlook are formed–and to maintain only those encounters that stem from professional, employment, economic, and political needs. On the cultural level (e.g. schooling, values), not only is there no continuum and no dialogue but the desire for them is decreasing. Is this not what we mean when we speak of alienation? Is it not correct to describe the dynamics of growing alienation and recurring dissatisfaction with the existing relationships, which impose excessive cooperation in the public sphere, as "polarization?"

In the light of all these, one must consider the finding, which indeed seems surprising, that more than half of the respondents expressed a belief in a divine power, in an ethical Providence over one's actions, and in the Torah as a revelation of divine authority. It is self-evident that individual and in-depth conversations are needed to arrive at the significance of this finding and especially to understand how these beliefs influence the daily life and behavior of those who are ostensibly nonreligious in the institutional sense, since behavior is the only reliable external test of the seriousness of such statements of faith. The opinion that I can express on this matter is therefore not anchored in the findings of the survey but in my personal experience and in conversations with Jews of various circles.

First, it must again be emphasized that a "generalized" belief in a divine power, who punishes sin and rewards good deeds, is not indicative of a religious attitude and certainly not of religious behavior. Paradoxically, the belief that the Torah is a divine imperative is also not such an indicator, so long as it is not expressed in a specific way of life that accepts the obligation of the Torah's commandments. One could claim inconsistency on the part of believers who do not fulfill the obligations of their faith. If this were so, then inconsistency would be the significant factor characterizing such nonreligious people. It would indicate that, despite their faith, these beliefs do not serve them as a value in determining their daily behavior. In practice (without being aware of it in their worldview), they prefer the authority of the society in which they were socialized as a focus to be imitated. The values of the secular society to which they belong are those that determine their behavior and way of life, and their faith is given emotional expression only so as not to exclude them from the conventions of the society in which they live. Conspicuous manifestation of their faith occurs only in moments of crisis, such as a dangerous illness, death of relatives or friends, accidents, catastrophes, or war. Such feelings of crisis motivate them to behave according to a different code, and generally their nonreligious environment, which tends toward "permissiveness," regards this with sympathy.

It is reasonable to assume that the faith of the nonreligious is, on the whole, the result of previous religious or traditional education. Maintaining their faith after leaving the religious framework, and after acquiring a general secular education, stems less from the strength of religious feeling and more from the fact that postmodern secularism is not ideological, inspiring, nor demanding of a certain world outlook. It creates a vacuum of faith, ideas, and spiritual values that people of various inclinations and education fill according to their training and preferences. In this regard we emphasize that religiosity is based frequently on characteristics of one's psychological makeup, especially among certain types of people. It certainly forms the basis for a religious-outlook way of life. However, as such, it will not be a religious position until it is conceived as a factor that determines behavior and that has become institutionalized.

Religious educators can therefore take this finding as confirmation of their claims that a vacuum is formed in secularism that only religion can successfully fill. They can also find confirmation of their belief that religious education or influence may lead to a reorientation toward religion among the secularist populace. Indeed, empathy may develop between the religious and the secular, and, if they so wish, they could understand each other's world. However, the fact that the secular community contains the potential for faith cannot be regarded as a barrier to the alienation and polarization that in fact exist.

There is thus no room for facile optimism on this issue. The findings of the present study show that the dynamics of the socialization process in the "general" Jewish society, with all its nuances, in the workplace, and in the promulgation of general education serve to separate the religious from the nonreligious rather than bring them closer to each other. In order to achieve dialogue, mutual understanding, tolerance, and empathy, we must work against the existing dynamic rather than with it.

Israeli Society and Secular-Jewish Culture

GERSHON SHAKED
Professor of Hebrew Literature, The Hebrew University

The social study before us confirms a number of accepted platitudes that exist almost as preconceptions among the Israeli public, even without their confirmation through social research. The study reveals, as one might have expected, that those who are observant and those who are not observant relate differently to the customs of the religion, the holidays, visits to the synagogue, and the Zionist experience (for those observant Jews who have nationalist tendencies). The study provides quantitative confirmation of phenomena that are more or less known to us in their substance and quality.

The findings of the study are acceptable to me, and they are consistent with common sense. However, it seems to me that in its general conceptualization, the study disregarded a basic phenomenon that explains both the contrast between those who follow the tradition and those who follow a different tradition, and a number of the elements of the identity and identification of the secular society, which, while they are an outcome of the tradition, are not its direct descendants.

My basic assumption is that alongside a culture based on faith and *mitzvah* observance, a Jewish culture has been created in Israel that is based on the tradition but is not a religious culture. The sources of this culture can be found in the Jewish culture, but the latter has undergone processes of secularization and sanctification that have changed its face—the sacred has been made profane and the profane made sacred. Israeli society underwent processes of secularization and sanctification (as a process that turned a religious community into a nation) in a polarized manner, such that it can be said that the Israeli secular society or the society that borders on secularity also was formed out of deep internal tensions.

The roots of the polarization within the secular community in the development of a "traditional" culture in Israel lie in the Jewish thought of the modern era. The polarization does not only reflect the ideologues but two main streams of thought, each of which had a broad base among the Jewish intelligentsia and the basic assumptions of which filtered down to wider groups. In the context of Jewish thought in the modern era, the conceptual platform of Ahad Ha'am stood opposite that of Michah Yosef Berdichevski. Ahad Ha'am tried to argue that the religious Jewish tradition has a total humanistic cultural message. Anyone who accepts it associates himself with the Jewish cultural community, and anyone who does not accept it is on the other side of the fence. The idea of absolute justice, as developed in *Priest and Prophet* and a number of other essays, emphasizes that Jewish identity means ideological identification with a (total) system of values that can be deduced from the Torah of Israel, from Moses to Moses (Maimonides). In order to continue this secular-cultural tradition (and in order not to assimilate into other cultural traditions), the Jewish nation must set up a spiritual center whose main role is to serve as a model for the entire nation of Israel of the possibility of realizing a Jewish secular tradition in a territorial framework (since the possible territorial frameworks in the Diaspora crumbled as a result of assimilation and the *haskalah).*

Berdichevski's assumptions were the exact opposite. He argued that neither the religious Jewish tradition nor any other Jewish tradition was total and that Jewish identity is not dependent upon identification with any fixed set of values. A Jew, according to Berdichevski, is anything that the Jews want to be. Any spiritual tradition created by the Jews is part of a pluralistic culture that was created by people who identified themselves as Jews. Therefore, the Samaritans, Karaites, followers of Elisha ben Abuya, Sabbateans and Frankists, Hassidim, *mitnagdim,* and *maskilim* could all be part of the Jewish people. The system of values and customs does not demand unequivocal identification with any agreed-upon order but only a willingness to identify oneself as a Jew in any situation from various and contrasting conceptual perspectives. Berdichevski came out against the world of values recognized by the dominant rational Jewish tradition and argued that the source of the spiritual exile was the Jews' identification with the tradition that, in Berdichevski's opinion, preferred the book to the sword, the house of study to nature, the spirit to the material, and the loser to the winner.

Under the influence of Nietzsche, he demanded a "transvaluation of values" (*Umwertung aller Werte*) and assumed that a spiritual revolution would lead to a social revolution. In practice, he attempted in his collections of legends to create a "countertradition" to the dominant tradition, and he argued, in accordance with his historical-philosophical assumptions, that if the countertradition that had been repressed overcame the dominant tradition, it would bring cultural and social redemption to a society that had repressed its life forces and voluntarily taken itself out of the course of history.

Berdichevski did not propose new existential systems or mandatory, permanent existential customs for a community that identified with its nature (without necessarily identifying with any permanent set of values). Living as a Jew meant identifying as a Jew and choosing a world of values according to one's individual preferences. Of course, it would be better if preference were directed precisely to those values that were not acceptable to the majority of Jews over the past centuries.

Ahad Ha'am's assumption is far-reaching, and its influence on Zionist culture was great, just as Berdichevski's assumptions also influenced this culture. It can be said that Ahad Ha'am's ideas influenced secular-Zionist ways of thinking, while Berdichevski's ideas influenced its content.

Ahad Ha'am's assumptions inspired Jewish society to secularize cultural traditions and to sanctify new traditions, with the new social-cultural values absorbing the power of the sacredness that was borrowed from the religious culture. The sacral link with the tradition finds expression primarily in a hidden internal aspiration to live a life of *mitzvot* (i.e., a life that charges the individual with collective tasks). Hayim Nachman Bialik's cry, "Give us *mitzvot*," in his essay *Halacha and Aggada*, is not a demand for the old or a renewed *Shulchan Aruch* (which Bialik kept as far away from as possible). Rather, it is a demand that the public and spiritual leadership charge the collective with *mitzvot*, in accordance with the new reality with which this society was grappling. It is a demand for a sanctification of the national act or the act that would create, in a community that had abandoned the 613 *mitzvot*, a unity based on deeds that would replace the *mitzvot*.

The idea of *hagshama* [realization] that was adopted by the pioneering movements represents the secular sanctification of a religious tradition. The standards that measure a man on the basis of the deeds that he performs for the collective can still be found in Israeli society, and the viewing of military service as a test of communal fitness is a descendant of this tradition. The granting of sacred meaning to new values, for which any connection to the original culture is purely random, is an expression of these sanctification processes. These processes try to maintain the unity of the community and the promotion of those values that may strengthen the community in its new environment.

Thus, there was the sanctification of work, the creative community (the *kibbutz*), the theater as the new temple (as Moshe Halevi referred to it), study as a replacement for prayer, as well as the sanctification of national sites (the *Kotel*, Massada). The ceremony in memory of Trumpeldor, who died in the defense of the homeland on the 11th of *Adar* (during the period of the *Yishuv*), and afterward Holocaust Remembrance Day, and Remembrance Day for those who have fallen in Israel's wars, became a sort of sacred reincarnation of the concept of *kiddush hashem* and of the sacrifice of Isaac. The experience of the Holocaust took on a central position as a sacred secular experience in Israel and the Diaspora. The pilgrimage to *Yad Vashem*, the "temple of the Holocaust," grants a sacred element to the basically secular identification with the fate of the Jewish people.

The secularization of the culture, which Ahad Ha'am saw as a secular solution for a religious tradition, found expression, first and foremost, in the educational system of the secular stream and in the idea of the renewed secular *kinus* (literally, "collection") of religious cultural traditions. The canonical book that is accepted by the secular (and semisecular) community in Israeli society is the Bible, and it serves as a cultural replacement for the study of the Jewish legal tradition, the study of the Talmud, which is the primary text in the *haredi* world. The Bible also serves as a literary text that is open to humanistic and artistic interpretations that are not dependent upon religious belief. It is also the source of symbols of identification and shared myths that allow cultural-semiotic partnership within the secular community. Concepts such as "a hero like Samson," "the wisdom of Shlomo," "David the King of Israel," "the golden calf," "Joseph's coat of many colors," "the binding of Isaac," "the sale of Joseph," "Jacob and Esau," and "Isaac and Ishmael" are not empty concepts, but traditions that create a system of connotations that is shared by secular and religious society, despite the fact that the meaning of these terms in secular society differs from their meaning in religious society. (For example, in secular society, there is also a soccer team called *Shimshon*–Samson.) The biblical tradition and the history of the Second Temple period (from the destruction of the First Temple and through the various periods of independence), and today modern Jewish history, as well, are additional focal points for cultural, social, and even ceremonial identification. The ceremonies that were designed around the Maccabean Wars and the stand at Massada are only two such examples. The Maccabean Wars gave birth to the torch race ceremony (almost an imitation of the marathon), while Massada generated various ceremonies from the pilgrimages of youth movements who swore that "Massada will not fall again" to the swearing-in of military units on the ruins of Massada. The biblical tradition and the historical tradition generated ceremonies that are in essence the secularization of religious ceremonies (a race on *Hanukkah* instead of lighting candles as a reminder of the religious miracle) and the sanctification of values (the Maccabean Wars, their military strength).

The new forms of *kinus* also created a shared secular cultural basis for the secular intelligentsia. Thus, the *Sefer Ha'aggada* of Bialik and Ravnitzky is based on the extraction of holy texts from their original religious contexts (*midrashim, drashot,* and legal tractates) and arranging them according to historical and moral-thematic principles (Jewish history from the Creation until the Second Temple period and various social and moral categories). The translation and "processing" of the *Zohar* by Tishbi and Lachover used similar methods, and many other "collected" traditional religious texts also serve as a secular cultural basis for the new national collective.

These are Ahad Ha'am–style attempts to create a secular culture on a religious basis and to mark this culture with a uniformity that is binding upon its followers in its ceremonies and its interpretation, just as the "mitzvot" that the community assigns its members obligate them.

Some of these social-cultural mainstays of the secular tradition have weakened over recent years. I do not want to get into the question of why these foundations of the secular Jewish-Israeli culture have begun to weaken. This issue is perhaps one that requires another study.

The tradition of Berdichevski had a fairly dominant influence on the content of the values of the new secular culture. The aspiration to create "the new Hebrew" who would replace "the old Jew," who had been subject to other traditions (or antitraditions), and who would create for himself new existential ceremonies, stems from the demand for a "transvaluation of values," which was made by Berdichevski, who also called himself Ben-Gurion. The image of the fighting Israeli, who is close to nature, who prefers aesthetics to ethics, and who is open to all ideas and does not rule out any stream in the name of Judaism because Judaism is whatever the Jews create–this image is the ideal figure of various streams in the new Zionist society and perhaps even of the streams referred to as progressive in Jewish society in the Diaspora. The strange combination of the demand for the unity of the community that must realize social tasks and the assumption that this demand may be fulfilled only if this community undergoes a fundamental change, is one of the main social-cultural contradictions of Israeli society. It is as if the society demands: Give us "mitzvot" as fighters, force upon us new "secular-religious" rituals that will distance people from the book and bring them closer to nature.

These demands are some of the dialectic contradictions that secular Israeli society tries to use in order to heal its breaches: *Tu B'shvat* as

Arbor Day, *Sukkot* as the harvest festival, and *Shavuot* as the reaping festival are three solutions for preserving collective ceremonies and injecting them with ancient pre-exile (and perhaps even premonotheistic) content.

These were solutions of the *Yishuv* period for shaping a traditional secular culture, which was supposed to be the mainstay in shaping the cultural partnership that was disbanded when the validity of the religious commandments was undermined. This tradition crystallized in the history of Israeli education, from kindergarten to high school and the youth movement. This was a way of inserting antitraditional Berdichevski-type content into traditional frameworks, in accordance with the forms of secularization outlined in the worldview of Ahad Ha'am. In this context, I could point out various contents that were realized in various forms of expression.

This trend reached its fullest expression in the world of values and images of the Canaanite movement and its various hidden extensions that are much more important than the movement itself. (The movement itself was very small in terms of numbers of members and was fairly limited in its direct influence as opposed to its indirect influence.)

The worship of the Israeli army, which for many years stood at the center of Israeli consciousness, and to which much of the time the main rituals of the society was devoted, is one of the transfigurations of this tradition, which, of course, became stronger as the physical and historical conditions required Israeli society to hold on to these values both voluntarily and against its will.

What I learn from this with regard to the issue under discussion–*Beliefs, Observances, and Social Interaction Among Jews in Israel,* is that secular Zionist society created for itself its own "belief" platform, which had a long chain of "positive" and "prohibitory" mitzvot (some of which were noted in the study). The religious-Zionist group shared some of these beliefs, ceremonies, and mitzvot. *Haredi* society, though, rejected outright the social and practical realizations of the secular Zionist thought of Ahad Ha'am and Berdichevski.

These "beliefs" were the true collective existential foundation of this group, and from it the group derived its main identifying marks. As long as these beliefs, with their canonic elements (the attachment to the Bible and to Jewish history, the belief in the new Hebrew, the keeping of ceremonies of place that replaced ceremonies of time), and noncanonic elements (Hebrew song, painting, and even the prose and theater that were tied to these traditions) were meaningful for secular society, they maintained its cultural identity, which expressed a fairly sincere attachment to the space of Israel and the time of Jewish-Israeli history. When these cohesive factors weakened for various reasons (which again are an issue for another study), a crisis of cultural and social identity in secular society ensued (or will ensue).

The preservation of the identity of the secular society is also very important to the religious-traditional society. This is because the links that connect the two social groups are traditions that the two groups interpret differently, even in opposing ways, but even polarized interpretations of the same tradition give a group more unity than the loss of the attachment of one of the groups to these links.

It seems to me that one of the roles of the secular Jewish educational system is to strengthen these traditional links, whose sacral or secular interpretation allowed and allows a shared platform of symbols within itself and between it and religious groups.

Comments on the Guttman Report

BERNARD (BARUCH) SUSSER

Professor of Political Science, Bar-Ilan University

What stands out in this very polished and professional Guttman Institute survey is the dramatically high incidence of Israelis who positively identify themselves with traditional Jewish practices, beliefs, and attitudes. Although previous surveys have reported broadly similar findings (surveys of the Guttman Institute itself included), the current survey is by far the most exhaustive and wide-ranging. These findings compel a basic reassessment of the 'conventional wisdom' that Israel is a fundamentally secular society saddled with an unfortunately troublesome religion/state problem deriving from the peculiarities of Israel's parliamentary system. A corollary to this 'conventional wisdom' has commonly been that religion/state issues are best dealt with through appropriate electoral reforms (to weaken the coalitional leverage of the religious parties) or by constitutional provisions that would insulate public life from religious intervention.

The sources of this 'conventional wisdom' are not difficult to locate. The greater part of the Zionist movement was secular, even militantly secular, in character. Breaking away from the life patterns of *galut* life entailed, for most of them, rejecting traditional forms of Judaism. Decades later, these ideas continue to have a certain residual normative appeal—whether as nostalgia or as ideology—despite the major changes that have overtaken Israeli society in the interim. Moreover, the Jewish State, since its founding, has been led by parties that, whatever their rhetoric, cannot be classified as religious. The impression of deep-seated secularism is only heightened by the antagonism of a great part of the Israeli population to what they see as 'religious coercion,' by the very broad popular animosity toward the exemption of *Yeshiva* students (and to a lesser extent religious young women) from army service, and by the revulsion of many from the machinations of the religious parties in regard to financial allocations.

Clearly, the image of Israel as a secular society is false. Even the popular picture of a large implacable secular community confronting a similarly barricaded religious community across an unbridgeable wall of enmity, is fundamentally inaccurate. As the survey indicates, traditional observances are practiced by the vast majority of Israelis–even by those who describe themselves as totally nonreligious. More Israelis understand themselves to be 'traditional' in some sense or other than the number of those who place themselves in the fully observant and secular camps combined. Indeed, if the definition of 'secularism' involves the rejection of all, or almost all, observances that derive from the religious tradition, there are very few secular Jews in Israel.

How are these findings to be interpreted? Do they mean that Israel qualifies as a religiously observant political community? This view is refuted outright by the relatively small number (no more than a quarter) of the respondents who observe religious commandments consistently and according to the letter of the law. The patterns of observance of those who follow 'a great deal' of the tradition and especially of those (the largest single category) who declare that they observe 'some of the traditions' is far too episodic and *halachically* incongruous to be counted religious in the common sense of the term.

Should we then conclude that Israelis, although not especially observant in practice, are, nonetheless, seeking religious enlightenment on a more abstract spiritual level? Are Israelis, in other words, seeking a form of religious self-expression, only without the encumbrances of practice? I doubt that this interpretation does justice to the accumulated data either. Truly spiritual activities, such as Torah study, are given scant attention by the respondents when compared to communal observances, such as circumcision, *bar/bat mitzvah*, marriage, and mourning rites. Prayer comes far behind familial practices like Sabbath candle-lighting. *Mitzvot* like donning *tefillin* and *talit* daily–more an individual than a communal act–are given far less weight than the social act of participating in a Passover *seder*. Consider as well the high incidence of *mezuzahs* on Israeli doors by comparison to the number of those who will, in even the most elementary ways, school their children religiously. Very notably, many of these ostensibly religious performances are observed by individuals who expressly deny them any divine or religious significance.

I doubt that any one simple interpretation can fully account for the voluminous, complex, sometimes contradictory data that the survey contains. Nevertheless these findings appear to support the thesis that an unprecedented and idiosyncratic pattern of religious practices, beliefs, and attitudes has become broadly constitutive of the Israeli national ethos. Whether or not one is 'religious' in the familiar sense of the term, these practices and beliefs are perceived as among the defining marks of Israeli national belonging. They are identity-performances rather than truly religious observances. In other words, they are performed in the context of national self-identification with Israel and the Jewish people rather than as theologically ordained commandments.

The term *civil religion* (Robert Bellah familiarized the concept in the American context and it was applied to Israel by Liebman and Don Yehiya) is often used to describe such patterns of belief and behavior that become almost mandatory elements of a national creed. In the Israeli case, the term is particularly appropriate because religious practices are indeed part of the content of civil affiliation. These religious performances are removed from their erstwhile theological context in order to serve civil/political objectives. They take on critical social functions, such as promoting national cohesiveness, providing a sense of communal support in an often stressful, beleaguered political reality, creating a link between the Jewish present and the Jewish past, and providing content and structure to Israeli national identity. Just as the Israeli civil religion has removed the Wailing Wall from its traditional, essentially religious significance and made it over into a national symbol that regularly provides the backdrop for military and political ceremonies, so has it 'nationalized' the Jewish religious tradition and transformed it into a central element of Israeli communal identity.

A *mezuzah* on the doorpost (as in the story of the Children of Israel in Egypt) indicates that here lives one who associates him/herself with the political community—again, more in the sense of a declaration of national allegiance than a declaration of faith. In much the same way, the very high percentage of those who report that they fast on Yom Kippur does not mean that they do so in order to beg forgiveness for their sins. Many of those who fast spend the day watching films they have borrowed from the video library. Others will devote themselves to projects around the house, such as painting or putting away summer clothing and taking out the family's winter wardrobe. Although there is no *halachic* difference between painting the interior of a house and painting its externally visible walls, Israelis will desist from doing the latter on Yom Kippur because the consensual national understanding mandates that the 'street' appear tranquil and nonworkaday. Similarly, the suspension of all motorized transport on Yom Kippur—even by those for whom the practice has no religious meaning—is an idiosyncratic attempt to fill this paradigmatically religious day with a visibly communal character.

The survey's findings demonstrate strikingly that there is little if any correlation between the practices that enjoy the highest degree of observance and their religious centrality. Indeed, that 'hard core' of *halachic* commandments and prohibitions are tellingly secondary to performances of a familial, communal, and national character. They are observed for reasons that have only peripheral relevance to what religious law enjoins. For example, it is *halachically* obvious that one ought not light Sabbath candles if this is done in violation of the Sabbath (i.e., after sundown on Friday). Yet many of those who are insistent on lighting Sabbath candles give no heed to the clock. Many for whom it is important to sit in a *succah* on *Succot* will not be concerned with whether the *succah* is *halachically* acceptable–a perfectly reasonable attitude if the *succah* is understood in a national rather than religious context. The Passover *seder*, although widely observed, is a time of family gatherings and social ceremony that is dedicated to commemorating national themes like the liberation of Israel from oppression by the gentiles. It often has more in common with the American Thanksgiving meal than it does with a religiously charged commandment.

Even the widespread practice of observing some aspect of *kashrut* often derives from sensitivity for national/historical traditions rather than from authentically religious motives. Apart from the community-defining qualities of *kashrut* as the normative national cuisine, refraining from consuming non*kosher* food is also part of a Jewish national and historical ethic and aesthetic. One often hears, as a justification for keeping *kosher*, remarks such as the following: "our fathers and mothers were often martyred because they refused to violate the various *kashrut* prohibitions. We would besmirch their memory and reduce their sacrifices to naught were we to voluntarily give up what they died to preserve." Here again, although religious commandments are the source of these practices, it is national sentiment that prompts traditionalists to observe them. Quite appropriately, different kinds of non*kosher* food are related to quite differently. Pig, with all its charged historical associations and its emblematic status as food forbidden to Jews, arouses considerably more intense popular aesthetic revulsion than, say, seafood or venison–even though *halachically* they are equally prohibited.

One particularly telling finding that supports the general tenor of the just mentioned suggestions is that the four leading elements comprising the Jewish self-identification of Israeli Jews are not at all religious in character. Respondents chose national foci of identification, such as living in Israel, the founding of the Jewish State, the history of the *Yishuv*, and the education they received in the home. These precede even communal religious performances, such as participating in the Passover *seder* and lighting Sabbath or *Hanukkah* candles. The Jewish religion was ranked only eleventh in this tabulation. Almost all of the sixteen leading elements that surveyors found encouraged the sense of Jewish identity in

Israel are either overtly national in character (e.g., living in Israel) or communal, life-cycle, familial events. On the other hand, Torah study, daily prayer, observing *halachah*, and so on—what we spoke of earlier as the 'hard core' of a traditional religious life—do not appear at all.

Admittedly more difficult to fit into my general interpretation are the findings related to the patterns of religious beliefs among Israelis. More than half of the Israeli population believes that G-d gave the Torah to Moses on Mount Sinai, that Divine will directs the world, that individuals are rewarded for their good deeds, and so on. These beliefs seem to point to a more basic religious character to the Israeli populace than I have been willing to allow.

But even here there are some glaring incongruencies that lead me to question how deep these beliefs go. Without, of course, doubting the findings themselves, it is difficult to conclude that beyond the, at most, 25 percent of Israelis who can be classified as Orthodox observant Jews (those who do not drive, turn on the electricity, or use the telephone on the Sabbath), these statements of belief reflect religious beliefs of a consistent, stable, or compelling nature. If these were expressions of such belief, it is difficult to understand why, for example, 50 percent believe that good deeds will be rewarded and only roughly 27 percent believe that not keeping the religious commandments will be punished. From a normative religious point of view the two are, of course, inseparable. (It would be interesting to see the data on how the 25 percent I classify as Orthodox observant Jews or the 14 percent who reported that they 'observe consistently' responded to these two options.) How is it that some 50 percent believe that the Torah and Mitzvot are Divine commandments and that G-d scrutinizes the actions of each individual, while only 14 percent report that they consistently observe these commandments? Can such vastly disparate responses be attributed merely to 'the weakness of the flesh' (i.e., to human failure)?

It is far more likely that, for many of those surveyed, these beliefs belong more to the category of 'folk religion' than they do to devout Orthodoxy. (The survey implies that these beliefs are more prevalent among Jews of Eastern origin.) This, of course, is not meant to belittle 'folk religion' but to point to its looser, less demanding character. As opposed to normative Orthodoxy, beliefs of a folk religious character are not necessarily bound up with a consistent or exacting practice. They are more easily permeable by other belief systems and social consensus than a codified normative Orthodoxy. It seems reasonable to conclude that folk religious beliefs have made a significant contribution to the development of Israel's civil religion. They have made Judaism available for popular national consumption by weakening the traditional links between these beliefs and the very demanding regimen of practice with which they have been normally associated.

One final parenthetical query of a methodological nature. Only Hebrew speakers were surveyed. Roughly 10 percent of the Jewish population of Israel are recent ex-Soviet immigrants. How many of these does the survey include? If few of them were included because of limited Hebrew, would this not tend to skew the results somewhat? Assuming that the vast majority of them are not at all religious, would their inclusion have changed the findings in a significant way?

The Time Capsule

EDDY M. ZEMACH

Professor of Philosophy, The Hebrew University

The conclusion of the study carried out by Levy, Levinsohn, and Katz (The Guttman Institute, December 1993) is that "there is no basis for the rhetoric that polarizes Israeli society into religious and secular Jews. It would be more correct to say that Israeli society has a strong tendency toward tradition, and that in terms of *mitzvah* observance, there is a continuum from the 'strictly observant' to the 'nonobservant,' rather than a great divide between a religious minority and a secular majority." Is this finding surprising? How should we interpret it? What can we conclude from it?

In second-rate American movies one may encounter the Englishman, complete with striped suit, a bowler hat, and an umbrella, who only talks about the weather and looks down on anyone who is not British; he is snobbish and conservative, keeps his cool when in danger, never exhibits emotion, is hypocritical in his social relations, reads *The Times*, quotes Shakespeare, and admires the royal family. One would seldom find that character in England. The British do possess some elements of this stereotype but usually not all of them. In fact, it may be impossible for an individual fully to realize the schematic image of the Englishman because it contains contradictory elements. There is (to use Wittgenstein's term) some family resemblance between Britons, but no fixed set of character traits need be shared by all of them.

Among the English who served in India, an enormous and foreign subcontinent, there was, however, a greater degree of uniformity, tending toward the realization of a schematic image by each individual. The need to maintain group cohesion among ex-patriats in a foreign land limits the possibility of each individual's developing a favorite strand in the "ideal" image of the gentleman differently. Under these special circumstances, free ramification and idiosyncratic variations along the schematic image of the sahib constitutes social deviation and is perceived as "un-British." Victorian India could not tolerate an Englishman who was not a pukka sahib (i.e., exactly matching the sahib schema). There, the choice was radical: either be a sahib or else get out.

The crystallization of a total system that covers family and community institutions; metaphysical and political beliefs; manners of individual behavior; public and private rites; a special diet; holy texts; patterns of education, dress, ritual, and prayer; and other elements into a coherent realizable schematic image is an emergency step. Such a step is only taken by a threatened culture, a culture that is in exile or is persecuted. A living culture consists of numerous varied characteristics that the coculturalists develop, each according to preferences and natural inclinations. Under normal circumstances, these characteristics will not be realized all together, cast into one schematic image; as mentioned earlier, features typical and/or essential to a given culture need not even be fully compatible with one another. Ironing out the variations, making one, monolithic image that can be assumed by every individual in that society occurs only as an emergency measure. Under conditions where a culture is too hard-pressed to sustain a plurality of versions it forgoes the variations and instead molds one coherent unit, a rigid core. Thus a binding formula, a codex, a canon, a schema that can and must be realized by every member comes into being. To maximize the chances of survival, whoever belongs to the group becomes a living embodiment of the embattled culture, a cell from which the whole body can, if necessary, be recloned.

This gambit can be described as the creation of a human time capsule: we forgo the development of the culture until the danger has passed and pack whatever we can into one capsule that we preserve by incarnating it. Therefore, the Jew in the Diaspora, like the sahib, incarnates a monolithic image that does not allow variations. The capsule cannot be opened because its sensitive contents will be lost, will be dispersed in the winds of seductive and/or threatening foreign cultures. The package must not be taken apart, one cannot choose and select among its contents, giving preference to certain aspects of the cultural heritage over other aspects. Different people cannot be allowed to specialize individually in aspects of the culture according to their tastes and preferences. No, it is all part of one package, because in the absence of a critical mass, and under heavy external pressure, neglect of an element will bring about its degeneration and eventual loss and may result in splintering the group and blurring its identity. Thin rivulets that split from the main stream will be swallowed in the surrounding sea of foreignness.

Several historical examples show that this grim diagnosis was valid for Judaism. The Hebrew enlightening movement, the *haskalah*, rose in the eighteenth century in Germany and disappeared with the assimilation of Germany's Jews, which it helped bring about. It then moved to Eastern Europe where it was a big success, but by the twentieth century it had reached a debacle—the periodicals closed down, the number of books published declined, and the number of readers decreased drastically. It seems that even if the Holocaust had not taken place, the Hebrew *haskalah* movement in Europe would have died out. The Yiddishist cultural movement started out from a broader basis and was more vibrantly alive than its Hebrew sister. Could it have constituted a lasting offshoot of the traditional religious-Jewish culture? We do not have a factual historical answer to this question because that subculture has been destroyed by external violence (the Nazis and the Communists). However, perhaps something can be learned from the fate of Yiddish culture in America (both in the United States and in Argentina), which flourished at the beginning of this century (workers' organizations, political parties, agricultural settlements, a ramified educational system, newspapers, books, theater), but within fifty years it died out, leaving almost no trace behind it. It seems then that under the conditions of the Diaspora, the monolithic approach of culture in a rigid framework was the only resistant option. It is no wonder, then, that the culture, so as not to be obliterated by multifarious change, took the most change-resistant form of all, that of a religious orthodoxy that cites transmundane sanctions for maintaining the old ways of life. The ideology that is created out of this necessity is total and extreme, and it allows only a binary choice—all or nothing.

That strategy is harsh and can allow only minimal cultural growth, yet it is very effective in achieving the goal for which it was conceived—preserving the foundations, salvaging the tradition until the danger blows over. What happens, then, when the danger does pass, say, when the British colonel returns to England, or when the nation of Israel returns to its land and establishes a state in which it constitutes the majority of the population and where its culture is dominant again? Two scenarios are unlikely to occur, and, indeed, the study before us confirms that they did not occur—despite the shallow slogans of politicians, and even, as this study indicates, the impression of the man in the street. These two scenarios are: (1) The entrenchment and victory of the traditional monolithic schema, which, in our case, is the prevailing of the orthodox norm in Israel (for comparison, England itself accepting the pukka sahib image as a binding norm after the dismantlement of the Empire), or (2) The rejection and discarding of the time capsule when the pressure is over—the Jewish state becoming entirely nonreligious. Both of these scenarios are based on a dichotomy (between those who are religious and those who are not), which was indeed valid in the conditions of emergency that existed in the past, when the Jews could not afford more than one way of being Jewish, when allowing the smallest crack meant opening the floodgates, where any horse brought in from the outside could be Trojan.

A digital description of religion is an error, however, even though that is how things seem to both sides. My point is this: although the description of oneself as more and less religious implies that there is a "full" amount of religiosity and an imperfect condition of practicing but a part of that "whole," in fact that is a very misleading way of looking at the issue. It is not as if the system of Torah and *mitzvot*, according to the *Shulchan Aruch*, is one unit that cannot be taken asunder, and therefore divides people into those who obey it fully, the *apikorsim* who reject it entirely, and those in the middle who are "partly religious," that is, fall short of perfect religiosity. The picture I have been trying to portray is that of many valid ways of maintaining the Jewish tradition, each such way being a "complete," not "partial," religiosity and/or a way of being Jewish. That the dichotomy of the religious versus the nonreligious is unreasonable and will not exist under normal circumstances can be seen by using a comparison. Would there be any validity to the dichotomous division of the English into "Perfect Christians" and "Non-Christians," with various degrees of imperfect Christianity in the middle? Of course not. There is no one way of being a perfect Christian, from which you can only tumble toward the condition of the atheist. Some people adhere to certain principles traditionally associated with Christianity, and there are those who believe in others, all with varying levels of certainty. There are those who hold dear certain rituals and customs, and there are those who prefer to keep others. In any event, there is no dichotomy here or a chasm between two approaches, not even a one-dimensional scale of being "more" and "less" religious. The picture we would get, were we to conduct a similar research in England, is probably similar to that which emerges from the study of Levy, Levinsohn, and Katz, if we conceptualize it correctly. I see it as showing a hodgepodge of more or less continuous functions across a variable space, with certain elements from the tradition more popular and/or perceived as more important than others, with varying levels of viscosity (i.e., high correlations between some variables and low correlations between other variables).

The true scenario, what really happens to the time capsule when its time comes to act (when the crisis has passed), is, therefore, that it releases its content into the bloodstream of the revived organism; the resuscitated culture absorbs the various components of the frozen schema and allows them to grow and change on their own. These components act separately, not as a complete package, and, thus, some catch on and some do not. For example, the study before us reports that a very high percentage of the respondents have *bar mitzvahs*, weddings, circumcisions, and burial rites according to the *halacha* (although it must be remembered that in the state of Israel it is difficult and sometimes impossible to have an alternative ceremony), while only about 20 percent of the respondents report that they observe the religious commandment to put on *tefillin* daily, do not to travel on *Shabbat*, and do not use electricity on *Shabbat*; even between these there is a difference of about 4 percent.

This means that the right way to understand the role of the religious tradition in Israel is not through the model that organized orthodoxy, as well as its opponents, propose. We can understand the situation better if we view religious observance in Israeli society as an interaction of traditional cultural and religious elements in a rich and varied social fabric, and not according to the usual *halachic* conception, shared by their archopponents as well, of religion as one indivisible package. In fact, it seems that the majority of Israel's residents do not accept the traditional approach of the Jewish religion as one corpus, such that whoever accepts part of it as valid must accept all of it. Most Israelis are willing to shape their lives in light of some religious traditions, without agreeing with the perception that the Torah, as interpreted by the rabbis in recent history, is all-holy and all-binding. The Israeli Jew evidently does not agree that to accept any part of the *halacha* is to concede absolute validity for all of its details.

This, then, is the most interesting conclusion of the study before us. Over the past thousand years Judaism perceived itself as a chain, the breaking of any of whose links results in the destruction of the entire chain. A structure such as this is typical to theories: in an ideal theoretical system, the conclusions are derived from evident premises; one cannot reject any of the theorems without contradiction. There is no room here for personal preference or style. If you accept the premises, you must accept what derives from them, all of what derives from them, and you cannot pick and choose without risking the validity of the entire structure. The reasoning was that the Torah sustains but one interpretation. If it is of Divine origin, then it is all-binding, and if it is not of Divine origin, then it is not binding at all. In any event, a selection of elements is not possible here. The Torah is not a supermarket. Culture, however, is precisely like a supermarket: many things in it have a lot to recommend them, but you need not and cannot buy them all. There is a certain homogeneity within a culture, there is a certain unity between religious tenets and practices, but that unity, as mentioned earlier, is one of family resemblance and not the unity of a theoretical system, in which one cannot remove one brick without undermining the entire structure.

The situation then is that the Jews in Israel, whether they are aware of it or not, do not treat their religion as its official spokesperson would have them treat it. They see their religion as less similar to a theory whose elements are inseparable and more similar to a living culture that has many related elements; people adopt items that are meaningful to them out of their cultural heritage, without deep commitment to the remaining ones. One may believe the existence of God but not the coming of the Messiah, or that one should celebrate *Pesach* without feeling too guilty about not fasting on *Tisha'a B'Av* or on *Tzom Gdalia*. Can Orthodox Judaism adjust itself to that change? Reform Judaism, which has not caught on in Israel, took a different path. It developed a new distilled version, a new time capsule, of Judaism. That was a more palatable version, perhaps, but still it took the form of a rigid theoretical system. It did not give the individual freedom to select from the rich religious tradition of the Jewish people those elements that were most significant to him or her. Outside of Israel, where the individual's access to the treasure of the tradition is minimal (partly through ignorance of the Hebrew language and literature, the history of the Jews, and their philosophical thinking), this path of the Reform movement was a highly reasonable one. Without it, most of the Jews would have found themselves completely cut off from their cultural heritage. Yet in Israel another path is indicated: given a complex mosaic, whose various strands were historically and theologically interconnected, the modern Israeli is invited to make a choice of motifs, those that one trusts to best shape one's life as a Jew.

Comments on the Guttman Report

RABBI A. YEHOSHUA ZUCKERMAN
Educator, Yeshivat Merkaz HaRav Kook, Jerusalem

I was given a copy of the interesting study carried out by the Guttman Institute, which dealt with beliefs, observance of *mitzvot*, and social relations between the various Jewish groups that can be found in Israeli society. These findings will be useful to those involved in efforts to improve the relations between Jews, especially with regard to the Torah and observance of the *mitzvot*, since often these represent an obstacle to mutual understanding among the people.

This study did, indeed, reveal some significant aspects of these issues (according to the *Highlights* of the full study), which I think are important to note because they will help me present my approach to the issue.

The common thread that runs through the findings is the desire for Jewish continuity that can be found among most of the people, with most types of Jews accepting a commitment to the Jewish nature of Israeli society. On the other hand, the findings indicate that the *apikores le'hachis* (deliberate apostate) usually only plays this role in order to raise the ire of the religious segment of the population. What this means is that what we are facing is more a social problem and intergroup tensions that find expression in this way.

The study also notes the commonly held stereotype that there are two blocs—the secular and the religious—and that the extreme secular bloc constitutes the majority. In actual fact the study reveals that the reality is quite different from this stereotype. Israeli society clearly tends toward the Torah's values and the observance of its *mitzvot*. Israeli society is also opposed to all types of extremism—whether antireligious or *haredi* [ultra-orthodox]. The study also attempts to clarify the degree to which Israelis identify with the "principles of faith" as formulated by Maimonides and finds a very positive attitude. An important finding is the public's historical approach in viewing the holidays as something they identify with—each person in his or her own way—a sort of personal actualization of the history of our people.

This approach was also characteristic of the observant Jew in the Diaspora, as Ahad Ha'am wrote in his book *Parshat Drachim:* [At the Crossroads] "More than Israel has kept the Sabbath, the Sabbath has kept Israel." It is an appropriate approach for a Jew who has chosen to return to the country that was the setting for the history of his people that he now wants to continue. In this context, it is typical that almost the entire nation makes it a practice to visit the Western Wall. However, the people would be happy to see the country less religious in terms of legislation, with regard to entertainment, transportation, and various other matters. The study also reveals that most of the people see rabbis only as the conductors of ceremonies or consultants for religious matters, but not as leaders who are supposed to deal with spiritual problems or decisions regarding matters on the public agenda.

Another finding that stands out is the polarity of two groups—the *haredim* and the antireligious. The paradox is that both of these groups base their philosophy on the same basic principle—a principle that disregards the holiness of the nation of Israel and its history. Their main concern is the individual.

Western liberalism raises the banner of individualism whose only goal is the success of the individual in a society which is there to serve him. Similarly, this study shows that the *haredi* is concerned about saving his soul, and for him nationality is only a profane framework that allows him to live a holy life. As mentioned earlier, the extremism of these two groups is generally rejected by the Israeli public.

Another important finding is the Israeli public's lack of familiarity with the various streams that divide American Jewry—Reform, Conservative, and Orthodox. It seems that most of the nation sees the Torah as belonging to the nation as a whole and not to religious sects. This is consistent with the study's finding that about 80 percent of the people identify with the *mitzvot* in some form or another, regardless of age or sex. These findings have remained stable across the studies carried out twenty-five years ago and those carried out today.

The findings of the study raise a certain contradiction. On the one hand, the study notes that the general identification with the commitment to a Jewish society is firmly entrenched in Israeli society. On the other hand, the prevailing belief is that there is significant polarization into two camps that divide the society—the religious and the secular—and that secularism has the upper hand.

It can be said that two main factors, among many, are responsible for this contradiction. The first such factor is the Israeli reality, in which almost every area is connected to political parties. Whether the issue is spiritual or material, social or personal, related to faith or related to technology, the platform of the political parties relate to it. Otherwise, it is difficult for the issue to exist, and there is no one who will fight for it in the Knesset—the seat of power and the source of funds. And it is only natural that parties fight against each other. Thus, certain parties find themselves fighting against religion even though they have nothing against religion, simply because a rival party has raised the banner of loyalty to religion; this rival cannot be allowed to become stronger and swallow up funds and perhaps even overshadow the achievements of the other parties. For this reason, there are rabbis who demand that religion and state be separated so that the Torah can remain above the political quagmire and retain an honorable moral and spiritual status, such as that awarded to the principle of justice. However, this is an attempt to run away from the problem, and this is not our approach.

The second factor is the extremism of the attitudes of the two groups—the *haredim* and the antireligious. And, as the study points out, each of these groups rejects the other because they see things in black and white terms, as a result of their individual demands. Because the extremists present their demands in such a vociferous manner, the impression is created that they have a monopoly on opinions and that the nation aspires to European-style individualism and to the abandonment of any idea of Jewish culture. It is also very easy for such ideas to fill the vacuum that, unfortunately, exists because education in the state of Israel is very shallow and weak on values, its only concern being to provide the student with a profession that can be used to earn a living in the future. Thus, the society is similar to the pit into which Joseph was thrown—as the Torah says "the pit was empty—it had no water." [According to the *Midrash*] it had no water, but it was filled with scorpions and snakes.

Our goal is primarily cultural-spiritual. And it seems to me that recent events clearly point out the spiritual problem. The antireligious Israeli Left weakens the foundations of the state by adhering to values drawn from European culture, and this is very dangerous. The *haredim* provide no answer because they themselves are trapped in a spiritual approach that is close to that of the exilic West. Their partnership with the antireligious element is complete.

The study notes the general public's distaste for these groups. This distaste stems from the internal instinct of the people to appreciate the internal strength that is shared by all Jews and that makes them one nation. Our role, then, is not to create an additional sect that is opposed to these two groups but, rather, to rise above and find the common denominator that will allow the inclusion of the extremists among us. The natural love for our fellow Jews should be cultivated in every way possible—radio, newspapers, television broadcasts, sports, youth movements—in short, in the manner that will reach the most people. At the same time, the existing spiritual vacuum must be filled—because every vacuum tends to be filled—by disseminating the positive values that unite the people around them and that give rise to a full consciousness of love for our fellow Jews. In addition, it must be shown that it is not possible to develop a feeling of social empathy toward ourselves without a return to our independent spiritual culture and a knowledge of our own value. A people that forgets its own value is pitiable.

This direction is diametrically opposed to that found in high schools and universities, which do not know how to separate the wheat from the chaff that is in European culture. This is prominent among the antireligious elements—in these circles, opposition to the Torah increases along with academic development. At the other extreme, the spirituality of the *haredi* movement is foreign to the spirit of Israel and its Torah, because for the *haredim* religion alone is the sought-after purpose.

> The holiness that mitigates against the natural world order is not complete holiness. (Rav Kook, *Orot*, p. 77, Sect. 28, Mossad HaRav Kook, Jerusalem 1950)
>
> There is no end to the physical and spiritual evils inherent in the shattering of the nation into factions. . . . This is truly an idolatrous thought that we are certain will not prevail. . . . This imaginary division undermines the very foundation of holiness, like the act of Amalek who cut off the meek. (Ibid., p. 74 till Sect. 20)

The previous section that I quoted was written by Rabbi Avraham Yitzhak HaCohen Kook in opposition to Rabbi Shimshon Raphael Hirsch's plan that attempted to separate communities and distance the observant Jews from the Reform Jews. This approach of isolation in order to uphold the Torah is based on the Christian approach that stresses the salvation of the individual and the saving of his soul. This approach has no interest in saving the entire world. The self-imposed isolation of those holding this approach is not just a defensive step to protect themselves from a permissive society, and the closing of windows in order to guard the embers of the Torah. Rather, it is a method in itself. In their eyes, the return to Zion does not represent the return of the *shechina*, the Divine presence. Only religious people have the power to "restore the kingdom," and at the moment they are not interested in the restoration of Jewish sovereignty in its present renewal in Israel. Their refusal to serve in the army reflects their lack of identification with the nation. In their eyes, the society of Israel is a secular framework that is no different from the nationality of any other non-Jewish country. The holiness of the nation of Israel without the observance of the *mitzvot* is nothing. Therefore, those of us who want to save our nation should not deceive ourselves by thinking that activities aimed at strengthening *mitzvah* observance are sufficient.

On the contrary, the problems that occupy the nation of Israel that is renewing its life in the Land of Israel and encountering a reality that is completely different from that which existed in the Diaspora are not even discussed in the *haredi* camp. The result is that the *haredi* camp does not produce any leaders who undertake responsibility for the lives of the entire nation, but, rather, it produces a leadership that is willing to restrict itself to dealing with religious rulings and the leading of ceremonies. And the attitude of the people toward them is similar to their attitude toward the people–as the study shows. These people come into contact with the rabbi at specific stages of the life cycle–from the *brit milah* (circumcision ceremony) through the *bar mitzvah* and marriage, and finally death.

The Jewish people await an Israel-Torah leadership with an independent spirit. Rabbi Kook thus describes the foreign attitude toward God, which is reduced to religious practice without any connection to the nation of Israel, its soul, and its ideals.

> This is the line that separates between the concept of divine worship which is embodied in the religious concept of every nation and language, and between the very same concept as it exists in the nation of Israel. The general understanding that was adopted by all of the nations . . . could not rise above a concept that in its essential foundation is pagan . . . denuded of all idealistic traits. Not so is the Israeli concept of divine worship that marks within it cosmic love for the divine ideals to nurture and increase them, and to rise up in them and through them. . . . He declareth his word to Jacob: His statutes and ordinances unto Israel, He hath not dealt so with any nation, And his ordinances they have not known. . . . Israel will rejoice in her creator the children of Zion will jubilee in their king. (Rav Kook, *Ikvei; HaTzon,* p. 147, Mossad HaRav Kook, Jerusalem, 2nd edition. 1967)

If so, in addition to the mass activity geared at fostering love for our fellow Jews and increasing the esteem that the nation has for itself, mutual respect, and respect for life–which will also reduce traffic accidents–

in addition, the nation must be presented with those things from their internal sources, through study in the appropriate frameworks, and the creation of the apex of the social pyramid around the ideals of the Torah of Israel—the lofty ideals spoken by the prophets to all of mankind. By doing so, we will make the people aware of that which is holy in the moral behavior of the *mitzvot*. And again, I will quote Rabbi Kook.

> The hunger is great in the land, Not a hunger for bread nor a thirst for water but rather to hear the words of the Lord. . . . The source of the hunger doesn't rest in the hunger itself but rather in the thirst of sons and daughters of the young generation. They are fainting with thirst. They lack a reliable source of water to revive the feeling and thought that has reawakened to life from the source of life. . . . This matter can not be fulfilled, except with the opening of the spring of Agaddah in its great expansiveness, and specifically through great holy Torah scholars who have acquired the Torah, the fear of G-d and the divine cleaving in the marrow of their bones, in the very blood of their hearts. The great spiritual questions that were once understood only by the special and outstanding scholars must be explained now on various levels to the general public, to lower the lofty and inaccessible concepts from their heights to the standard level of the masses. For this a great enriched spirit is needed, and only with its regular practical involvement, will knowledge expand and language attain clarity to express the deepest matters in a simple popular style to revive the thirsting souls. (Ibid., pp. 144–45)

The country's youth thirsts for spiritual values, and their answer will come from our cultural origins. And this will be accomplished by great Torah scholars, with their fear of God and with their knowledge of the Talmud and the foundations of faith and the spiritual values stemming from it. They have the power to impart the basic values that uplift the heart, that raise one to lofty ideals, and that fill life with happiness and fortitude.

All of the practical steps implied by my comments must be developed at length, and surely this is not the time or place for doing so. However, if the general direction appeals to those attending this forum, we can sit together and formulate a detailed plan reflecting the spiritual policy outlined earlier. The greatness of Rav Kook was that he was able to rise above the various divisions among the people, and to concentrate on the principle of "Love of Israel," and the idea that each section legitimately reflects a different aspect of the people. Because he was certain that every group sought only the good of the people, he respected its opinion. I therefore will propose another step that Rav Kook said must be taken—the elimination of the labels that divide the nation of Israel into those who are "religious" and those who are "secular:"

> It seems to me that we are divided into two camps. People frequently use the two names which together make up our entire nation—*haredim* and *hofshi'im* [literally, "those that are free"]. These are new names that were never used in the past. We have always known that people are not equal in all respects, especially with regard to their spirituality, which is the foundation of life, but to have special names which limit and describe factions and parties—there never was such a thing. In this respect, it would certainly be reasonable to say that things were better in the past. If only we were able to eliminate these two names which threaten the strong and pure life which we hope to have restored to us, with God's guidance. The emphasis given to these two names, and the imaginary agreement which links the individuals within the two camps—as if one person says "I am from this camp" and the other says "I am from this camp," and each is happy with his status—blocks the path to improvement from both sides. The *haredim,* i.e., those who see themselves as belonging to the camp known as the *haredim,* look down from above at the other camp known as the *hofshi'im.* And when it comes to repentance and spiritual betterment, the *haredim* look at the second camp with its lack of observance of the *mitzvot,* and they think to themselves that it is they who must repent—they and not he. And one of the *hofshi'im,* i.e., those who see themselves as belonging to the camp which uses this modern term, will certainly think to himself that the whole idea of repentance is a *haredi* concept which is not relevant to him at all. This basically means that we lose both ways, so where will our spiritual healing come from? . . . We have no choice but to get rid of these names. . . . Have we not learned from God that every person, even if the whole world says that he is righteousness, should see himself as an evil-doer? Everyone should look at his own deeds and consider his spiritual weaknesses, while giving others the benefit of the doubt since we do not know their thoughts. We should refer to everyone as members of the nation of Israel, rather than using the name of some camp or party." (Rav Kook, *Articles,* pp. 76–77, Katz Publications, Jerusalem. 1980)

Index